# What others are saying about
## A Philadelphia Catholic in King James's Court

"This book gives a taste of the depth and richness of Catholic thinking. In a very enter-taining story, our most deeply-held beliefs are confirmed."

**Terry Werner**
**Rancher**

"The rich scenes of Amish farm life took me back to a simpler time, when people used horses, kerosene lamps, and their own know-how instead of high-tech gadgets and machinery. It made me think hard about my own family's lifestyle."

**Sharon Adonzio**
**Homemaker**

"What a terrific story! And what a great way for students to prepare for the challenges to the Faith which will inevitably confront them in college and beyond."

**Anna Micko**
**Catholic school teacher**

"Amazing, how much I never knew about the Bible. I wish this book had come out years ago."

**Catherine Kocs**
**Grandmother**

"It's not always easy to defend the claims of the Catholic Church against Scripture-quoting fundamentalists. Michael O'Shea, the main character, is a wonderful of example of charity and patience."

**Helen Lansinger**
**Businesswoman**

"This is a modern-day *Outlaws of Ravenhurst*. Young Catholic readers will be inspired and instructed by Michael O'Shea's spirited and engaging defense of our Faith."

**John O'Brien**
**College history instructor,**
**Retired Infantry Officer, and father of nine**

"I learned a lot and the story was great!"

**Peter O'Brien**
**High school student**

"Masterful! This book portrays the mindset of fundamentalist Christians with uncan-ny accuracy. It's chock full of insights about how people fall into error — and how to prevent it from happening to you or someone you love."

**Bruce Sullivan**
**Convert and former fundamentalist preacher**

A Philadelphia Catholic in King James's Court

By Martin de Porres Kennedy

Published by
Lilyfield Press
W5180 Jefferson St.
Necedah, WI    54646

Copyright © 1999 Martin de Porres Kennedy

This book is a work of fiction. Names, characters, places, and incidents either are the product of the author's imagination or are used fictitiously, and any resemblance to actual persons, living or dead, events, or locales, is entirely coincidental.

Bible quotations are primarily from the New King James Version and the New American Bible.

Cover illustration by Mark Covell

Printed in the United States of America
Second Printing

ISBN:  0-9671492-1-5

# A Philadelphia Catholic
# in
# King James's Court

Martin de Porres Kennedy

Lilyfield Press

Luke 12:27 - 31

# *Acknowledgments*

I first thank my wife Nancy for all her comments, insights, and encouragement. She endeavors to strike a balance between building me up and keeping me humble, and does so masterfully.

I thank also those who gave me a vote of confidence and support so that this book might become a reality, especially the Iepson family.

Editor Larry Montali deserves praise for cleaning up the text and providing many helpful recommendations. Tom Brophy I thank for his superb layout work.

The folks at Envoy magazine and Catholic Answers, plus Dr. Scott Hahn, Patrick Madrid, David Currie, and Karl Keating have all "learned me" a great deal in the past couple of years through their many books, magazines, and tapes.

Many people read the manuscript and provided good feedback, including the Werners, the O'Brien family, and especially Bruce Sullivan.

I am grateful also to those Christians here in Kentucky who strove to "rescue" me from Rome, thereby initiating the process that resulted in this book. I pray they persevere in their search for truth.

As a member of the Church Militant, I also thank the Church Triumphant, the communion of saints on whose constant intercession we rely for help.

*Martin Kennedy*

## Author's Note

King Henry VIII's divorce and remarriage triggered what is commonly referred to as the English Reformation. Later King James of England commissioned an English translation of the Bible. It was introduced in 1611 and until fairly recently was the translation used by the vast majority of non-Catholic Christians. The King James Version does not include all the books in the original canon of Scripture.

*For the Church Suffering, those who have died and have yet to enter the heavenly Kingdom.*

*"I plead with you to live a life worthy of the calling you have received, with perfect humility, meekness, and patience, bearing with one another lovingly. Make every effort to preserve the unity which has the Spirit as its origin and peace as its binding force. There is but one Body and one Spirit...There is one Lord, one faith, one baptism, one God and Father of us all..."*

Ephesians 4:1-5

# 1

Michael O'Shea had been sleeping peacefully for hours, then the dream returned. It was the same dream that had visited him each night since the fire. He couldn't escape the images — his father running inside the row home which was already engulfed in flames, totally focused on rescuing the man whom neighbors insisted was still inside. The roar of fire was deafening, a loud and boastful profanity encroaching on the souls trapped within. The flames licked his father's shoulders and mid-section, a sick pre-torture warm-up, or maybe just a way of tempting him... *Forget the man trapped inside. Get out. Save yourself, before it's too late.* Finally his father spotted the man on the floor, tied to the recliner.

By this time in Michael's recurring dream the scene became maddening and pathetic, his father working furiously to free the unconscious man from the chair while the fire burned his skin and the smoke filled his lungs. Upon freeing the man, he placed his overcoat around him and began dragging him toward the front door.

Michael's nightmare was almost over now. Every night it was the same — he had gotten to know the dream like a film buff gets to know an old Humphrey Bogart movie. In his dream, Michael would be out by the front stoop, as he was on the night of the fire, praying feverishly and nearing panic as the crowd gathered behind him. The fire engines and paramedics, with horns blaring, were just rounding the corner. His father, burned and dazed but still dragging the unconscious man, emerged and collapsed on the stoop. Michael and a couple of the bystanders dragged both men out to the street, just as they had that night. From there the paramedics, efficient ministers of modern medicine, went to work right on the blacktop. Michael was left stunned and helpless. Just fifteen minutes before, he had been driving home with his father. They had been discussing where he might go to college.

Each night Michael woke from this same dream weeping quietly. It was even more vivid this night, perhaps because his hospitalized father had become unconscious during the day and was not expected to make it through the night. Michael was watching, like the film buff, knowing what was going to happen next but engrossed in the events nonetheless.

Then the strange thing happened. The ending changed... at the part where he stood by the stoop waiting. The fire roared, just like before. The smoke was billowing out of the front door and the open window, just like before. But when his father emerged this time, he wasn't dragging the man behind him. Instead a lamb leapt from his arms to safety. The lamb was spry and alert as if it had just jumped through a gate that led back to a lush, green pasture and not an inferno.

Michael quickly looked back, but his father was gone and Michael awoke.

Unlike the other times, he was not sobbing. He was at peace. Was it because he was more intrigued and startled by the surprise ending, whereas before he could only feel sad and helpless? Yes, that was it in part, but the peace went beyond that. There was a supernatural element involved. It was as if he were a little boy again being cuddled, cradled, and consoled by his mother.

He was also wide awake now. Then he remembered something his grandmother had once said. She had been fussing one morning about not being able to sleep as soundly as in her younger days. In the middle of her complaint, she had stopped short, and with a smile gently rebuked herself: "If you wake up at night without knowing why, it's usually the voice of an angel to your soul calling you to pray for someone in need."

His grandmother — his father's mother — was a beautiful and unusual Italian woman. Though thoroughly modern in many respects, she had not cast off as old wives' tales all of the ways of her ancestors as so many her age had done. Michael thought to himself, *Then who am I to cast them off? Is there truth in some of those ways? Even if they are just tales, would it hurt to pray for someone in need right now?* Almost despite himself, Michael decided to pray. The one in need was obvious. Michael began to pray for his father with the very same prayer he heard his father pray for others:

> *Hail Mary, full of grace, the Lord is with thee, Blessed art thou among women, and blessed is the fruit of thy womb, Jesus. Holy Mary, Mother of God, pray for us sinners, now and at the hour of our death....*

Michael continued to pray in the darkness of his room. The shapes of his little brothers in their bunk bed were barely visible by the light of the moon. They slept peacefully. The baby slept in the small room, and in his parents' bedroom slept his grandmother.

They lived in a snug row home on Dawson Street, right off Ridge Avenue in the Manayunk section of Philadelphia. It was the safest neighborhood in the city. Not only was it a stable community, but many of the city's cops and firemen made it their home. Michael loved his house and neighborhood — the street hockey in winter, stickball in the spring, basketball in the summer, and football in the fall. And there always had been plenty of kids to play with throughout his childhood. His fellow shipmates, cowboys, and "armymen" of youth grew up to be his teammates as running backs, defensemen, and outfielders in his early teens.

For the world, he wouldn't trade places with his cousins, who lived out on the Main Line in Bryn Mawr and Valley Forge. Like his dad, he couldn't understand how anyone could want to leave the old neighborhood. There weren't as many kids to play with and you had to depend on your parents to drive you around. Often if they were at his uncle's house on a Sunday they ended up playing TV video games. Michael's dad would insist on starting a soccer or volleyball game out in their spacious yard which everyone ended up loving. He knew his cousins enjoyed coming to Manayunk, walking down to "pretzel park" across from St. John the Baptist to play team sports. They loved going to Cheek's for a soda and soft pretzel after the game, then walking back up the steep Manayunk streets to Michael's house on Dawson in time for dinner.

Michael was still lying in bed praying to the Blessed Mother when he heard the front door open. *It must be Mom*, he thought. He waited awhile longer in bed, but did not hear his mother come upstairs. He was aware that she had the latest update on his dad, but Michael still felt no hurry to go downstairs. *Better to let Mom sit awhile and collect her thoughts*, he reasoned, showing wisdom beyond his years.

After 15 more minutes he pulled the covers back and made his way downstairs. His mother, Tammy O'Shea, was sitting on the edge of the couch in the semi-darkness. The light from the kitchen range threw enough light to cast one side of her in a sort of glow. Strangely, Michael was able to appreciate the remarkably youthful appearance for which his mother was known. She didn't seem like his 39-year-old mother, but rather like a beautiful child with the weight of the world on her shoulders.

"Hi, Mom," he quietly spoke as he approached where she was sitting. He remained standing next to her.

"Your papa went home to Jesus tonight, Michael." Her accent, the "backwoods preacher accent," the one his father would sometimes tease her about, was more pronounced than usual.

"I know," he responded. The news only confirmed what he had learned from his dream. He moved a step toward her and put his hand on her back just below her neck. She gently leaned into him and began to cry, slow at first but with increasing passion. She made no great noise and was not demonstrative; rather, it was a private and personal grieving. It was as if she realized that by sunrise she would be a mother again, husband or not, and that this was her time to grieve. By tomorrow she would be grieving with her children, who had lost a father; with the extended family, who had lost a son and brother; with friends, who had lost a buddy and fellow fire fighter. This was her time to grieve as a wife, and her eldest son's warm hand on her back opened the floodgates.

To accommodate the enormous crowd that was expected for the wake, Willie O'Leary suggested holding it in the large banquet room at Kelly's, the local caterer. They set up the casket in the part of the room where the wedding party would typically be seated. Flower arrangements surrounded Mick O'Shea's casket and were many rows deep. The casket, because of the facial burns, remained closed.

The O'Sheas arrived first, accompanied by Mick's parents, Mick's brother Mathias and his family, and Lester McGuffey, Tammy O'Shea's brother. Soon others began trickling in. The trickle quickly turned into a steady flow of additional family members, neighbors, cops and fire fighters in their dress uniforms, old high school friends, and parishioners from St. John's. The stream of mourners continued for hours. The quiet murmurings that struggled to fill the large room in the first ten minutes turned into a constant buzz as they all gathered.

Michael's younger siblings had stayed at home with their grandmother. Michael, on the other hand, ventured out amid the company of the adults. He enjoyed his relatives, especially his Uncle Mathias. "Matty" O'Shea, his father's older brother, was renowned as the sharpest, most skillful defense attorney in all Philadelphia. Norm Epstein, head of Kaplan

5

Epstein, the most prestigious law firm in Philadelphia, had tried unsuccessfully to lure Matty to his firm. "Brains I can get, chutzpah I can get, but blarney I gotta import," he was quoted as saying. And, no one doubted the story, even though it was Matty himself who reported it.

Uncle Matty was naturally endowed with a keen intellect and quick recall. Over the years he had developed that perfect balance between sincerity and animated flamboyance, between humility and righteous indignation. He connected well with both juries and judges.

Michael's father had taken him to see Matty in action once. Young Michael had been spellbound. He had since gone all by himself a few times to watch his uncle. He enjoyed the drama and theater of the courtroom, and afterwards the star of the show would treat him to a hot dog, soft pretzel, and soda lunch right out in front of the court house steps. His uncle knew all the vendors by name, the ones who made their living feeding the many courthouse employees, center city business people, and whoever else happened to be passing through.

In the courtroom with Uncle Matty, Michael would watch time and again as the prosecutor would establish a crucial point, say "I have no further questions at this time," and move coolly toward his seat. Everyone in the courtroom would be fully convinced that the defendant sitting next to Mathias O'Shea, whoever he was, was guilty. The prosecutor didn't need any "further questions." He had his man. The courtroom would be hushed as Matty paused a moment in his seat. Like Gary Cooper in High Noon, he faced insurmountable odds and the hour of reckoning had arrived. You could almost hear the train whistle off in the distance.

*He has nothing to say*, Michael would think, feeling panicky for his uncle. *He's cornered!* Then Matty would rise slowly and approach the witness stand. He would begin to probe. *What's he getting at?* Michael would wonder. Uncle Matty would dig some more. Then Michael would begin to see where he was going with his questions, how he was raising doubts. Finally, like Harry Houdini in an expensive suit, Matty would wriggle free, or rather provide the narrow opening that would allow his client to squirm out. He would return to his seat, the humble hero.

"How are ya, laddie?" Matty bellowed. He often put on his Irish accent in social settings.

"Okay, Uncle Matty," Michael replied.

"Why, he's a fine lad, I'll tell ya," Matty continued, as he reached out, pulled Michael toward him, and held him with his right arm wrapped around Michael's neck. His other hand held a mug of beer.

"Are ya busy with your storytellin'?" Michael asked, putting on a bit of the brogue himself.

"An' what else would ya 'ave me be doin' lad? When a'm not so busy makin' a bloody livin' with my mouth a've got to keep it well exercised spinnin' yarns." With his mouth and theatrics, Matty could have someone think he was at a 19th century Irish wake. You could almost hear the howling of the Banshee on the foggy moors outside the building.

"Now tell us, Mikey, what would ya be doin' for schoolin' next year, lad?" A serious question, despite the continued brogue.

"I've got another year of high school," Michael reminded him.

"And so ya 'ave, lad. And the year after?"

"I don't know, Uncle Matty. Dad and I were just talking about that the night of the fire." Michael knew that his uncle didn't think his brother, Mick, placed enough emphasis on his children's education. That night they had indeed been discussing the possibilities. They had been talking about St. Joseph's University locally, versus the possibility of going to Christendom, Steubenville, or even Thomas Aquinas out in California — schools that actively promoted their strong Catholic identity. Michael had been surprised his father had even mentioned Aquinas and the others. He realized that his going there would entail a significant sacrifice for his family.

"We were talking about St. Joe's and LaSalle." Michael thought better than to mention the possibility of the other schools. Uncle Matty would pooh-pooh such a notion. St. Joe's, on the other hand, was where Mathias O'Shea had graduated, as valedictorian.

"Ah, and fine schools they both are."

*He really can get carried away with this Irish thing*, Michael thought. He wondered if Shakespeare knew someone like Matty O'Shea when he came up with the "all the world's a stage..." line.

"The Jebbies at St. Joe's are a fine bunch. You might not learn much Church history, mind you, but they'll do a good job preparin' you for the bar, they will. If it's good basketball you're wantin', then LaSalle might be a consideration."

Michael had heard his Uncle Matty refer to the Jesuits as "Jebbies" before.

"I'll be needin' to talk with your mum about all this, Michael," Matty said as he drifted toward the restroom.

Matty O'Shea saw potential in young Michael. He was insightful, mentally agile, and reflective. He had always been impressed with the boy's critical thinking and problem-solving ability. He recognized the raw talent in his nephew and felt that it wasn't being developed or challenged sufficiently in the local diocesan school. It was no secret that Matty and his brother had had their differences with regard to educational philosophy. Matty stood outside the men's room and considered those bittersweet memories. The most polished attorney in the city on one side of the room and his fire fighter, younger brother on the other. The fire fighter would hold him at bay time and again with different versions of the same argument...

"What does Scripture say, Matty? 'Seek ye first the kingdom of God... and a good school system?' 'Seek ye first the kingdom of God... and a lucrative career?' 'Seek ye first the kingdom of God... and a Ph.D. program?' No! 'Seek ye first the kingdom of God and all other things will be added unto you.'"

Matty the marvelous, who earned his bread with his words, would be left groping for them. His brother would continue by claiming that even many of the so-called Catholic schools were "sell-outs." "They put out fancy brochures trying to convince parents how well they would prepare their children for the future, but only in a temporal sense. They insist on competing on the world's terms. They're like a team that chooses to play all 'Away' games," Mick would cry in frustration. "They should advertise their intention to pass on the Sacred Deposit of the Faith. They should start playing some 'Home' games."

Matty never had the heart to inform his idealistic and well-intentioned brother that most parents who happened to be Catholic didn't even know what the "Sacred Deposit of the Faith" was. Matty thought back to a stand-up act he had caught down in Florida a few months back. He had been there because one of his client's kids had been busted for drugs down there. The comic mentioned a beautiful church and synagogue located in Palm Beach, then asked, "Why do they need those there? All *their* prayers have been answered!"

Matty was in a position to appreciate the irony in that crack. His mind flitted to his many professional acquaintances. They all had beautiful cars. Some had nice swimming pools, one a private tennis court, another an airplane. Yet he could think of no one he had ever known who seemed as spiritually content and fulfilled as his younger brother, who lived in a humble city row home.

The flash and shine of worldly wealth, toys for grownups, often came at a high price. Some who possessed them had chronic medical problems, others were in loveless marriages or divorced. He knew some who were thankful they could afford to farm out their children to the best schools and camps money could buy. And, after meeting some of the kids, he could see why. Certainly not all who had done well were like that, but he had seen enough to conclude that there was no correlation between material wealth and fulfillment. To so many it was not about "seeking first the kingdom" but about making enough money to buy into that elusive kingdom, even if it were on a time share deal. Matty was wading around gently in his thoughts when activity on the other side of the hall caught his attention.

"Good friends of Michael O'Shea," boomed the mayor who had perched himself on a chair. Matty would have been thoroughly disgusted with this – politicking at a wake – but he was always somewhat in awe of the mayor, if only for his sheer chutzpah. Bernie Gross was small in stature, but scrappy. He was a skinny little, unassuming, junkyard dog type. He reminded Matty of one of those pathetic-looking, emaciated mongrels who were fear-biters. The kind that will back away when you extend a gentle hand and then take a pound out of your rear end the minute you turn your back.

Bernie tapped Matty for contributions, both for himself and for other candidates, on a regular basis. For Matty, politics was not about ideology but business, and periodic contributions were merely a cost of doing business. Matty thought about his dear brother. For Mick, politics was strictly ideological. The fire fighter's union held no sway with him. He believed it sinful to vote for, much less contribute to, any candidate that was not in favor of stopping abortion. Mick would have flipped had he known some of the creeps to whom Matty had sent money.

"...I grieve when any of those charged with the protection of life and property in our great city pay the ultimate price as a result of their dedication to service...," Gross continued.

*Ultimate price*, mused Matty. *He can't* <u>not</u> *speak in euphemisms*, Matty marveled, as his revulsion began to grow. *Bernie Gross is grieving because there's one fewer voter to woo.*

"...How much more, then, when Mick O'Shea, who was off-duty, laid down his life to save life..."

*Even the life of a guy who was in debt to a low-life drug dealer,* mused Matty, thinking about what the investigation had pieced together about the fire. It turned out that the guy Mick saved was long overdue on a drug debt. The "Man" had likely hired some young punks to rob the guy, tie him up, and set the house ablaze. Such techniques proved extremely effective for the expeditious collection of other overdue debts.

"...I intend to recommend Michael Patrick O'Shea for the prestigious Medallion of Courage...," Gross droned on.

*Hold on,* thought Matty. *Michael is probably puking in his coffin at this nonsense.*

Matty jumped onto the nearest chair. "Thank you, Mr. Mayor," he bellowed in his best Irish, cutting the mayor off mid-sentence and capturing everyone's attention, "but Mick O'Shea never voted for you when he was alive, and you've already got all the dead people who vote pullin' your lever."

Nervous laughter broke out in the crowd. It happened so fast that the assembled mourners didn't know quite what to think but were appreciative that something — or rather someone — had cut the mayor short.

"But we appreciate your thoughts, Bernie," added Matty politely as the mayor stepped down from the chair. After all, he didn't want to humiliate the man, if that were even possible with someone like Bernie Gross. From that point Gross worked his way to the door shaking hands. He couldn't help that. It was second nature to him.

After a few hours, the banquet hall turned funeral home emptied just as it had filled up, slowly at first. Before long, there was a steady stream toward the exit. Then, just as it had begun, the closest relatives of Mick O'Shea — his father, wife, son Michael, brother Mathias, and brother-in-law Lester McGuffey — were again alone with the casket. As they also drifted toward the door, a couple of men from O'Leary's began to load up the flowers and prepare to transport the casket.

◆ ◆ ◆

The funeral the next day at St. John the Baptist was huge. Father Anthony McBride gave the sermon.

"...In life, Michael O'Shea was a friend, a son, a father. In death he becomes our brother. What does it mean to have sisters and brothers? It means to be part of a family, a family that shares the same flesh and blood. How can we do this on earth? We do it every time we take the Body and Blood of our Lord and Savior into our body as he commanded us..."

*How on earth can people listen to this blasphemy?* Les McGuffey asked himself in disgust.

Les stood in the back, not because he could not have gotten a seat earlier but because he was afraid of the contamination. He had traveled from Kentucky to support his sister Tammy as she grieved. It was just as bad as he had read and heard about, the priest in his colorful capes, the candles, the altar boys, the incense. *How could so many still be willingly led by this religion of the Dark Ages? They call the reverend "Father" in direct contradiction of Scripture. Practically everything they're doing is unbiblical.*

Nevertheless, he struggled to separate the people being deceived from the religion itself. He could not be too hard on them for falling prey to myths and fables. They had grown up with it, been indoctrinated with it. It's all they knew. His own sister, though, was a different story. How he had grieved for her these so many years since her conversion to Catholicism. It only made more poignant what Les was preaching in his own church regularly, that those faithful to Sacred Scripture had an obligation to reach out and save those held captive by Catholicism.

The few Catholics he had ever known were decent people, he had to admit. He even agreed with much of their teaching on some of the controversial issues of the day...their opposition to abortion, assisted suicide, and even contraception, which he had more recently changed his position on. He had sincerely liked his recently deceased brother-in-law, and thought back to the Catholics he had known in the Marine Corps. Peter Rodriguez had had a colorful picture inside his locker at boot camp down at Parris Island. He had called her "The Virgin of Guadalupe." Rodriguez was one of those Marines you'd want on your side in a fire fight — tough, loyal, and cool under pressure. Then there was Ken Bartuziak. He was the kind of a guy no one could dislike. Les remembered how thrilled Bartuziak had been when Pope John Paul II was elected. "Finally a Polish Pope," he had bellowed with a wide grin.

Les, still Presbyterian at the time, had taken part in the informal Bible studies that emerged when the Christian Marines got together. Indeed, that was where Les, the descendent of the Scotch-Irish Presbyterians who had settled and tamed the rugged mountain region that included eastern Kentucky and Tennessee, had abandoned his Presbyterian roots. His heroes still included Davy Crockett, Andrew Jackson, and Daniel Boone, but he had abandoned John Calvin.

He had come to realize that even though Calvin left Romanism, that it did not leave him completely. The Presbyterians still clung to all sorts of unbiblical practices. They were still under the yoke of Rome. They just didn't realize it. Some of the Christians had helped him to see that and he was thankful, though it had been painful to shed a part of his heritage. Those who clung to the Bible were a devout and zealous lot. Some, Les came to view as a bit self-righteous and proud, but most were "lay-down-their-life-for-you" Christians who taught the Bible and lived what they taught.

Throughout his enlistment, though, he had never met even two Bible Christians who agreed with one another in all areas. Discussions about what Christ meant in a given discourse or about a certain doctrine became passionate at times. It impressed him all the more that earnest study of Scripture was essential "that the man of God may be complete, thoroughly equipped for every good work," which had become one of his favorite verses.

The Catholics, he had observed, were not like the Bible Christians. He knew that Catholicism had doctrines that all Catholics were supposed to agree on, but the individual Catholics he knew seemed utterly uninterested. He was anxious to hear what they had to say, but they remained oblivious.

Only Rodriguez had he seen reading the Bible, and then not to discuss it, but seemingly for its own sake. The Catholics never seemed particularly opposed or hostile to the Christians getting together, as were some of the others. The Catholics, though, would sooner get together over a pitcher of beer at the E club, tell stories, and laugh. Les had seen this many times before he himself had given up drink, another surrender of his heritage.

The sermon continued... "No greater love can one have than to give up his life for another. It is tempting to question God. How could you let this happen? This is fair? That a good family man dies saving the life of a man wrapped up in the illegalities of drug use!? ...But perhaps we should be asking instead, who are we that Christ suffered unto death to save us? Are we not guilty of sin? Was Christ guilty of any crime? Was it such a shame then or a tragic irony that Christ died to save us? Lord, protect us from pride and grant us the wisdom to recognize that your ways are not our ways. Mick O'Shea would have us pray for that man he saved. Pray that he may find that 'pearl of great price,' the faith that Mick had found in his life, instead of shaking our collective heads in wonder at God's heartlessness...."

Michael thought back to his dream... the lamb jumping from his father's arms. *Whatever you do to the least of my brothers, that you do unto me...* Mother Teresa had often quoted that verse. She used to speak of finding Christ disguised as a poor man, a wretchedly sick woman, a malformed child. *Who was that man my father rescued?* Michael asked himself.

*Dear Father in heaven, have mercy on these people,* prayed Les McGuffey. *They are good people, but they don't know what they're doing.*

14

*Help me reach them.*

*I guess he's rebuking me,* thought Matty, as he considered what the priest had just said. He was bitter that his brother had died saving a worthless wretch.

*I know my husband didn't die in vain, Lord,* thought Tammy, *but I need Mick's help to raise these children.*

"...I think it one of the great aspects of our faith that we do not give eulogies at funerals. We don't focus on all the earthly accomplishments and career milestones of the deceased. All of that is for the obituary page and it is as nothing to the mind of God. Our Heavenly Father cares far more for the small things done with great love — the thoughtful words spoken to a mother, the gentle encouragement given to a child, the anonymous courtesy extended to a complete stranger.

"You see, all the professional accomplishments in the world, all the earthly recognition that we may receive, and all of our accumulated material wealth is of no use when it is our turn to face judgment. Salvation can never be accomplished on our own. That is why God sent His only Son — to show us how to live, to open the gates to all those who endeavor to imitate him. That is why we come together to pray for our brother Mick O'Shea, and to offer the holy sacrifice of the Mass."

*That's right,* thought Les, as he considered the priest's words about not being able to be saved on our own. He liked the way Fr. McBride had articulated their belief. *Why do they have these great eulogies at funerals? The Catholics might have a point there,* he conceded, as he promised himself to think about this more on the trip back to his home in Kentucky.

The recessional was beginning...

Music from the pipe organ filled the old stone church, escaped through the windows, and spilled out onto the streets and alleys of Manayunk. The hymn was joyous, not any sort of a dirge.

15

*And I will raise you up on eagles' wings, bear you on the breath of dawn, make you to shine like the sun, and hold you in the palm of my hand...*

The words of the chorus were triumphant, Les noted with interest; they were positively exultant. The church bells could be heard for miles around. The spring sun had risen high enough to illuminate the beautiful stained glass windows. The colorful scenes were magnificent. The casket and procession made its way back towards Les and the others standing in the back. The sweet smelling incense filled Les's nostrils as he gazed up at the stained glass.

*This is beautiful*, he marveled, as he indulged his senses. *No wonder so many follow and are taken captive. It's all so sensual, so seductive.* He thought to Revelation 17:

> "...the great harlot who sits on many waters, with whom the kings of the earth committed fornication, and the inhabitants of the earth were made drunk with the wine of her fornication...the woman was arrayed in purple and scarlet, and adorned with gold and precious stones and pearls...I saw the woman, drunk with the blood of the saints and with the blood of the martyrs of Jesus..."

*If they just read the Bible, their eyes would be opened*, he lamented, redoubling his commitment to reach out to Catholics. *We've got to get them to read God's Holy Word.*

He caught sight of his sister Tammy right behind the casket weeping freely. He noticed her oldest boy, Michael, beside her, carrying on with remarkable composure. He remembered Michael as such a sensitive boy. His calm surprised Les.

The doors behind Les were flung open by two of O'Leary's men and the cool air of the mid-March morning flooded the back of the church. Out in the street the hearse waited to receive the casket. Willie O'Leary himself was directing this funeral. He had known Mick (or rather Mick had known Willie, as did everyone in town) and was fond of him.

Les made his way out just before the procession.

"Good morning, Mr. McGuffey," O'Leary said in an upbeat but professional voice. Les sensed that Willie O'Leary was one of those guys who couldn't help but be upbeat. "I'm sorry for your loss." It was one of those lines that funeral directors must use a few thousand times a year, yet Les sensed it was genuine.

"Thanks," replied a slightly startled Les, "and thanks for all you're doing." His response almost surprised him. He had met O'Leary briefly the night before. He seemed to be at the wake not so much in a professional capacity, but because Mick was part of his life, as were all those gathered. *An undertaker who loves his job,* mused Les.

Les had sized up O'Leary the night before, after observing him for about 15 minutes as he held court with many of the men. He was full of life, mischief, and profanity (although he checked the profanity whenever a lady was within earshot). He was obviously financially successful, yet unimpressed with worldly wealth. The only time he spoke in hushed tones, as if discussing hallowed things, was when someone asked him if he thought Notre Dame could rebound next year after the tough season last fall.

The tiny graveyard adjacent to the church had been long since filled with many of the parishioners who had seen the great church built. A few headstones bore the O'Shea family name. Mick O'Shea would be buried just across the Schuylkill River at Calvary Cemetery. The interment would be a sad affair. There was always something brutally jarring about seeing the casket perched aside the pile of dirt and over the hole in the earth.

Tears flowed freely. Forty-one year old Mick O'Shea, father of four, was truly gone. He had lost his life rescuing another man from a burning row home. Never again would he catch a baseball with his son. Never again would his shadow fall across the dinner table. No one could come over and have a beer with him. No, it was time to put Mick O'Shea in the ground and move on without him.

"... And may the souls of all the faithful departed rest in peace. Amen." Fr. McBride finished his priestly duty.

"Are we going home now, Mom?" one of Tammy's children asked her as they loaded back into the limousine.

"Not yet, sweetie, we're going back to Kelly's for a reception," Tammy answered and smiled at her child as she stroked his hair. "I know you're tired."

Tammy was exhausted herself. For days it had been totally draining. It must be part of the tradition, to get you so absolutely exhausted that it takes your mind off how miserable you feel.

The reception was a blur for Michael. He too was tired. He did have a short conversation with his Uncle Matty who still seemed particularly interested in talking about Michael's future, especially with regard to educational plans.

Michael talked also with his Uncle Les, his Mom's brother, who let him know he would do anything he could to help the family. With Uncle Les, such words were not just polite courtesies. He was well respected as a man of his word. He was a Scripture-quoting, Bible-believing Christian. Mick had said more than once about Uncle Les that not only did he "talk the talk," but unlike many others, he also "walked the walk."

Les McGuffey, like Michael's Uncle Matty on his Dad's side, was concerned for the future of his nephews and niece. Les's concern was a bit different, though, than Uncle Matty's. He considered it his responsibility to provide spiritual leadership and guidance. Much as he disagreed with his brother-in-law's brand of faith, he had always respected and admired Mick O'Shea's sense of responsibility with regard to being the spiritual head of the household. He had taken it seriously and had been faithful.

Les did not want to be presumptuous with regard to assuming the role and responsibility of spiritual leadership, but he realized that the formation of his children was crucially important to Mick. *It isn't that I am trying to shimmy my way in,* thought Les, *rather it's more a matter of filling the vacuum.* He was sure that none of Mick's siblings were even considering how they could provide spiritual guidance. Les's only dilemma was how to deal with the Roman flavor of their Christianity. Was it his right as an uncle to unteach that? Wasn't it his responsibility under Christ to retrain these children? He consoled himself with the realization that such a decision was not needed in the next couple of weeks. He'd ask the Lord to guide his actions and not become anxious now. *Today has troubles enough of its own,* he decided, as he meditated on that verse.

◆ ◆ ◆

That night at the O'Sheas', Michael helped his mom get the younger ones ready for bed. He could hear her talking to his two-year-old sister, Kate, short for Kateri, in the adjacent bedroom.

"You had a long day too, didn't you, Kate? It's going to feel so good to get down under those covers tonight."

On the inside, Tammy O'Shea was broken-hearted. This was the first night that she had gotten Kate ready for bed since the fire a week ago. She was anguished for Kate's sake. Never again could she ask with excitement "Do you want your Daddy to come in and tuck you in tonight?" She had developed that ritual and Kate would respond with giddy anticipation.

"Would you like to go to Kentucky, little girl?" Tammy asked little Kateri. "Do you think that would be fun? I think they'd like you there, yes they would."

Michael's ears perked up. He remembered Kentucky, his mom's home state. As much as he liked his own neighborhood in Philadelphia, for him Kentucky was a dream. Philadelphia was Ben Franklin, but Kentucky was Daniel Boone. Six years had come and gone, but he remembered his Uncle Les's farm well. He remembered the barn, the hayloft, the smell of horses and manure. He remembered the Trammel Creek, which bordered the property, the tree-lined ridges, the meadows, and the rows of crops, especially the strawberry patch. He remembered his cousins, playing "king of the hay bales," wading into the creek for crawfish, going to town, and the homemade ice cream on those warm summer nights.

*I like the country...,* thought Michael. *I like the city, too. I guess what I don't really like much is where my other cousins live, the suburbs.* To Michael, the suburbs seemed to include most of the disadvantages of the city, and few of the advantages of the country. The yards there were much bigger, but there were no cows, goats, or sheep grazing on them. There were no corner stores and markets, but also no strawberry patch or blackberry brambles where you could collect berries for your breakfast cereal. There was a nice pond out where his cousins lived, but you weren't allowed to swim in it or even fish in it. It was just to look at, his aunt had said. In Kentucky, ponds were for swimming, fishing, or paddling around in on a makeshift boat. Whoever heard of a pond just for looking at? To Michael, like his father, the suburbs represented not the best of both worlds, but the worst. A place where it was "always winter but never Christmas," just like in Narnia, that land created by C.S. Lewis that he loved so much.

"You heard me talking about Kentucky?" His mother interrupted his dreaming as she entered the room.

"Yeah," he replied, wanting to sound casual.

"Your Uncle Les has invited us down to his farm. He has a cottage on the property that's not being used."

Michael sensed that she was probing as well as informing him.

"How long would we stay?" he replied directly, not sure if he would ever want to move to Kentucky permanently.

"I don't know, a few weeks at least, maybe through the summer. We could leave soon, though. Everyone's doing well enough in school. I don't think missing a few months would set anyone back."

"I like Uncle Les's farm," he said, already thinking of the fishing, swimming, and the homemade ice cream.

That settled it in his mother's mind. She wanted to get away, to sort through the boxes of Mick's belongings, and to finish grieving in peace.

"I'll need to take care of a few things before we go, but I'll stop by the travel office on Ridge Avenue tomorrow," she said before leaving the room. Michael always liked that about his mother. She was so efficient once she had settled on a plan.

*Martin de Porres Kennedy*

**2**

In a week's time they were boarding the train at 30th Street Station in Philadelphia. Michael had figured they would go by train. His father had not liked to fly and insisted that efficiency should not be the only measure of judging a means of transportation. "Trains are far more enjoyable, if a bit slower," he would argue. So perhaps as a tribute to their father, they traveled by rail.

There was no direct train to Kentucky, so the O'Sheas first traveled south to Virginia and then west through West Virginia and into Kentucky. In Bowling Green, Uncle Les would pick them up.

Michael's younger siblings were giddy with excitement. He, too, was thrilled, but tried not to let his demeanor reveal it. Indeed, his role had already changed since his father's death and he considered his actions more thoughtfully now.

En route they played board games, observed the varied countryside and urban landscapes, and talked about what they would do first on the farm. At night, while the others were asleep, Michael and his mom would read and talk. Michael was reading *The Chronicles of Narnia* by C.S. Lewis. He had begun to read it to his younger brothers before bedtime, and had become so captivated that he read ahead on his own. His mom was reading a book by the late Archbishop Fulton Sheen. His essays seemed that much more profound due to the torment she was feeling.

Michael paused in his reading and thought about the conversations he had had with his Uncle Matty this past week. Matty was keenly interested in Michael's future. He had asked if Michael knew what he wanted to pursue as a career — if he had ever evaluated his strengths and weaknesses, likes and dislikes.

Uncle Matty had been relieved to learn that his brother's family would not be staying in Kentucky, but would come back in time for Michael to finish high school next year. Matty couldn't help but view Kentucky and people like Les McGuffey as a bit backward and unsophisticated. He didn't dislike Les McGuffey personally, but culturally they were worlds apart. People like Les clung to the Bible, but failed to appreciate that other literature existed in the world. They made the Bible a lifelong study at the expense of so much else. Studying the Bible was fine, but not everyone had the time for it. *That's what monks are for*, Matty opined. When he was not working as a lawyer he was trying to unwind from his work, and that could not include intense Bible discussions. He worked hard and made good money so that his children would be afforded the best schools, the best music lessons, and the best sports equipment. He could pay for Bible lessons for his children. It's just that he never did.

Michael had picked up over time that his father was the "odd man out" in his family. The O'Sheas were endowed with great intelligence and used it in their various careers. They were all professionals — except for Mick. His father was plenty smart, Michael knew, but he was different than his aunts and uncles. Michael thought of the relationship he had had with his father and cherished it.

"Uncle Matty is real interested in where I go to school next year," Michael offered.

"He's a good uncle to be so concerned about you," his mother responded, lowering her book. His mother always assumed the best in people and believed charity to be the virtue that was most scarce in the world.

"He thinks I'd be a good lawyer."

"I'm sure you would, Michael," his mother smiled. "Is that what you'd like to be?"

"I'm not sure. It's exciting how he stands up there and defends a man in public. A good lawyer not only needs to know the law, but really understand it and be able to explain how it should or should not be applied."

"There is an excitement to it, Michael. No one can deny that," his mother agreed.

"I've seen Uncle Matty practically pull a rabbit out of a hat in front of a jury," Michael continued with a note of awe in his voice.

His mom laughed softly. "And he'd be the first one to give you the blow-by-blow account of how he worked that magic trick," she joined in, recalling Matty's flair for self-promotion and storytelling.

"Why did Dad become a fireman?" Michael queried rather suddenly. It wasn't something he had planned to ask. He could have asked his Dad himself just two weeks ago, he realized sadly.

His mother sat quietly for a moment, returning in her memory to a time before she was married. They had met when Tammy had visited her brother Les out in California when he was in the Marines. Les had been in the habit of going to a formal Bible study program at the Protestant chapel on Wednesday evenings, and Tammy had tagged along one night. Afterward, Les had been happy to see her mingle as they broke for soft drinks and cookies. Little did he know that his sister had chanced upon the only Catholic who ever attended the Protestant Scripture studies — Mick O'Shea.

Neither Les McGuffey nor anyone else had known that a Catholic was ever in attendance. The chaplain who presided welcomed those from all denominations, but the rhetoric was a bit critical of Catholicism at times. The undercurrent of much of the discussion was the great reform which had been started by men like Martin Luther, Calvin, Zwingli and others, and that was still underway today.

Les first had assumed that Mick was struggling to come to grips with the Catholic faith tradition with which he had grown up. He suspected that Mick was trying to discover the real truth from Scripture, much as Les had had to do with regard to his Presbyterian roots. He soon learned, though, that Mick had no intention of leaving the Church in which he had been raised.

Mick never countered anyone's interpretation of a Scripture passage, nor did he seek to defend the Church to which he belonged. When Les had asked him about this, Mick replied that he'd have been happy to discuss any area of Catholicism but was never asked directly. Besides, Mick had suggested to him, at a Protestant Bible study it would be better for Protestants to engage one another. He had just come to learn, sensing that many Protestants had a command of Scripture that was truly impressive and that he sought to acquire. Mick was aware, too, that his grounding in Scripture was not firm enough to debate anyone well versed. Had he ventured to offer the Catholic perspective, it was quite likely that someone would have run circles around him, thereby exposing him as another loyal but misguided Catholic.

"Your Papa told me a few days after we met that he wanted to be a firefighter. Just said he felt called to rescue people from fire. That's what he set out to do as soon as he got out of the service, and he never uttered a word of regret for his decision."

"I wanna save people too, Mama," Michael said, almost as an automatic response. He really had not thought of his future that way, but the words sprang forth from his lips.

His mom smiled as she thought how her oldest boy wanted to follow in his father's footsteps. Yet Michael had no specific intention of being a firefighter like his Dad. The excitement of saving people had seized him, but he wasn't thinking of doing it as a firefighter.

"Are you looking forward to Kentucky?" Tammy asked, bringing him out of his thoughts.

"Yeah, there'll be a lot to do. I have some good memories from six years ago, and it'll be great to see my cousins again."

Michael's thoughts turned back to his uncle's farm. It was on the edge of an Amish horse-and-buggy community. His uncle farmed with horsepower like the Amish. He thought about those big Belgian workhorses plowing up the field, bringing in the hay, or dragging a tree out of the wood lot.

"I hope things are as nice as you remember them," his mom smiled.

Michael saw no reason why they shouldn't be. What he didn't realize was how, with the passage of time, the differences in his own outlook and experiences might color his view of life in rural Kentucky. When he was eleven years old, he got to know the farm and the little world contained therein. He now looked forward to getting to know the whole community better, to meeting more people, and to seeing how and what they farmed. He was excited about getting acquainted with rural America as it could be found in Akin County, Kentucky.

Michael O'Shea was about to drop into a different world — a land of tobacco farming, bluegrass music, and Bible Christianity — the same world his father had dropped into to finish courting his mother twenty years before.

◆ ◆ ◆

Les McGuffey leaned back against his old truck, a 1978 Chevy Suburban, just outside the railway station. He saw the train approach from a distance. He prayed in thanksgiving for the safe trip of the O'Sheas and for continued guidance in being a good comforter and brother in the coming months. By this time he felt led to a way to provide spiritual guidance and leadership, without insulting and undermining the memory of his brother-in-law. Like most of the contentious issues with which he had grappled in his life, the right path lay well marked once he had located the trailhead, which often times was a bit obscured.

Les was in awe of how God, once consulted, could take care of everything. His very life was a reflection of how he had been led by God. Les had undertaken to simplify his family's life ten years earlier and had been richly blessed because of it. First went the TV set, and the time spent with his children increased. Then, he and Pam had begun to homeschool. The children's interest in learning increased and they began to provide more help around the farm. They cut the electricity to the house and used kerosene lamps, much like their Amish neighbors. He sold the tractor and other mechanized equipment, and in came the horsepower. As a result, they were free from debt, worked in a safer and more peaceful environment, and were profitable as a farm again, which enabled Les to leave his off-the-farm job.

It had started to come to Les on his long morning walks. He bounced the idea off his wife as he always did.

"I'm just going to preach the Word as I always do and let God do the work," he began. "Reading and studying the Word is sufficient; what could I possibly add to it?"

"So you're not going to address those areas where they follow unbiblical teachings?" Pam asked. She felt a bit relieved on the one hand to learn that no feelings would get hurt and there'd be no misunderstandings. On the other hand, she knew that they were called to witness to the truth, as painful as that could sometimes be. There were plenty of times it had been uncomfortable and unpleasant, but the Lord had blessed them for it.

"I'm not going to bring them up. I don't have to. The Bible will 'bring them up.' As always, we'll read and discuss the Bible during devotions, and it won't be *me* bringing them into line but the Word of God laid before them. That's how it should be. We only have an obligation to present the truth. The Holy Spirit can handle things from there."

"That makes sense, Les. I pray that we present the truth clearly and compassionately," she responded. She grieved for the O'Sheas and so resisted the idea of admonishing and instructing them directly. She was thankful that the Spirit had led her husband to what appeared to be the better path.

"I do hope they come to accept the Lord," she continued sincerely. She so liked the family and hated the idea of such good people being held captive by a faith tradition so steeped in idolatry. She didn't feel that Catholics could not be good Christians as some others did — only that their ritual worship, their layers of hierarchy, of bishops and the Pope, and the various rules they had to follow all combined to form a denial of the blood of Christ, the blood that saved man from the bondage of sin.

Pam had been raised in the foothills of Kentucky and had never had much contact with Catholics. She remembered seeing a pope on television once and she also recalled following the news of the cardinals, some sort of special priests, going to Rome to choose a pope after the one she remembered seeing had died. It was like the royal wedding with all the pomp and ceremony, and she found it all fascinating. It was impressive in a way, but no one discussed anything about it. She found herself drawn to it, but as time went on the images faded. Later she learned that the Catholic Church still clung to many medieval customs and traditions. They still practiced these ways as a means of keeping many of their followers happy. They needed the revenue that the masses provided for them.

Les was there to greet the O'Sheas on the railway platform. Michael noticed the great bear hug of an embrace Uncle Les gave to his mom. It was genuine and it struck him. He could not think of anyone on his Dad's side who was like that. They weren't inclined to such strong displays of affection. Neither was he, for that matter.

The family loaded up in the old Suburban, and the luggage — half of which contained Mick O'Shea's belongings — rode in the rickety old trailer behind.

In less than an hour they pulled off Route 100 onto a side road that curved back and forth as all roads in Kentucky seemed to, then quickly turned again onto Trammel Branch, a gravel road. There was a sign on a huge oak tree that read *Lilyfield Farm* with an arrow pointing down the gravel road. Trammel Branch continued about a half mile through a cedar forest and stopped short right in front of the McGuffey farmhouse. Les turned and drove to a narrow passageway that led, after a quarter mile, to a rustic cottage. It was tucked just beyond a hill and a wooded area. A babbling stream that flowed into the Trammel rolled by about a stone's throw away.

"Welcome to the guest quarters of Lilyfield Farm," Les announced sheepishly as he parked.

"It'll do, Les," responded Tammy, looking relieved to have finally arrived. The level area of land was a lush carpet of fresh green grass.

"The sheep will be here off and on to graze as we rotate the pastures," Les informed.

Tammy was already thankful for this quiet little hideaway. Her mind was directed almost by reflex to consider that most famous of Psalms:

> He makes me to lie down in green pastures: he leads me beside the still waters. He restores my soul...

Eli McGuffey, Les's eldest son, stepped out of the cottage with broom in hand and began unloading the O'Shea luggage. Michael stepped in to help, and the other boys half-helped, half-explored the immediate area.

"Elijah's a grown boy," Tammy marveled. She hadn't seen Eli in years and had failed to consider, as seems to be a natural tendency, the inevitability of his growing into a strapping young man.

"Yeah, says he's headed off to the Marine Corps when his eighteenth birthday rolls around in September," Les answered, not so much with pride as with resignation.

"They did all right by you, big brother," Tammy responded, trying to relieve the anxiety she perceived in her brother's tone.

"Well, I'm not so sure about what we're trying to defend anymore," he said.

"What about 'God, Country, and Corps?'" she said lightheartedly, in an effort to lighten the subject.

"That's right, Sissy. As long as it's in that order," he responded with a smile.

Tammy knew that her brother was disgusted with the same things that she and Mick had found so incomprehensible. Mick had often given one of his "discourses" to those who seemed interested, even remotely, in his thoughts and ways. Sometimes, she thought, he'd say something a bit provocative just to get a good discussion going. She could almost hear him now mixing it up with a few of his brother's neighbors out in Matty's back yard in Bryn Mawr.

Once she remembered him trying to convince a few of Matty's neighbors, who were in disbelief, that while it was illegal for a school nurse to administer aspirin to one of their teenage daughters, that it was perfectly legal for the nurse to refer her to an abortion clinic. At the clinic, an abortion could be performed without any parental consent or notification, the only medical procedure to enjoy such leeway when dealing with minors. Ironically, one of the men who was shocked to learn this was an attorney. Another was the head of the Republican Party in that township.

Once Mick had provoked a heated discussion with a law school dean at Matty's Christmas party over China's one-child per family policy. The dean defended China's right to impose such a policy on her people. Matty asked the dean if he believed that the words of the Declaration of Independence were universally true or just true for Americans: "... we are endowed by our Creator with certain unalienable rights, that among these are life, liberty and the pursuit of happiness."

The dean dismissed Mick as a radical even though Mick was

always gentlemanly and logical, if a bit passionate in what he said. Some considered him contentious, more because he did not limit himself to the innocuous, country club chit-chat that tended to dominate so much conversation, than because he was actually confrontational or disagreeable. Matty enjoyed his brother and did not mind it at all when he engaged people like the dean. Such men, Matty knew, were not challenged often enough, simply by virtue of their position.

Tammy knew that her brother Les felt much the same way about the "issues of the day" as she and Mick had, and that was why he was reticent about Elijah joining the Marines. After all, the freedom defended by American servicemen all over the globe included the freedom to terminate a perfectly healthy baby even in the third trimester.

"Now, Eli can come by and pick Michael up to help with morning chores, if that's all right with you, Sissy," Uncle Les suggested as they prepared to load up in the truck. Michael was thrilled to join in the daily farm schedule.

"He's a grown boy, Les. I expect him to pitch in as much as possible," Tammy answered.

"Whatta ya think?" Les said, turning to Michael, "I've heard a lot about lazy city boys likin' to sleep in," he ribbed.

"When will you be by?" Michael asked Eli directly.

"Oh, I get started about dawn or so," Eli answered.

"See ya then. And thanks for being concerned about me getting enough sleep, Uncle Les," Michael smiled to his uncle.

"Don't mention it."

Michael looked forward to being with Eli over the next couple of months. He was different from the high schoolers Michael knew back home. He was polite and mannerly, yet not at all soft. On the contrary, he carried himself with confidence; he was self-assured, but not boastful or profane.

Uncle Les and Elijah turned to leave in the old truck.

"Les," began Tammy, trying to be matter of fact in tone, "we'd like to go to Mass tonight if it's possible for us to use the truck or get a lift?"

"Sure," responded Les without expression. "I'll have Elijah drive it back after supper."

"Thanks," Tammy said smiling, but her brother was already backing the truck out.

# 3

Michael was up and ready to go a half hour before dawn. He was excited and didn't want to be late on his "first day." From the front window he spotted Elijah approaching through the early morning gray. He came out the front door and met Eli at the porch steps. Eli was a bit startled by his cousin's sudden appearance and it didn't take long for him to appreciate Michael's enthusiasm. In fact, Michael's energy rejuvenated Eli. As they proceeded out from the cottage, Eli stepped a bit more lively and was ready to approach his chores as more of an adventure than as the daily routine he took for granted.

"Ready to be a farmer!?" Eli asked cheerfully as they approached the pasture.

"Ready to try," Michael responded. "Just tell me what and how."

"First we'll milk the cow, then we'll get along to some of the other things. Shouldn't be much to do before breakfast, and I try to keep chores to a minimum on Sunday of course." It was little things like that which impressed Michael, the level of respect Elijah accorded the Lord's Day in a matter-of-fact fashion.

"I think Papa's ready to start disking and harrowing the fields this week," Elijah mentioned.

Michael decided not to ask his cousin what "disking" and "harrowing" meant just yet. He thought of Mark Twain's advice... *Better to keep your mouth shut and be thought a fool than to open it and remove all doubt...* and held his tongue.

"Ever milked a cow before?" Eli asked as they arrived at the pasture fence. Michael saw the big brown cow lumbering her way over when she noticed them approaching. Her bell's tinkling gently announced the sunrise.

"No."

"It's a piece a' cake, once ya get the hang of it." Eli's words washed away some of the anxiety Michael felt, another thing that drew him to his cousin.

"First you go in the stable and get her a half bucket of grain," he continued, as he headed for the small, rustic-looking barn. "Doesn't take much to keep ol' Genny happy. A little grass and some grain is a small price to pay for fresh milk, butter, cottage cheese, and ice cream."

Eli caught hold of Genny by the halter and led her over to the post. There was a leather line on the post and he fastened that to her halter. He reached over, grabbed a five-gallon plastic bucket that he set upside down near her udder for a seat, then brought the bucket of grain under her nose. Genny inserted her nose appreciatively into the grain. Elijah began working his hands and the milk dinged as it struck the empty stainless steel milking bucket.

"See how it's done?" Eli asked, still milking away. "Just grab the teat first with your forefinger and thumb then work your hand kinda like an accordion," Eli went on as he more slowly pinched with his thumb and forefinger then applied pressure with his middle finger, his ring finger, and pinky in succession. The milk shot out into the silver bucket. "Just remember to relax all the pressure after each squirt to allow more milk to come down to the teat." He concluded his tutorial with a half dozen quick squirts of milk. "Piece a' cake," he assured, as he released his grip and stood to make room for Michael.

Michael assumed the milking position and began trying to imitate his cousin, but with little success. *It might look like a "piece a' cake,"* he thought to himself self-consciously as he struggled to get any milk out. Elijah stood back like a violin instructor trying not to cringe in too obvious a way as his student proceeded with the lesson. Genny let out a howl of protest.

"Easy, girl," Eli assured her, patting her on the side, "Don't be afraid to talk to her. I'll get some of the other things done and let you finish milking her... Don't worry, you'll get the hang of it. Maybe she'd enjoy hearing about life in the city," he joked as he slapped Michael on the back and hustled away. Michael was left to grapple with his new cow friend.

Back at the cottage, Michael's two brothers were just waking while Tammy struggled with the oil lamps. She soon learned that if the flame was too high, caused by too much wick being exposed, the glass chimney got black. *What's my brother's big objection to a little electricity?* she thought with mild frustration. Finally she got two of the lamps lit that shed some more light in the dim kitchen area. She began rustling up breakfast, but was presently interrupted by a gentle tapping on the front door. She opened the door for her nephew Eli and was thrilled to be handed a little brown basket of farm fresh chicken eggs.

"A little something for Sunday breakfast, Aunt Tammy," he said, handing the basket to her. "Michael's milking the cow. I better go rescue him." He was off as suddenly as he had appeared.

*Now that's something I like about country living,* thought Tammy, as she admired the simple beauty of the handmade basket full of fresh eggs. She forgot about her frustration with the oil lamp.

"How ya makin' out, partner?" Eli announced his arrival back at the small stable.

"Still workin' on it." Michael had not even managed to get half the milk out of Genny.

"You'll get better each time," Eli assured, indirectly informing

Michael that this was to be his chore from now on. "She needs to be milked at dawn and around dusk." He stood back and observed that Michael had improved a little bit in just the twenty or so minutes that he had been gone. "I'll finish up here, since it's Sunday and we usually try to get to church by nine-thirty or so."

Michael made room for Elijah to milk. Again the milk started to flow as if from a spigot. It was all the more impressive to Michael after having tried it himself.

"How much do you know about cattle?" Eli inquired, still milking away.

"Not much, I guess."

"Well, there's not a whole lot to know for our purposes around here, but I'll tell you a few things. Genny here is a Jersey. They're a brown, mid-sized breed. Not as big as the Holstein... you know, those black-and-white milk cows that are the most popular. Now, Genny's calved, or has had youngins, at least three times now. If y' hear someone say that a cow or goat has 'freshened,' that just means that they've calved or kidded and are now giving milk. So if someone were buying a milk cow at auction, they would want to know when the cow would freshen."

Michael was soaking it all in and humbly realized that there was much he could learn from his "country-boy" cousin.

"Now before a female has calved," Eli continued, "she's called a heifer. A male of course is called a bull — unless it's been castrated, which most are — and then you call it a steer. No good livin' around these parts in ignorance of some of the basics," Eli smiled, as he stood up and released Genny. "Good girl, now go out and eat some grass and make some more milk," he commanded as he gave her a soft swat on the rump.

"What's an ox, then?" Michael queried.

"An ox is a castrated male, a steer, that's been trained as a draft animal. They work in teams and are yoked at the neck. The plain folks, the Amish that is, don't use oxen but that's what has been used for draft power throughout the ages. In most of the world where animals are still used in agriculture, they use oxen 'stead a' horses.

"This milk's gotta be brought to mama so she can strain it, so tell your mama I'll deliver a gallon of it as soon as that's done." With that, Eli was off toward the McGuffey home.

After a breakfast of fresh eggs, smoked bacon, toast from home-baked bread, and juice, Michael found himself packed into the McGuffey "bus" again. He had accepted his cousin's invitation that morning to attend church services. After just a five-minute drive that followed a curving gravel road alongside the creek, they pulled up to the tiny white church.

"Normally we'll just walk up to the church from home," Les informed Michael.

Michael nodded and got out of the car tentatively. The plain looking sign out front just read:

*Church of God's Word*
*Worship and Scripture: 10:00 AM Sundays*

Michael followed Elijah. He had already decided to keep his eyes open and his mouth shut, lest he do or say something wrong or commit some offense without even knowing it. There were just a few cars in the tiny lot and as they approached they could hear piano music from the open church windows. It was just 9:20 now, and Michael wondered why they had come so early. Maybe the church had a ping pong table or foosball game in the basement like the Catholic church did, and there would be some mingling and socializing before services started. Perhaps his Uncle Les had to prepare somehow before presiding over the service, though he couldn't imagine how. As they entered the church through the front door (there was only one door), those already gathered exchanged hearty greetings with his uncle.

"We're just between hymns," informed the man at the piano. "Have a request, Brother McGuffey?"

"Well, hold on now, Floyd," someone interrupted from the left, "looks like they got a new face with 'em today. It'd hardly be polite to jus' go on singin' without a proper welcome... My name's Walter Gent," he said, as he reached out his hand to Michael, "glad ya could join us today."

Then in turn, all those gathered made their way over to Michael to introduce themselves and welcome him to the church. Michael was a bit overwhelmed. It was like nothing he had ever experienced when going into a Catholic church he'd never been to before. Even in his home parish, St. John's, there were often faces he didn't recognize, and not all parishioners knew or even expected to know one another.

"Michael is my nephew from Philadelphia. He and his family will be staying with us for a while over at Trammel Branch and we hope they'll join us here whenever they can," Uncle Les explained.

The McGuffey family and Michael took their seats in one of the pews and the hymn singing continued. As the congregation continued to arrive, Les introduced his nephew to the many who paused at the McGuffey pew to greet Les. The singing, intermixed with some prayer intentions and personal testimony, went on until 10:00. At that point Floyd, at the piano, stopped, looked to Les and simply said, "Brother Preacher!" to announce the transition in the service.

Les McGuffey rose and proceeded forward to the podium, which was on a carpeted platform about one foot higher than the church floor. The congregation was quiet. First he seated himself on the lone wooden chair on the platform behind the podium. Michael was impressed at the sheer austerity of it all, from the simple box-shaped church itself to the absence of anything superfluous on the platform. There were no candles, no altar, no statues, no expensive marble, no kneelers, and no intricate carvings or huge paintings. It was utterly unlike any Catholic church to which he had ever been. It was small and intimate compared to the big stone churches he knew back home. Even his Uncle Les up front was still just 30 to 35 feet away from the last pew. Though foreign to him, the whole set-up and atmosphere reminded him of someplace he had been or maybe a scene from a movie he had seen.

Brother Les remained in the chair silent, seemingly in deep prayer, for the longest couple of minutes Michael could imagine. The anticipation grew. The little building had grown ever stiller as if all assembled were hushed, listening for a mouse between the walls or under the floor boards, but there was only the sound of uninterrupted quiet.

Finally the creak of Les's chair broke the silence. He rose and approached the podium, Bible in hand.

"Did you know, brothers and sisters, that you can go right to Christ when you want to?" he asked rhetorically, in a casual voice. "Right to Christ when you need to?"

*A pause...* "You can go right to Christ to thank him."

*Still casual...* "Right to Christ to ask what you need to do in your life when you're confused."

*Pause...* "What do you think about that?" *Again rhetorically.*

*Pause...* "And when you sin..."

*In a low voice...* "When you stumble and fall... When, as that old song went, tears are in your eyes..."

*In a sad whisper...* "When we're at the end of the proverbial rope... Who can we go to then?"

*Pause... In a forceful and assertive voice...* "We can go to Christ, our Lord and Savior, yes!"

*Now booming...* "We can go to him, our brother, and he will hear us, and he will act on our behalf before God the Father!"

*Animated and theatrical...* "You might say, 'Well I knew that,' or you might wonder, 'What's the big deal? That's the way it's always been...even way back when I was just a little boy or back when I was a little girl helpin' grandma bake pies.' You might even go to first Timothy

41

chapter two and say, 'Gee whiz, Brother Les, it says it right here in black and white...

> For there is one God, and one mediator between God and men, the Man Christ Jesus.

*With booming voice...* "And I'd say, Amen, brother, Hallelujah, sister! It does say that, and that's how we know that there is *no mediator* between God and man save Jesus Christ!"

*Pause...* "But it was not always so, brethren! Let's look at Exodus thirty-two..."

Les opened his Bible, as did all those in the congregation. "We know what's going on here. Before Moses could even get down off of Mount Sinai, the Israelites, God's chosen, the ones he had led out of the bondage of slavery in Egypt, insisted that a god be made for them. Aaron made the calf out of the jewelry that the women were wearing in verses two to four. And why this young golden bull? Was this really their new god or did they just want an image of the one true God, an image of the strong and powerful God of Abraham, Isaac, and Israel?

"It didn't matter!"

*Booming voice...* "God wanted and commanded that there be *no* images and he has not yet loosed us from that commandment as some churches might think."

The barren, statueless platform re-impressed Michael.

"Now let's read on and see what became of these idol worshippers. It says right here, Exodus thirty-two, that God was fixin' to destroy them all if it weren't for Moses beggin' on behalf of the people. Moses then came down the mountain, tablets in hand — I'm lookin' at verses fifteen and sixteen. These were tablets made by God himself, that were engraved by God himself! But when he heard their revelry, their wild partyin', their boozin' and cruisin', their smokin', jokin', and tokin', he smashed God's tablets on the ground in his fury."

Heads nodded in affirmation in the congregation.

Michael's eyes scurried across Exodus 32 for the description of the wild party. *Where does it say they were drinking?* he wondered.

"Go down now to verse twenty-seven. Moses called all those who were 'for the Lord' to come to him. I'll read now what Moses said:

> "Thus says the Lord God of Israel: 'Let every man put his sword on his side, and go in and out from entrance to entrance throughout the camp, and let every man kill his brother, every man his companion, and every man his neighbor.'"

*Now he spoke deliberately, with each word pronounced for effect...* "Three thousand fell that day, my friends. Wasn't such a good idea to go makin' idols, now was it? Then Moses said to those who had slayed their kinsmen, I'm at verse twenty-nine now...

> "Consecrate yourselves today to the Lord, that He may bestow on you a blessing this day, for every man has opposed his son and his brother."

"Who were those ones who carried out this bloody command? Verse twenty-eight tells us that it was the Levites, those from the tribe of Levi."

For Michael it was spellbinding. It was a sermon and a tutorial on the Bible. He had never heard such a presentation.

"And you'll remember that Levi was the third son of..." Les looked for someone to answer from the congregation, which quickly happened.

"That's right — Jacob, whose name was changed to Israel by God. He was Levi's father. But who was Israel's father and grandfather?" Many from the congregation answered, but Michael could not hear it clearly and did not know the correct answer himself.

"That's right, Isaac was the father of Jacob and Esau, and Isaac and Ishmael's father was Abraham, with whom God made a covenant." Les continued... "This was how the Levites merited the privilege of assisting the priests. Let's look at Numbers one, verses fifty to fifty-three. The Lord commanded that the Levites be responsible for the Ark of the Covenant and the meeting tent, the place where God came to dwell amongst his people. They, the Levites, pitched their tents around the meeting tent when the Israelites were encamped. Numbers three, verses six through ten shows us that the Levites were set aside by God for this sacred responsibility.

"An even smaller group of Levites was chosen to serve as priests, those who carried out the ritual sacrifices and such. It was only the descendants of Aaron who served as priests. What happened to anyone who tried to change or otherwise not abide by this divinely established system? Numbers one, verse fifty-one tells us that anyone who came *near* the Ark, would be put to death. Seems pretty severe in our day and age. Why should God make such a big deal out of it? So what if a non-Levite helped pack up the meeting tent or helped pitch it in camp? God was only exaggerating for effect, right?

"Let's look to answer that question in second Samuel chapter six. Here we have the Ark being transported under David's authority. One of the Levites helping was Uzzah. When the cart began to tip at one point he reached out his hand to the Ark, *merely to steady it.* In verse seven the Lord strikes Uzzah dead on the spot! For trying to steady the Ark! Being a Levite, he could help transport the Ark, but not being an Aaronite he was not authorized by God to touch it. God doesn't lay out commands, decrees, and practices for 'grins and giggles.' We serve a God who says what he means and means what he says."

Les continued with Scripture and commentary from Leviticus, then to Deuteronomy, to Ezekiel, back to Exodus and so on...

"By what right, then, do we just go straight to God? We're certainly not sons of Aaron. We're not of the tribe of Levi. We're not sons of

Israel at all in the fleshly sense. I'll tell you how... The *blood of Jesus* made the earthly sanctuary obsolete. Paul the great evangelist tells us in Hebrews nine. He describes the sanctuary set-up to the Hebrews. He explains how only the high priest could enter the innermost tabernacle, the Holy of Holies, and that but once per year with the animal blood that was offered in expiation for the sins of the people. This was on the Day of Atonement that we saw back in Leviticus.

"But Christ the Son, Paul writes in verses eleven and twelve,

> ...came as High Priest of the good things to come, with the greater and more perfect tabernacle not made with hands...but with His own blood.

"And when Christ gave up his Spirit, I'm at Luke twenty-three, verse forty-five now, 'Then the sun was darkened, and the veil of the temple was torn in two.' Brothers and sisters, that was symbolic of our invitation to go directly to God — the Father of Abraham, Isaac, and Jacob — through his one and only son Jesus, the only mediator we'll ever need. The only mediator one should ever use. The holy word of God makes it abundantly clear that those who rely on intermediaries, especially any sort of priestly class, do so in error."

The assertion struck Michael like a sledgehammer.

"When that awesome day of the Lord's judgment comes upon our land, those many will plead that they did not know... or that nobody told them... or that this was the denomination that I grew up in. None of those excuses will be acceptable..."

*Les lifted the Bible in one hand...* "It is laid out for us in His Book for us to read, study, and follow."

With that, Les backed away from the podium, sat and closed his eyes. After a few moments a hymn was sung. There were some prayer intentions, tithing (Michael had never heard that word before), and other church business. Finally the worship was finished at 11:25. A two-hour service — including a one-hour sermon — was something totally foreign to Michael.

As Les made his way back to where his family was sitting, he prayed that his sermon would serve the will of God with regard to leading his young nephew to righteousness. He had tried to be direct and pointed toward what he knew were the fallacious teachings and traditions of the Catholics and some of the other denominations, but knew that he had to be compassionate and gentle.

"Didn't put ya to sleep, did I?" he smiled as he greeted Michael.

"No! Not at all, Uncle Les, I really enjoyed it, especially your sermon," Michael said. "I thought the way you explained Scripture was great!"

Les was a bit surprised by that response, and was excited that Michael's road to accepting Christ would be much smoother than he had anticipated. The relief he felt was rejuvenating.

Michael, though, was responding more to his interest in the delivery and staging of the sermon and the repeated citing of Scripture, which was not typical of the sermons of the vast majority of priests, than he was to the challenge of the message itself.

He had recognized the message as being contrary to what he had been taught, but didn't even consider the notion of asking his uncle about such matters. Frankly, he was intimidated by how well his uncle, and the other folks, seemed to know the Bible. He knew that any biblical discussion would only serve to illuminate his profound ignorance. Again he thought of Twain's advice and refrained from asking anything that would lead to a discussion on the Bible.

On the way home, though, Michael did think of a question to ask. It was a safe question, he thought, one that wouldn't give away how little he knew the Bible. He asked it as much to show interest as out of curiosity.

"Why did Christ choose twelve apostles?" he asked from the back seat.

"Beg your pardon?" responded Les, as much out of surprise as anything. It caught him off guard.

"I mean, you spoke about there not being any need for anyone to act as a 'go-between.' Why would Jesus then go and choose twelve men when he began his ministry?"

"Well, the twelve apostles were sort of a fulfillment of the twelve tribes of Israel," began Les, still unsure of the exact question. "You'll remember that Abraham, the first Patriarch, was the father of Isaac."

Michael did not exactly remember that, but was glad for the lesson.

"Essentially, God promised Abraham three things: that his descendants would inherit their own land, that Abraham would have a multitude of descendants, and that nations would stem from him. Isaac received the blessing and fathered twins, Esau and Jacob. Jacob received the blessing from Isaac even though Esau was older."

Michael vaguely remembered seeing that in a movie.

"Jacob fathered twelve sons and the second to youngest was Joseph. Remember, he was the one given the cloak of many colors by his father, then was sold into slavery by his brothers, and was later re-united with his family down in Egypt, where he had achieved great honor and authority."

Michael was amazed. In minutes, his Uncle Les could give a synopsis of an entire biblical period, something he had never heard from a priest, or any Catholic he knew, for that matter.

"God changed Jacob's name to Israel. So the twelve sons became heads of twelve extended families or tribes of Israel. The twelve Apostles chosen by Jesus were a fulfillment of the twelve tribes. The original twelve tribes ushered in the very formation of the people of God and bore the name of God's people, Israelites. The twelve apostles were the foundation for the 'New Israel,' the people of God not by virtue of birth and bloodline, but His adopted sons and daughters, the ones who accepted His Son as their brother. Does that clear it up for you?" Les asked, thrilled at Michael's interest, and excited by the opportunity to explain the Bible to him.

"I guess so," Michael responded, a bit overwhelmed with the breadth of the answer. "Thanks." He was indeed thankful for the explanation of how the New Testament was a fulfillment of the Old, but his question went beyond that. *Why the Patriarchs, the twelve tribes, and the twelve apostles at all? Why did God need or at least use all these people? Aren't they all mediators in a sense? But Uncle Les must be right — since Christ died and rose, we don't really need anyone now. It's right there in the Bible that Christ is the only mediator we need.*

As darkness descended that first Sunday night, Tammy lit the oil lamps and adjusted the dampers on the wood stove. The late March air was a bit chilly. It was just their second night there, and already she was settling into a bit of a routine, taking life without electricity for granted. Sitting around the table after sundown, she appreciated the soothing effect of the soft glow the lamp flame produced. It was evident to her that not much in the way of work could get done in the dim light, and she rather liked that idea. Suddenly the idea of bright incandescent light at night didn't seem like the great invention people always assumed it was. Tammy thought about how often she stayed up and worked on things after the children were in bed. Then she would go to bed exhausted and not at all in a state of peace. Nature's way seemed to suggest that the gradual dimming of natural light was a cue that work for the day should come to an end.

The children seemed enamored with the whole idea too. Tammy remembered the occasions when electrical storms would knock out power in the entire city, or maybe just in their neighborhood. They'd break out the candles. Neighbors would talk with one another out on their front stoops after the rain was over while they waited for the electricity to come back on. It was quite the little adventure and the children loved it, as did she and

Mick in their way. When the power came back on, people would say their good-byes and scurry back into their little homes, quick as mice fleeing the house cat.

She remembered her mother-in-law talking about the "old" South Philadelphia. Warm summer evenings were a time when people gathered on their stoops. Neighbors visited, talked, ate Italian water ice, and listened to the Phillies on the radio. The boys played stickball in the alleys or right out in the street while the little girls played hopscotch and jacks on the sidewalk. It was too hot to stay cooped up in those snug little row homes. People really knew one another.

Of course, everyone knew everyone else's business. There was plenty of gossiping. Some people didn't care much for the company of others, but just like family, you learned to tolerate one another, accept the good and bad in people, and even grow attached to one another. There was never even a notion of moving out of the neighborhood because you didn't like your neighbors.

Then came the advent of air conditioning, like some weird bomb that killed all the people but left the buildings standing. Now men could watch the Phils in the comfort of their own homes. Visiting took place inside the home — by invitation only — which meant the spontaneity of it all was lost. Now you could control and limit visiting to just those you really liked. With that, the notion of "neighborhood as family" waned.

"It's just not the same South Philly," Tammy's mother-in-law would sigh, even though any outsider could plainly see that the neighborhood still had very distinctive features. It was still considered to be the capital of Italian-Americanism, at least by those who lived there. The homes were still neat as a pin. The aroma of stewing tomato sauce still wafted out front doors and through the streets on Sunday afternoons. You could still get a cold, juicy, and authentic Italian water ice at the corner market on a hot afternoon, or a warm soft pretzel on a cold one.

On-street parking, the only kind of parking there was, still looked third worldish in design, and was still governed solely by tradition. That tradition, the unwritten parking code, still worked and promoted good order. Such ways of doing things, by mutual understanding and submission to the community good rather than by external enforcement, would only be workable among people in the same family. And despite air conditioning, television, and other forces that eroded the very core of the culture of Italian South Philadelphia, that sense of family had not been totally obliterated.

*Maybe these Amish have something here with these oil lamps,* Tammy laughed to herself. *Mick would have liked living without electricity.*

"Did you enjoy the service today?" Tammy asked Michael, who was sitting across the table from her peering into the Bible. Michael did not typically open the Bible on his own.

"I did," he answered, "I'd like to go again if that's all right with you."

"You're a young man now, Michael. Your father couldn't teach you everything, but he taught you well, and you have enough understanding now to be able to search and find out about any areas that you think you need to."

Tammy realized that her son was at an age where he could not be told what to believe and what to reject as if he were a small child. Far better, then, to give him a vote of confidence by respecting his free will and his ability and desire to seek truth, and to pray that he be led to all truth.

"Our Lord founded his Church and commissioned preachers and teachers to pass on the true faith. You have two thousand years of scholarship at your disposal," she said. Tammy couldn't resist sending him off into spiritual adulthood without one last plug for the Church, the one she was received into just before marrying Mick, the one her husband loved, and the one that so many misunderstood and denigrated.

Michael appreciated his mother's posture towards him. Her confidence in him fueled his own confidence and made him feel more mature.

"Would you mind if I looked through some of Dad's books? We did bring some, didn't we?" Michael inquired.

"Sure, they're in some of those boxes up in that walk-in closet. We'll wait 'til your siblings are in bed," she said, as she pointed to them with her eyes. Michael's two brothers were busy playing a board game in the tiny living room area, and two-year-old Kate was still toddling around.

Less than two hours later, Michael and his mother retreated to the storage area in the cottage where he, with Elijah's help, had stacked the boxes containing his father's things. *Did Mom really pack everything that belonged to him?* he marveled. His clothes she had already packed away back home and they fit easily into one closet. What struck Michael was the sheer lack of things. There were only four boxes: one marked "hunting gear," another "mementos," and two boxes loaded with books.

"You ought to take your Dad's hunting clothes," his mom said as she opened the box. Michael nodded, seeing the camouflage jumpsuit and large hunting knife inside.

His father had started taking him bow-hunting two years ago. In his mind he traveled back to upstate Pennsylvania last October. He and his Dad were walking from the car across a cleared field toward the woods, which they knew was filled with deer. The afternoon sky was wild with sunshine. The tree line was ablaze in reds, yellows, oranges, and many shades of brown. The sky itself was the color of sapphire. *This must be what heaven's like*, Michael remembered thinking.

"You can look through these books here," his mother continued, as she finished opening both boxes. "Maybe you'll find something."

Mick O'Shea had not been a voracious reader and hadn't read much fiction, but there had always been a book opened on his nightstand. Michael glanced over and saw his mother picking through several books. He noticed a few titles by Fulton Sheen, one by Thomas Merton, and a couple by a Dr. Scott Hahn. The one his mom picked up, entitled *Rome Sweet*

*Home*, caught Michael's attention. He reached out for it. He quickly perused the cover and summary. It was about an Evangelical Protestant minister and Bible scholar who had converted to Catholicism. He had converted, it appeared, because of what he had learned from the Bible. *This is where I'll start*, thought Michael.

"Why don't you take this now, too, Michael," she said, handing him a medal from the box marked mementos. He took it in his hands and examined it while his mother closed up the box.

"Your father wore it for years, and I pinned it to his hospital gown when he lost consciousness." Her voice cracked just a bit. The emotion that had been welling up inside her was about to spill over.

"Thanks," he responded, still carefully studying the medal and noting his mom's struggle. For some strange reason the medal captured Michael's imagination. It seemed fairly basic on one side, an image of the Blessed Mother. Her fingers had what looked like rays of light coming from them. Stars encircled her head. Words outlined the whole image: *O Mary, conceived without sin, pray for us who have recourse to thee.*

The other side was more mysterious. It was outlined with stars. There was a large "M" with what looked like an upside down cross sort of interwoven with it. Below the "M" were two hearts. The heart on the right had a sword through it.

"That's called a Miraculous Medal, Michael," his mom said, regaining her composure. Michael put it around his neck as he stood up with his mom to leave the room.

Tammy was just about to blow out the kitchen lamps when there came a booming "Hello" followed by a tapping at the door. She opened the door to her brother Les. Michael came down from his bedroom.

"Sorry about the loud hello, but out in the country it's a good practice to announce your approach once the sun goes down," Les explained. "You can give people quite a fright by suddenly appearing at their front door."

"That's okay," Tammy responded. "The children are asleep, and Michael was just getting ready for bed."

"I'm going to head back up now," Michael began, "unless you need me for anything now, Uncle Les."

"No! No, go on up and get some sleep. I know Eli'll be around early tomorrow morning to get you for chores, then we'll start some of the fieldwork with the horses after breakfast. It'll be a pretty full day, so go up and get your sleep."

"See ya tomorrow then." Michael ascended the staircase.

"He's a fine young man, Tammy. You and Mick did well by him."

"Thanks, Les, he sure is. I'm thankful to have him," Tammy answered.

"Just came by to see how you were makin' out, Tammy. Is everything going all right here? Gettin' used to livin' with oil lamps?"

"Oh, we're settlin' in, brother, and don't you worry for a second about our comfort. I don't know how we'll ever be able to repay your generosity." Tammy knew he would not accept her money, so didn't even bother to offer. "Now you just don't hesitate to let me know what we can do to help out. I'm thankful you've got Michael involved, but let us contribute, too," she gently challenged him.

"I will, I will," he assured her, "but I thought I'd let the younger ones have a couple days or so to mess with the crawdads down at the creek and play in the hayloft. You know how boys like to explore. I'll get some regular chores for them soon enough."

"Don't forget me. Or maybe I should say don't forget Pam. This could be a nice break for her, havin' someone around to help with meals and things. And thanks for letting us use the truck to get up to Glaston for Mass last night. I insist on paying for the gas."

"I'll let you do that, and I do appreciate your enthusiasm, Sis. Les paused, and walked over to look out the window. He avoided looking directly at Tammy, and with a hesitation that was not typical of him, he spoke.

"That kinda' brings up what I wanted to talk to you about. Of course, you know Michael came to services with us today, and I just wanted to assure you that I'm not trying to undermine your authority by invitin' him. Strong as I am in my beliefs and biblical convictions, it would be wrong of me to ignore your, both yours and Mick's, efforts to instruct him."

Les McGuffey's sense of Christianity so impressed Tammy. He didn't dare approach her as the "big brother" and insist on doing what he felt was for their own good without consulting her. He was speaking to her not as a blood brother in the biological sense, but rather as a spiritual brother, a fellow Christian who respected her. He dealt with her in charity, kindness, and love.

*You would make such a great Catholic!* she almost blurted out. *The Church needs men like you, Les! What could I say or do to bring you home?* She was saddened at realizing he was likely thinking much the same thing about her. After all, it was she who had converted, but she knew that she was home now. It would be impossible for her to convey such a feeling to her brother.

"I've considered all that, Les, and I thank you for having the respect to come to me." She paused, thinking how she would articulate what was in her mind. "Michael's daddy taught him well, and I pray every night that I may provide a good Christian example to my children. Adult responsibility will come more quickly for Michael because of Mick's death. That's just the way it is, and I have to accept that. Part of being an adult is deciding what you believe in."

Les listened patiently to her answer. It was obvious that she had considered this whole area since Mick died.

"You know we've had all our children baptized into the Catholic Church. When you do that you make a commitment to teach them the Faith. I'll carry on without Mick in teaching the younger children, but

Michael has been taught well. He has all the tools to search for answers that he might be confronted with. I can't do more than that except pray for him and be a good mother to him as long as I continue to live.

"You know, Mick used to say that all people as they grow up must face a challenge of belief that becomes a turning point in their lives. For some it comes when they go to college, for others when they enter the work force full time or some other transition. They either tenaciously embrace what they believe in, abandon what they once held fast to, adopt some other philosophy, or decide not to really decide and become lukewarm. Mick thought most just go the 'lukewarm' route, and that those were the most pitiable."

"I'd have to agree with him, Tammy," Les asserted. He continued in a low voice, not looking at his sister, "The seventh church in Revelation, Laodicea: 'but because you are neither hot nor cold but lukewarm I will vomit you out of my mouth.'"

"Some of what Michael's been taught is going to be challenged if he goes to your church. I realize that, Les, but this is his transition, his time to embrace or abandon," she concluded, almost shivering with anxiety with the thought of his rejecting what he'd been taught by his father. "I am comforted that he'll not tend toward lukewarmness from anything you have to say, Les," she smiled, trying to lighten the mood for both their sakes.

"Thanks for sharing that with me, Sissy," he said as he got up to leave. "You feel free to come and talk with me anytime about this or anything else that might go on out here that I might be able to help with or whatever." Les was at the door. Tammy embraced him tenderly.

"Thanks, Les, thanks for everything."

That night, as he was climbing under the covers, Michael's thoughts hearkened back to his uncle's sermon. *I know that priests are important... How else could you have the Mass or have your sins forgiven?... But Uncle Les said — and the Bible seems to say — that we don't*

55

*need anyone between God and us except Christ.*

He wished he could have asked his Dad. His Dad would have been able to explain it all. *What if the Bible says one thing and we do another? In that case, I guess our traditions overrule the Bible? But that doesn't seem to make sense. Dad read the Bible every day and he thought everyone should study it. How can Uncle Les and Dad read the same Bible but believe different things?* These thoughts haunted Michael until he drifted off to sleep...

Into a dungeon Michael descended. It was dark. He could barely see the stone walls that surrounded him. There was only natural light, and that from a barred window at least fifteen feet off the ground. Just under the window, at about the height of a basketball rim, there was a balcony about ten feet long with a solid stone parapet. There was no way for him to escape this enclosure. He was barefoot and wearing solid brown pants and a long sleeved, brown shirt. The corners of the cell were too dark to see and he feared walking over to investigate on account of his bare feet. *Maybe there are rats in here,* he thought, as if that should be his greatest concern.

He stayed put in the middle of the rectangular-shaped cell. The scene unnerved Michael and made him feel vulnerable. *Where am I, and what in the world is going on?* he nervously asked himself. He stared up at the window and parapet above and considered a strategy for getting himself up to that level. He could not see any opening except the barred window, but wanted at least to be able to see out the window and call for help or find out where he was.

As he gazed up at the window, there suddenly appeared a snake slithering between the bars. It was long, thick, and dark. It quickly slithered out of sight onto the stone balcony.

*That thing could make its way down here in no time,* he thought, *and in the shadows I wouldn't even be able to see it.* He was paralyzed with fear, unable to think of a way to get out.

Tammy O'Shea began readying herself for bed. She couldn't help but be concerned for her son. Especially after seeing him flipping through the Bible after dinner and asking for some of his father's books. What he saw and heard at her brother's church was challenging him. With his father taken so suddenly, she knew he would be asking some big questions, even questioning the sense and justice of life itself. She restrained herself from offering unsolicited answers. Instead, she committed herself to prayer. She prayed that her son be led to all truth.

Ready for bed, she took her Rosary out of her small travel bag. She had prayed the Rosary on their trip every night after all the children were asleep. Kneeling beside the bed, she collected her thoughts. She would pray especially for the soul of her husband, for her big brother Les (for whom she always prayed), for spiritual protection and guidance for her oldest son, and for the strength and wisdom to be a good Christian.

Michael remained standing, suspended in that foreboding feeling that immediately precedes panic, when a small door opened out onto the balcony. He had not even noticed the door before, so dark was the wall. A figure in a dark cassock ducked under the door lintel and emerged onto the balcony. He centered himself on the balcony in front of the window and appeared to be looking down at Michael. A hood on the cassock covered his head like a monk and the sun shone right over his shoulder into Michael's eyes. Michael struggled against the sun and the contrast of light and dark to identify the man, but it was impossible to see his face. The man stood, peering down at Michael. For Michael, he was a welcome distraction from the snake.

"Why don't you believe and follow what's in this book, young Michael?" the man asked in a voice that was deep, clear, and compassionate. He was holding a book out as if he were presenting it to Michael. Michael identified it as the Bible because it was black and because the

57

sun shone across enough of the cover to illuminate the words *New King James Version*.

"I do believe what's in that book," Michael responded.

"'We have been sanctified through the offering of the body of Jesus Christ once for all.' So wrote Paul in Hebrews ten, verse ten," the man stated. "'For one offering he has perfected forever those who are being sanctified...' verse fourteen. How much longer will you continue to sit through the 'sacrifice of the Mass?'" he asked, trying to disguise the disdain he evidently felt. "This 'Mass' of yours makes a mockery of Sacred Scripture. Why do you insist on crucifying your Lord over and over again?

"In the book of Hebrews" (the robed man had the book open as if prepared to read), "it clearly says that:

> Christ was offered once to bear the sins of many. To those who eagerly wait
> for Him He will appear a second time, apart from sin, for salvation.

"The Messiah has been offered, Michael. It's blasphemous to offer him again and again as your tradition does."

Michael was overwhelmed and at a loss for words. The man sounded so hurt by what was being done to the Messiah. Michael didn't know what to say or how to respond to all the charges, both those from this robed man and from his uncle. Though he felt ill equipped to present a biblical explanation, he was somehow confident that there *was* some explanation, some way to reconcile Scripture with the Church his father had embraced with all his might. He felt ashamed at his inability to defend all that his father had taught him, and in his humility stood and prayed that he might be forgiven for his shortcomings. He stood there under the eyes of the questioner and prayed silently for forgiveness.

Tammy lifted up the Rosary just before starting to pray and said,

"O Mary, conceived without sin, O Mother of our Savior, I bind my children to you. I pray that you protect, guide, and care for my babies like you did for your son..."

"I don't know," Michael admitted. "I think there's an explanation, but I'm not sure how to explain it."

"You can't explain it and yet you partake every week?"

"Yes," he answered humbly. He looked up at the figure, who stood there motionless with the snake laying on top of the stone parapet. The silence was deafening.

"Do you need more than Jesus Christ as a mediator?"

*I'm caught*, thought Michael. *If I say yes, then I'd be contradicting the Bible, what my uncle just talked about today. If I say no, then I'll have to explain why we have the saints and Mary and why we think they're important.*

"The Bible says no..."

"And you believe that?"

"I believe in what the Bible says, it's just that we have a different view than Protestants about that kind of thing."

"Can you explain it to me?"

"Not really." *How humiliating*, Michael sighed. *If there were any question before about my being a complete jackass, I think I've removed all doubt.*

"Christ founded one Church," began Michael lamely.

"Enough!" the figure shouted, and then with the flick of his hand knocked the snake off the wall down into the chamber where Michael stood.

Michael jumped to avoid the falling snake, and with that he awoke suddenly to find himself in bed, slick with sweat, his heart pounding inside his chest.

*Martin de Porres Kennedy*

# 4

E lijah came around again early in the morning, and he and Michael went off into the pre-dawn black to do chores. Michael thought he was a bit more efficient, if not totally comfortable yet, milking Genny. Elijah found that he enjoyed his cousin's company and looked forward to the next couple of months. They finished up quickly and Elijah repeated his pre-diction from yesterday, that he thought his Dad would begin working the fields today.

Michael arrived back at the cottage with some fresh eggs and milk. Everyone was up. His mother was starting to put water on the stove for breakfast. They ate oatmeal and some homemade biscuits, which was to become the standard weekday morning meal. Tammy had talked to Pam about their family's eating schedule and found that it made sense — a sim-ple hardy breakfast, a large dinner or noon meal, followed by a siesta in the warmer weather, and a simple evening meal a few hours before bed.

Tammy marveled at how frugally the McGuffeys lived with regard to food. Not that they didn't eat well — quite the contrary. They ate the best of food and maintained a fairly healthy diet, but produced the great majority of it right on their little homestead. Breakfast foods included eggs from their own chickens, milk from their cow, and cornmeal from corn grown on the farm and milled at the local Amish feed mill. On occasion they'd have sliced apples that they'd canned themselves or dried bananas.

The apples came from a local orchard where the McGuffeys had bartered for them. The bananas they had purchased cheaply in bulk and had simply dried them.

At lunch there was either a meat dish — pork, beef, venison, or chicken — or a stew. The meat was raised or hunted on the farm. The stew they had canned last fall — it was a thick mixture of potatoes, green beans, and corn in a base of tomato juice or chicken broth. Pam would just add some meat when it was warming up. For supper they'd have bread and cheese, jam, or apple butter – again all home made – or maybe just some popcorn.

The O'Sheas would come to realize, too, that over the course of the growing season their diet would change dramatically depending on what was "coming in." Any food that was not conducive to canning, drying, or smoking was gobbled up while it lasted. Pam had explained that they learned much from their Amish neighbors both in terms of food storage and preservation, and way of life.

Michael devoured his breakfast. He was amazed at how good oatmeal with brown sugar and milk could taste after less than an hour's worth of morning chores. He sat for awhile playing with Kate and then his two brothers before heading out to meet his uncle and Elijah at the main barn.

Michael saw his uncle leading one of the workhorses out of the barn as he approached. Les fastened the animal's halter to a short line on the side of the barn and went back inside the barn to lead out the other. As he re-emerged from the barn, he was startled to find Michael right there waiting for him.

"Mornin', Michael, I didn't notice you approaching," he greeted. "You can get the collars, lines, and all the other gear we'll need from inside the barn."

Michael entered the barn, unsure if he'd even recognize what the appropriate "gear" looked like, but hoping somehow that it would be so obvious as practically to jump right out at him. He was relieved to find Elijah in the barn. Before he could even ask Eli for help, his cousin asked if he could give him a hand carrying the tack out. His uncle provided a quick tutorial on the gear while he put it on the horse.

"The collar goes around the horse's neck first. It's got to fit properly because this is where all the pressure of pulling is felt by the horse." He snapped and fastened the collar onto the horse efficiently. Then he picked up the two curved, metal bars. "The hames fit right here on the outside of the collar. The tugs, fastened to the hames, are what's actually used to do the pulling. So the chain or tug that pulls the plow or disk is linked to the hames here," he explained, pointing to that spot on the curved bars. "Finally, you got the lines," he continued, preparing to secure the leather-leash looking thing. "Each end of the line goes here in the horse's bridle. This is how you drive the horse, by applying pressure to its mouth, through the bit, with the lines, simultaneous with a voice command." He finished outfitting the horse.

"Now to review," he smiled, "before you're tested on Maggie." He gestured to the other horse.

Anxiety welled up within Michael. *I'm going to make a fool of myself,* he thought.

"Three basic components: the collar, the hames, and the lines. The collar is where pressure is put on the horse, the hames hold the tugs in place so you can actually pull things, and the lines enable you to drive and control the animal. There are names for all that other stuff on the hames, but don't worry about that. You can call all of that the harness.

"Elijah," Les continued, "you help him out and I'll check Maude's feet here." Les turned away. He appreciated his nephew's nervousness and knew his observation would only intensify it.

Michael was thankful that his uncle wasn't watching, and was unaware that it was by design. He approached the horse with trepidation. As he closed in on the huge chestnut-colored animal, his nostrils were filled with the beast's smell and he was captivated by the texture of its beautiful coat. Not only did he not know where to begin, but he was practically paralyzed with fear of the big animal.

Elijah came to the rescue. Michael fumbled his way through helping Elijah harness up the big animal.

Every time the horse moved, Michael's anxiety level skyrocketed. He remembered hearing that animals could smell fear in humans. *This animal should be absolutely overwhelmed with the odor I'm producing,* he nervously laughed to himself. So anxious was he that he couldn't really focus on the harnessing, but his fear of displaying his trepidation to his cousin was more powerful than the fear of the draft animal itself. *Better to be stomped on by a 1500-pound draft horse than to let a country boy know you're deathly afraid of a horse,* he figured. He wanted to get it done quickly so that his uncle wouldn't find out what an absolute klutz he was. It seemed so easy when his uncle did it. Presently they finished up, and just in time for Michael's sake, because his uncle's attention was back on him. Michael breathed a sigh of relief.

"Okay, now harness Maude up," Les commanded. Michael wheeled about to see the first horse completely unharnessed. "I needed to check something on her collar but it looks like everything's okay. I'll check Maggie's feet while you get that done." Les proceeded to position himself to lift up the hoof. *Education the Marine Corps way,* chuckled Les to himself, as he picked up Maggie's hoof and began cleaning it.

Michael braced himself, and with cousin Eli's help, accomplished the mission. He noticed that he was slightly less anxious this time and could even concentrate a bit on the mechanics of how the tack went on.

"Looks like this collar's all right, too," Les announced as soon as they had finished, "better get this girl harnessed back up." Michael was the only one not aware of what his uncle was doing, but this time he actually looked forward to re-harnessing the horse. His confidence and comfort level were growing, which was exactly the point of Les's whole exercise.

"Repetition is the mother of all learning," Michael smiled, "at least according to the Jesuits." It was a line his Uncle Matty used often.

"I'm sure those Jesuits were right smart about some things," Les replied. *I wonder if that's who taught the Marine Corps drill instructors?* he joked to himself.

The harnessing lesson concluded, they proceeded out to the field, Elijah with the lines.

"Now, Michael, there's really only a few things that the horses do when it comes to fieldwork," continued Les.

*Maybe he's going to explain what "disking" and "harrowing" mean,* hoped Michael. He was too embarrassed to ask.

"It's all pretty basic. The first thing to be done in the early spring or really the late winter is plowing."

Michael continued to be impressed with his uncle as he taught. He was a tall, powerfully built man with a slightly intense personality. His stature commanded attention and could even intimidate, yet his manner was also gentle and understanding. You sensed from being around him that you could count on him, that he was trustworthy and loyal.

"Now, when you plow a field, what you are doing is literally turning the soil over, about the top five to twelve inches." He illustrated with his hands how the soil was sliced and flipped as the plow worked.

"What that does is bury the growth on the surface of the field. That does two things. It exposes bare soil that can be further prepared for planting of course, but it also incorporates the green growth of the field into the existing organic matter of the soil. Have you had basic chemistry yet?" he asked, instead of assuming that it all made sense to his pupil.

"Yes, sir, but nothing about soil science."

"Okay, well plants are somewhat like us," Les began with his crash course in organic chemistry. "They need water, light, and food to live. The food they get is from the soil, and soil is composed of minerals and organ-

65

ic matter, mostly minerals. Now, organic simply means that something is alive or was at one time alive. Inorganic matter, like minerals, does not have life. Plants use both organic and inorganic matter. You've heard of food having lots of vitamins and minerals?"

Michael nodded. He knew that Les didn't have any college education, so figured that all this must be self-taught or from experience. Michael noted the contrast between Uncle Matty on the one hand, who always *talked* about education, and Uncle Les, who actually spent time teaching him. They had arrived at the field that needed to be worked.

"Whoa," Elijah gently commanded in a deep voice to stop the horses.

"Now without getting too complicated, the organic matter that is still alive, the micro-organisms in the soil, feed on the organic matter that is dead — grass, leaves, manure, banana peels, whatever. Through that process," his uncle manipulated his hands like a professor delivering a passionate lecture, "food is made available to the plants. The how or the exact mechanics of that process is still being studied by soil scientists at big universities," he informed with awe in his voice, trying to impress upon his nephew the magnitude of complexity involved. "But they'll never figure it out," he concluded in a matter-of-fact voice.

That comment captured his student's attention, just as it was intended.

Les continued, "What we're dealing with here..." He leaned over and grabbed a handful of soil. Michael noted its dark color, and rich, crumbly texture. It looked almost like a light, airy piece of chocolate cake. "There are literally millions of tiny organisms in this handful of soil," Les said parenthetically, not finishing his thought.

Michael, of all things, could only think of that Dr. Seuss children's book *Horton Hears a Who*, in which the elephant, Horton, finds a speck floating in the air. The speck, he learns, contains an entire village — complete with houses, stores, roads, schools, and most importantly, a healthy

66

population of Whos inhabiting Whoville. Horton assumes responsibility for the speck containing Whoville, and saves it from destructionn. *Uncle Les is a Hortonesque character,* Michael thought.

"The mystery behind this stuff," Les continued, letting the soil fall through his fingers, "is at the core of the mystery of life itself. He paused. "Jesus says in Mark chapter four...

> "The kingdom of God is as if a man should scatter seed on the ground, and should sleep by night and rise by day, and the seed should sprout and grow, he himself does not know how. For the earth yields crops by itself: first the blades, then the head, after that the full grain in the head. But when the grain ripens, immediately he puts in the sickle, for the harvest has come."

"...And that mystery," he continued, "is unknowable, for it is of God." He finished his short course in hushed tones and paused momentarily.

"Now let's get this disk working, 'lijah. Can't be sittin' around here all day flappin' our gums." He was back to the simple country man persona in an instant. "You learn Michael here how to prepare a field for plantin'." With that he walked off. "I'll be back out to check on ya in an hour or so," he called over his shoulder.

Michael was relieved at the abrupt close to his lecture. He wouldn't have known how to respond. Did his uncle have the entire Bible memorized? He thought of his father and compared him to his uncle. His father was a fireman through and through. It was not only his work and livelihood, but was something of a mission for him. And in the unique way firemen enjoy their work, his father certainly did. Uncle Les, though, did not merely like his work, nor could one even describe it as a love for his work. Rather, to Les, tilling the soil was *holy* work. To do it poorly, not to appreciate the mystery, or to poison the soil with toxins, was not merely being sloppy and negligent, but it was a desecration, the profaning of something holy.

"Okay, cuz," Eli started. He had already hitched the team to the disk. "This is called disking.

"*Geeeeet up*," he bellowed in a deep voice. With that the horses pulled the disk — with Eli standing on top — to the other end of the plowed field, about a football field and a half away, and came back along the opposite edge.

Michael watched, thinking of what his friends back in Philadelphia were probably doing today after school. *Nothing like this,* he laughed to himself.

"That's disking!" Eli called to him, as the horses approached the starting point again. "Now it's your turn," he said, as he jumped off the disk.

By this time Michael was not surprised. This seemed to be the McGuffey way of instruction, heavy with "hands-on" experience. This, however, seemed to be too much too soon. The anxiety again welled up in him. Before this morning, he had never even been close to a huge draft animal, and now before noon he would have harnessed and driven a 3000-pound team.

The disk was a simple-enough looking piece of equipment. It had a platform for standing on, over a network of metal saucers that actually served as its wheels. The saucers or disks were slightly larger than Frisbees and were positioned straight up and down to slice the soil as they rotated.

"You're gonna help me out with this, right?" Michael asked Eli, as he approached the team slowly. Faking normalcy was one thing when harnessing a horse, but Michael was ready to resist verbally the notion of actually driving the team. He had never dealt with horses at all before this morning.

"You ride standing next to me a turn, then see how ya feel," answered Eli, seeing his cousin's reluctance. "It's not real hard or anything."

Michael realized that Eli, who had been working horses for years, didn't have any idea of how new and different and scary this could be to a greenhorn like himself.

Michael jumped up next to Eli. They stood right next to each other, as there was very little room. Michael was relieved to be only two or three feet off the ground. *"Bailing out" is definitely an option if these horses decide to gallop off somewhere,* he reassured himself.

"Dad didn't really explain why a field needs to be disked," began Eli, before starting the horses. "We plowed this field about five weeks ago. We had it sowed in winter rye and turned that under."

"Why did you sow it and then just turn it under?" Michael asked. "You harvested the rye first, right?"

"Well, the winter rye was what you call a cover crop," smiled Eli, realizing he was assuming too much in his explanation. "That field was sowed in cantaloupes last year. After they were harvested we planted rye, a type of grass, to cover the field. That prevents your loose topsoil from being washed away in the rain or from blowin' away when it's dry and windy. It also provides the soil with a lot of organic matter once it is plowed back in or 'turned under.'"

Michael nodded. There was a bit more to farming than just planting seeds or milking cows, he was starting to understand.

"So not only does the green grass, which is very high in nitrogen, feed the soil, but all the roots break down, too. Again that becomes feed for the micro-organisms in the soil," Eli said, trying to draw a connection to what his father had explained. "Soil like this," he pointed down to the fluffy, black, chocolate-cake looking stuff, "takes years to build. Now by disking, we're just accelerating the breakdown. After plowing we let the millions of little buggers in the soil go to work for four to six weeks, then we hit it with the disk."

He paused to let it sink in, then continued, figuring he'd may as well extend his explanation, "Finally we harrow it, to smooth it out more before planting. That's what we're trying to get done in the end, prepare a nice smooth bed for seed or for transplants."

"Where'd your dad learn all this about farming?" Michael asked, amazed that there was a fair amount of know-how and management involved in farming and knowing also that his grandfather had made his living in the coal mines, not as a farmer.

"Just picked it up over time, I guess, and the Amish folk are real helpful. He's learned a bunch from them." Michael couldn't help but compare his cousin with the college-bound high schoolers back home. Plenty of them were smart guys and good athletes, but none of them had the practical know-how in their family's business or the level of responsibility that Elijah had. Elijah was more a junior partner to his father than an employee or a son just helping out once and a while. He seemed like a grown-up in a teenager's body.

"Broaden your base a little bit," instructed Eli, pointing down to his own feet which were spread wider than shoulder width, "this is gonna exercise your balance."

"*Geeeet up,*" in his deep bellow, and the horses responded. Michael felt the jolt of the start and instinctively reached out to grab something to steady himself. The only something there was Eli's shirt. "Told ya it'd work your balance," Eli laughed. As they proceeded down the field, Michael acclimated himself to the perch atop the disk. He remembered the fishing trips with his father off the South Jersey shore and how it took awhile to get your "sea legs."

"Now I'm okay," he informed his cousin. "Just had to get my sea legs back." He looked behind the disk at the ground they were riding over. Sure enough, it was being sliced down and broken up.

◆ ◆ ◆

The first week was full of new learning opportunities for Michael. He learned a bit about carpentry as he helped shore up a support on the stable. He helped doctor up some of the animals and learned something about their breeding cycles.

On Saturday of that first full week on the Kentucky farmstead, his Aunt Pam showed them her "kitchen" garden. In Amish fashion, she had a small garden just outside the house to supply the family with fresh produce. The tour was the result of Tammy's wondering aloud how it was they were being supplied with fresh greens every day when she knew no one had gone to town that whole week.

"These are my 'cold frames,'" Pam said, pointing down to a couple of three-foot by five-foot Plexiglas boxes with wooden frames. The tops or lids to the boxes were on hinges. "I plant greens in here in middle fall and late winter. At night, when the temperature dips, this lid is closed," she told them, pointing to the lid which was now ajar. "I think it keeps the temperature inside about twenty degrees above the outside temperature. Then as the sun climbs in the sky, even on a fairly brisk day, I open the frames so the plants don't get burned up."

She noted the look on Tammy's face. "It's really not that hard to manage, and believe me, I've had my share of plants burned up over the years. Planting the right variety is important too," she continued, making it even more of a mystery to Tammy, who never realized how easy it was just to pick out what you wanted from the grocery store.

"Chards, spinach, and kale like the brisk weather."

What impressed Michael was the management involved. Pam had to decide when and how much to sow so that she'd be able to harvest what she needed when she needed it. In that way it was actually a more sophisticated form of farming than what her husband engaged in, which consisted of three or four cash crops, plus hay and feed corn for the animals.

"Many people think that the way of the plain people is dominated and controlled by the menfolk," Les began when they were seated around the table for supper that evening. "They maintain very separate and distinct roles between men and women both in work and when socializing, but the responsibility for the smooth working of the farmstead is equally shared by husband and wife." He took a breath to continue his thoughts.

"Now don't you start in to preachin', Les McGuffey," Pam started, "let's make sure we get everything finished up and squared away before sundown."

"By golly, you're right, woman," Les bellowed, with a big sheepish smile on his face, "but I'd like to invite our kin over for singin' tonight... Whatta ya say, Sissy, popcorn and hymns after you're finished with supper tonight?"

"That sounds just fine, brother," Tammy said, then to Pam, "You'all finish up around six o'clock or six-thirty?"

"Six-thirty'll be fine. That'll give me a chance to straighten up around here," Pam replied.

"See ya then." The O'Sheas made their way out the door and proceeded on the ten-minute stroll down the lane to the cottage.

"Are you plannin' to go to your uncle's church tomorrow, son?" Tammy asked, trying her best to sound neutral.

"They invited me again this week." There was a pause, then realizing he had not answered her question, "Yes, I'd like to, if that's okay with you, Mom?" Michael sensed that this whole area was a sensitive one for his mother, not only because she was concerned about him, but also because it was her own brother's church.

"You may go," she confirmed. "That means we'll go to the vigil Mass tonight," she announced to the family. She didn't ask him if he were going to Mass with them. She wouldn't give him that option. "Michael, you run back and tell your uncle that we'll be need'n the truck at about four o'clock to drive to Mass. I expect you're not gonna be working with Eli this afternoon?"

"No, Eli told me that Saturday afternoons are just a wind-down time. He'll just be squaring things away to keep 'til Monday."

"Okay, then, get along and tell them we still should be over by no later than seven o'clock."

Glaston was a thriving little city, but St. Anne's was a tiny parish compared to what the O'Sheas were accustomed to. They passed scores of churches on their way to Mass: Ramble Creek Missionary Baptist Church, First Methodist Church of Dunstan (Michael saw another First Methodist Church and wondered why they had two of the same churches within a few blocks of each other), the Tenth Street Church of Christ, the True Tabernacle of God Church, Antioch Baptist Church (*Were they the same folks as the Missionary Baptist Church?*), and finally, the block just before St. Anne's, there was an Assemblies of God Church.

Mass went along smoothly enough. The Gospel reading was from Matthew. It caught Michael's attention.

> At dawn, as Jesus was returning to the city, he felt hungry. Seeing a fig tree by the roadside he went over to it, but found nothing there except leaves. He said to it, "Never again shall you produce fruit!" and it withered up instantly. The disciples were dumbfounded when they saw this.

Michael was anxious to hear the sermon and see how the priest interpreted the Gospel. *Why was Jesus so angry with the tree? Was he in a bad mood? Wasn't it a bit extreme to lose patience with a tree? What was the whole point of the story?*

The sermon, however, did not explain the Gospel and didn't even seem related. The priest spoke of our duty to try to be good neighbors and citizens. The priest was actually a pretty good homilist.

After the sermon, the bread and wine were consecrated, people received Holy Communion, and the closing hymn was sung as the priest left the altar. Michael noticed some people leaving right after receiving the Eucharist. Actually there were not as many "early-leavers" as at St. John's back home.

He remembered how his Dad had felt about that. After Mass one day, his father had hit the roof, bewildered at what he saw week after week. "Why don't priests say something when people behave disrespectfully? Can't they at least put a word of instruction in the parish bulletin? What are they afraid of? They're not doing anyone any favors or any great courtesy by remaining silent. Maybe people need to be reminded once in awhile that the only apostle to leave the Last Supper early was Judas."

Mick O'Shea had had great respect for the priesthood, which was why such abuses by parishioners were particularly hurtful to him. Michael thought about how his father had impressed upon him the great sacrifices made by various priests throughout the ages.

"They have consecrated their lives totally, both priests and nuns, to serve God," he had once said, voicing his frustration at someone who was complaining about his priest. But he empathized with him, too, and said finally in a soft, tender voice, "We shouldn't expect them to be perfect, and I appreciate as well as anyone that some can really test your Christian charity, but we should help them and support them in their effort to be holy and worthy men and women. Try praying for them and offering up your frustration as a sacrifice." It was such talk, Michael realized, that had earned his father a reputation for being eccentric and hopelessly old-fashioned.

The O'Sheas were filing toward the back of the Church. Father Buchan was shaking hands at the door as people exited. Michael thought for awhile, then decided he would ask the priest about the Gospel reading.

Tammy O'Shea exchanged greetings with Father Bucham. She

mentioned that they'd be attending regularly through the summer.

"Great to have you," Father Bucham smiled. "Enjoy southern Kentucky," he said, sounding more like a travel guide than a priest.

"Why did Jesus curse the fig tree?" Michael blurted out.

"Excuse me?" Father Bucham replied, bending slightly closer to Michael. He had heard the question, but was taken completely off guard.

"Well, I was wondering about the Gospel reading today," Michael began a bit self-consciously. "Why did Jesus curse a fig tree and make it die?" It was as if he were unaware of the book of "unwritten" rules in which it was understood that such questions were not asked as one left Mass. Once you'd fulfilled your weekly obligation, it was considered appropriate to thank the priest and otherwise exchange pleasantries.

Tammy blushed slightly. It was as if one of her young children had said something socially embarrassing. She saw that the priest was uncomfortable, but she struggled to control her initial reaction. Her son certainly had every right to ask about something he didn't understand. Frankly, she didn't understand either why Jesus had bothered to curse the fig tree either or what it symbolized.

Father Bucham was still collecting his thoughts. People who bothered to ask such questions, that is, questions of substance and gravity, often ended up being troublemakers, as far as he was concerned. They never seemed satisfied. They would question further. His experience had been that such people tended to be more zealous and devout than the average parishioner. Some ended up leaving his parish unsatisfied or leaving the Church for another denomination.

"Well, the answer to that could take you a couple years in the seminary to understand fully," he laughed, trying to avoid an answer. He noticed his young student's lack of expression.

Michael didn't get the humor. Besides, he was more intent on hearing a serious answer.

"Well, we're all born with various talents, gifts, and abilities. It's up to us to use them, to bear fruit if you will. Because the fig tree had borne no fruit, Jesus condemned it," the priest summarized, with the only interpretation he thought remotely plausible. He, too, was a bit mystified with the Gospel reading. He thought it better, though, not to admit his own lack of understanding about any deeper meaning. *Why a fig tree? Why then? It didn't seem to fit in with the surrounding text in Matthew.* He just didn't know. He smiled, hoping the boy would move on.

"Thank you," said Michael, and he began to leave. It was no time to dig deeper for a more thorough explanation, and he sensed that Father Bucham was not overly enthusiastic about giving one. But still he felt unsatisfied. *Could Jesus have been in a bad mood and taken it out on a poor defenseless fig tree? Didn't Jesus teach forgiveness, charity, and long-suffering? Then he goes and curses a little tree just to teach us a lesson about using our talents?* Michael O'Shea didn't buy it, but was at a loss to offer an alternative interpretation. *I know who could explain it,* he concluded, thinking of his Uncle Les.

"Have you been up to Mammoth Cave yet?" Fr. Bucham called to them before they were out of earshot.

"Excuse me?" asked Tammy. *Did he ask if we'd been to Mammoth Cave?*

"Mammoth Cave isn't far from here," he explained. "It's a huge network of underground caverns. The kids would love a trip there." He wanted so much for people to like him and somehow to let them know that he was a nice guy. But he cringed at the thought of getting questioned about the readings every Sunday.

"No, haven't been there yet," Tammy answered, unsure whether to walk back to ask him about the caves. She was not particularly interested at this point and didn't know quite how to respond. There was an awkward pause as she waited for him to explain why they were so good or how to get there or whatever he wanted to offer.

"About an hour's drive north of here, just off I-65," he called. "The kids'll love it." He took his nieces and nephews there every time they came out to visit. He liked it because they could explore the caves all day and entertain themselves. He had difficulty relating to his brother's kids and they seemed to enjoy the caves.

"Thanks, have to take a drive up soon," Tammy said, and waved goodbye. She was relieved to have concluded the exchange. Tammy's younger boys were wondering when they would be going.

Back at the McGuffey house, the singing had already started. Some were seated around the dining room table while others were on folding chairs or chairs pulled out of the living room. The kerosene lamps glowed, and huge bowls that had been full of popcorn and apple slices were nearly empty.

"Looks like we missed the party," Tammy said as they entered the room.

"Just gettin' warmed up, sister," her brother assured her, as he hopped up to help them get seats. "You just come right on in."

Once settled, Les introduced his sister to the other guests. "And you'all remember my nephew Michael from church services last week." The people nodded and smiled.

Michael recognized only one man but didn't remember his name. He smiled back. They were dressed casually in plaid shirts and blue jeans, the women mostly in simple jumpers. Everyone looked so clean and dressed up, mostly because Michael had grown accustomed to seeing his uncle and cousin in dirty work clothes all week with matted down hair from the hats they wore. He had learned this past week that the Saturday night bath was still a way of life around here. During the week, one just washed up face and hands, underarms, and neck. It was apparently deemed sense-less and a waste of time to shower everyday when you worked under farm conditions.

"*Just a Closer Walk*," someone called out. There was a slight pause while people nodded and looked around to see if that was agreeable to everyone, then it began...

> *I am weak, but thou art strong.*
> *Jesus keep me from all wrong.*
> *I'll be satisfied as long,*
> *as I walk with thee, let me walk...*

Michael only knew the song from the movie *Cool Hand Luke*, one of his father's favorites. Listening now, he heard some angelic voices and he heard some weather-beaten, back-country-roads type voices. Together they somehow complemented one another. They sang prayerfully, with depth, and as an offering to the Lord. It was a soulful rendition.

> *... Just a closer walk with thee.*
> *Grant it, Jesus, is my plea.*
> *Daily walkin' close to thee.*
> *Let it be, dear Lord, let it be...*

Michael could hear his mom singing. She was one of those with an angelic voice, but hymns like these Michael decided sound more authentic with some rough voices. The hymn was as different from what would typically be sung back at St. John the Baptist as was the brand of Christianity that would be preached from the pulpit.

> *... And through this life of toils and snares,*
> *if I stumble, Lord, who cares?*
> *Who with me my burden shares?*
> *None but thee, dear Lord, none but thee...*

*The song makes sense,* Michael concluded, as he considered the lyrics. *It reflects the personal relationship you should have with God that Uncle Les talked about last week.*

He glanced over at Elijah's younger sister, Lori, who was sitting on the other side of the room. She had long, straight brown hair which she usually wore pulled back away from her face. She wore a brown, freshly cleaned dress. She was singing without self-consciousness right near her father. She was very pretty, Michael had decided during that first week. She was not strikingly beautiful, but her countenance seemed to grow on you. She looked more attractive every time Michael noticed her. She was always cheerful, and he would hear her sweet laugh each time he had reason to be around the McGuffey house.

After the hymn, one of the men started in with a story.

"Earlier this week one of my heifers calved. Well, you know how those first-time mothers can have some difficulty. The little calf — it was a bull calf — came a bit too early. He lived nonetheless and struggled to his feet, but I knowed he was weak and wasn't sure if he was gonna make it. I looked down at that hardy little calf as he struggled to stand and figured 'if you gonna give it your best shot, I'll do everything to help that I can.' And I babied that little calf this past week. Every morning as I went out to the barn I thought I'd likely see that calf dead. Each night as I went in I looked at 'im and didn't even think he'd make it through the night. But there he was each morning, strugglin' to get his feet under 'im and standin' up to greet me."

He paused, then continued with sadness in his voice... "Just this mornin' I came out, and sure enough this time he didn't make it through the night. I stood there starin' at that game little bull calf and asked why? Why are some babies born into the world with sickness and disease? Why do some die so young without a chance to live a full life? It seems from everything you can figure that there's sometimes no rhyme or reason why some people suffer while others don't seem to be afflicted with any great suffering.

"Well, I can't begin to answer all those questions, those mysteries of this life, but that little bull calf taught me a good lesson. The Lord spoke to me through that calf. That little animal struggled and fought for life 'til the very end. And that's just the example Paul the Apostle gave to us..." He reached for his Bible and opened it. "When Paul wrote to Timothy, it's in second Timothy four, verse six:

> For I am already being poured out as a drink offering... I have fought the good fight, I have finished the race, I have kept the faith...There is laid up for me the crown of righteousness.

"O' course, our struggle is a spiritual struggle, nonetheless there is a lot out there that can beat us down, discourage us, keep us low, weaken and even kill us spiritually."

He continued in a more upbeat voice. "Just like that little bull calf, we gotta fight. We gotta struggle. We gotta keep clawin', scratchin', and strugglin' to the end. If we do that, fight the good fight, we can walk with Paul in the Kingdom someday, walk with that crown on our head. And this much I know, that when Christians come together like this to pray, and sing hymns, and witness to one another, it's like a spiritual boost. Those early Christians 'exhorted one another daily.' We've got to help each other persevere in love, kindness, and charity. We've got to bear each other's burdens, suffer wrongs and offenses with patience, and strive to love and pray for our enemies."

Finished with his discourse, he quietly sat down.

"I appreciate that witness, George," Les responded on behalf of those listening.

Tammy considered what the man had said. It made an impression on her, as she thought about how people such as George were viewed by many "sophisticated" people whom she knew back east. The typical attitude was that devout Christians in the South and Mid-West were self-righteous, bigoted, extremist imbeciles. Even otherwise good Catholics often regarded such "Bible Christians" with similar disdain, eyeing them with great suspicion. It was assumed that they were both judgmental and anti-Catholic. Tammy, however, knew better. She realized that while many of them were guilty of anti-Catholicism, they tended to be tremendously charitable when it came to dealing with people on an individual level. Most of these people were like George — humble, devout, responsible, and thirsting for God in their lives. Most would not lie, cheat, or steal from you, regardless of your faith or ethnic background.

Michael again noted the glaring difference from the religious culture in which he had been raised. His father had been an altar boy, Uncle Matty had been one, he had been one, and next year his brother would become one. They were Catholic through and through, in their experiences, their ways, and their thinking. However, it was impossible for Michael to imagine his family, Uncle Matty's family, and other families from the old neighborhood getting together to sing hymns on a Saturday night. *Would never happen, especially if there were a Flyers game on that night.* Nor could he envision his Uncle Matty relating an everyday experience and tying it in some way to a passage in Scripture, as George had just done. That *really* would never have happened.

"This baby needs to go down," Tammy said to her brother, as she rose to leave.

"Eli'll drive you back," Les offered.

"It's a nice evening, we'll walk," she insisted, "Tim and Dante will make sure no wild animals sneak up on us... Come on, guys," she called to her two younger boys. "Don't be too late, Michael," she said as she left the room.

Michael was glad he could stay. It made him feel more mature. After all, he had been working all week with "the men." It wouldn't be right to be treated like a boy now.

More hymns were sung. Michael was not familiar with them and had to consult the hymnal. He wasn't much of a singer, he had decided, and therefore justified his not putting forth too great an effort.

Between hymns someone brought up "the tobacco issue," as they referred to it. It was discussed briefly and decided that they'd hold a council about it this coming Wednesday night. After an hour or so of singing, the guests started to make their way to the door. Then the McGuffeys began heading off to bed. Michael, too, started to leave. He remembered his mom's final words, about not staying too late, but his uncle would have none of it.

"Stick around, Michael. We'll have a cup of coffee." Michael smiled and stayed put. Elijah was also tarrying awhile longer. *It really isn't late — only nine o'clock*, Michael said to himself.

"I'll put some water on to boil on my way up to bed," Pam said.

"Thanks, we won't be too long," Les replied, as he winked at Michael. "Don't worry, we drink decaf around here."

Michael hadn't been worrying about the caffeine. He didn't even drink coffee at home, but the invitation to have a mug with his uncle was a nice boost. It was as if he were being invited into "the club." He had reached a good comfort level with his uncle and cousin over the past week and this "after-hours" coffee drinking was like a ritual ceremony that acknowledged the bond that was developing.

"Whatta ya got to say for yourself after a week on the farmstead?" Les threw out, as a way to get the conversation rolling.

"Well, I've enjoyed it, Uncle Les. I really have." He thought back to two weeks ago when he was back home in Philadelphia. The novelty of life on the farm was still there, yet he had been able to settle in over the past week. They proceeded to talk about the farm and the upcoming growing season. Their mugs were about half empty when there was a lull in the conversation.

"What was the 'tobacco issue' thing all about?" queried Michael.

The notion that he was prying or presuming too much on his uncle's treatment of him as a young man quickly emerged in his head.

"Oh, that's interesting, Michael," Les began, "let me give you a little background. I don't know how much you know about our little church, or my history as a preacher, but it all has something to do with that. I originally left the Presbyterian denomination years ago, when I was still in the Marines, and started going to a Baptist service. When I got out and came back home, I started going to Dunstan Baptist. I thought of myself as a good Baptist, even became an elder — or what the Presbyterians call a presbyter — and later became a minister. That was almost ten years ago."

Les sipped from his big mug, then continued. "Then I asked a couple questions, things I was interested in, things that we were doing that didn't seem on the surface to square up with the Word." He tapped his Bible, which lay on the table, three times with his index finger. "Now all that was fine by me. I was just seeking explanation and clarification. I wasn't assuming, at that point, that I was right and the way the Baptist church did it was wrong. I really thought that one of the elders or other ministers could give me a good interpretation of the things I didn't understand, and that's all I was looking for. I mean, we were members of the Middle Southern Baptist Alliance. We had hundreds of member churches in a couple different states and hundreds of thousands of individual members. Surely we all weren't doing something that was just flat out wrong."

Les paused for a moment at this juncture and considered how to explain all that happened so that it would make sense to a young man completely unfamiliar with such things. *This can be made to fit in with the situation Michael's in,* he thought. *What happened to me is pretty much what'll happen to him in his church.*

"Let me give you an example." Les picked up his Bible. "Go to first Corinthians eleven." There was another Bible on the table and Michael paged through quickly. He didn't really know where the book of Corinthians was in the New Testament.

"Starting at verse four, it says that any man who prays with his head covered brings shame upon his head. Then the very next verse says 'But every woman who prays or prophesies with her head uncovered dishonors her head,' then it goes on to say 'For if a woman is not covered, let her also be shorn.' Now we know that can't be a good thing because a few lines down, Scripture tells us that the long hair of a woman is her glory. A woman ought to have her head covered while at prayer is what it says, right?" Les knew that the Catholics did not require women to cover their heads in church.

"Sure enough seems to," Michael answered, realizing exactly what Les was thinking about Catholic women and their lack of head coverings. *The women in his uncle's church did cover their heads during prayers last Sunday*, Michael remembered, *then they took them off for the preaching and singing*. He remembered, too, that his grandmother always wore a veil at Mass and that most of the older women did. He had no idea how to explain the Catholic practice, but knew there must be an explanation. He glanced over at First Corinthians 11 and continued reading further down to see...

> I received from the Lord that which I also delivered to you: that the Lord Jesus on the same night in which He was betrayed took bread; and when he had given thanks He broke it and said, "Take, eat; this is My body, which is broken for you; do this in remembrance of Me." In the same manner, He also took the cup after supper, saying, "This cup is the new covenant in My blood. This do, as often as you drink it, in remembrance of me." ...whoever eats this bread or drinks this cup of the Lord in an unworthy manner will be guilty of the body and blood of the Lord... For he who eats and drinks in an unworthy manner eats and drinks judgment to himself, not discerning the Lord's body.

It seemed that way to me, too," continued Les. "I asked about this whole head covering issue and some of the other things that Paul wrote about, like women being teachers. I got some answers to my questions and for a while they satisfied me. Then the more I considered what Scripture actually said, the more uncomfortable I got and asked some more. Before long, I was just thought of as a troublemaker." There was a remnant of pain in Les's voice. "'A contentious man' is what one of the ministers called me."

Michael was amazed that his uncle was telling him all this, and obviously Elijah was familiar with the whole story.

"Y'see, Michael, I was not thought of as a sincere brother in search of a deeper understanding. No, I was a *troublemaker*." He emphasized that word but his voice was stronger now and assertive. "Well, what was happenin' to me can be found in Scripture." He paged through his Bible until he found what he was looking for. "Second Timothy four, verse three reads,

> For the time will come when they will not endure sound doctrine, but according to their own desires, because they have itching ears, they will heap up for themselves teachers.

"In the end, I realized that they, and so many of the Protestant churches, were doing the same thing that they criticize the Catholics for doing. They were placing the traditions of man on the same level as the Word of God," his hand came down flat on the table with a slam. "That's when we left the Baptist church and just home-churched for awhile. It was in those times that we changed our lifestyle and felt called to live plainly, made a commitment to study the Word, and just asked for the Lord to guide us along His way.

"Then the Lord began sending people in our path. Everyone in this little county knew what had happened to us. Many of them were having the same things going on in their churches and were frustrated. They were being called out by God, out of the churches and denominations many had grown up in, been married in, buried their parents in."

Les paused a moment, then began his summation. "We don't identify ourselves as Protestants, I mean the people of our church. We call ourselves Christians and we endeavor to follow the Word of God. I believe the Lord is calling people out of their various denominations to love and serve Him and follow His way as was laid out for us in Scripture. The Lord didn't want all of this denominationalism, this forty flavors of Christianity. He has but one flock the world over that needs to re-discover the ways of the early disciples."

Michael sat there dumbfounded. His uncle had reached yet a new level of passion in this discourse. *Does he think I'm being called out?* wondered Michael. *How do you know if you're being "called out," or just making a judgment that feels right or seems to make biblical sense?* He didn't dare ask such questions.

"Now what does all that have to do with tobacco, you're probably wondering?" he took up where he left off.

Michael had indeed forgotten his original question.

"Well, the early Church had disputes and areas that needed clarification and interpretation, and what did they do?" Sensing that it was a rhetorical question, Michael didn't even attempt to answer.

"They came together in a council," Les continued, while leafing through his Bible. "There were some in the early days insisting that the Gentile converts had to be circumcised in order to become Christians, said they had to start following the whole Mosaic ritual law. Remember this whole movement of Christianity began amongst the Jews. Christ didn't have Gentile apostles or disciples. He told them first to preach to the house of Israel. Acts fifteen begins:

> And certain men came down from Judea and taught the brethren, "Unless you are circumcised according to the custom of Moses, you cannot be saved."

"This created dissension among them," Les explained as he looked up. "They determined" – *He was reading from Scripture again* — "that

86

Paul and Barnabas and certain others of them should go up to Jerusalem, to the apostles and elders, about this question.

"Now if you go down to verse six it says: 'Now the apostles and elders came together to consider this matter.' They settled matters by meeting in a council. That's not the way the Baptists did it when I was at that church. No, those in authority decided to settle issues how they saw fit."

*Weren't the ones who met in Jerusalem those in authority?* thought Michael. *Everyone didn't travel to Jerusalem to address the issue — just Paul, Barnabas and some others.* Michael read on as his uncle got up from the table to refill his mug. He found where his uncle had stopped and began reading at verse seven:

> And when there had been much dispute, Peter rose up and said to them: "Men and brethren, you know that a good while ago God chose among us, that by my mouth the Gentiles should hear the word of the gospel and believe. So God, who knows the heart, acknowledged them by giving them the Holy Spirit, just as he did to us, and made no distinction between us and them, purifying their hearts by faith. Now therefore, why do you test God by putting a yoke on the neck of the disciples which neither our fathers nor we were able to bear? But we believe that through the grace of the Lord Jesus Christ we shall be saved in the same manner as they." Then all the multitude kept silent...

*Seems like Peter was the one who settled that matter*, thought Michael. *Doesn't sound like they voted on it.*

"Now, growin' tobacco is big in Kentucky. We produce more tobacco than any other state, except North Carolina. Some families have been growin' tobacco for a couple generations. Some of their earliest memories is of settin' tobacco plants with their grandpappies, then cultivatin', harvestin', strippin', dryin' it out in the barns, then finally drivin' the harvest over to the big auction. I don't know if you can really appreciate what tobacco means to some of these farmers. I don't know if I can. You know your Granddaddy was a coal miner, not a farmer."

Les continued, finally addressing the original question directly. "Some of the folks in the church are thinkin' that Christians shouldn't be farmin' tobacco. They say that smokin' cigarettes does nothing but harm to the body and that's not what we should be about. Of course, tobacco's been discussed so much in the past couple of years about how bad it is, and how young kids get suckered in and so on, but the farmers growin' tobacco in our church are pretty simple folks, just tryin' to make a livin' and carry on a tradition. Are they responsible for spreading disease and ill health? I guess that's the question. That's what this upcomin' council is goin' to address, whether sincere Christians can grow tobacco."

"That's coming up this week?" Michael asked. Again he was amazed at the contrast between the little independent Christian church and his own parish. Things like this just didn't happen back home at his church. The parish council concerned itself with the budget and deciding when the gym floor needed re-finishing or the parking lot some patch work.

"What is it, like a debate or something?"

"Well I wouldn't want to call it a debate, but each side gets to present their position using Scripture," Les explained.

"How do you determine who wins?"

"Well, a Christian shouldn't be interested in winning or losing, Michael." The question struck Les. "Our responsibility is to be led by Scripture. We're interested in the truth."

"Sorry," Michael began, realizing his choice of words was not the best, "I didn't really mean to compare it to a pick-up game of basketball."

Michael still didn't quite understand how such issues would ultimately be resolved. *Did the truth just become obvious to everyone? Did the best debater win? They must have some real 'knock 'em down, drag 'em out' showdowns*, he thought.

"You're welcome to come along on Wednesday night," Les said, excited that his nephew seemed to be interested.

"I'd like that. You're goin', Eli"?

Eli nodded.

They talked some more, then Michael walked back to the cottage. He got ready for bed by the light of a dim oil lamp his mother had left burning for him in the kitchen.

Tammy had just finished her Rosary when she heard her oldest child come in. She thanked God for answering her final prayer and drifted off to sleep.

# 5

A fter chores and breakfast the next morning, Michael headed off with the McGuffeys to the church service. He thought back to First Corinthians 11 and wondered if they ever had anything like the Eucharist at his uncle's church. He thought about what he had read the night before...

> This cup is the new covenant in My blood... whoever eats this bread or drinks this cup of the Lord in an unworthy manner will be guilty of the body and blood of the Lord... he who eats and drinks in an unworthy manner eats and drinks judgment to himself, not discerning the Lord's body.

He had read First Corinthians again before falling asleep. He knew that Protestants celebrated what they called "the Lord's Supper," but that they didn't consider the bread and wine to be the real flesh and blood of Christ, that Jesus was only using a metaphor.

*Pretty strong language if it's just symbolic,* thought Michael as he considered it all again, but he could see their point. How can Christ be present in that tiny wafer and in red wine? Michael couldn't admit that he really believed, only that he knew what he was supposed to believe as a Catholic. *How do we know Jesus meant it to be taken literally? Maybe I would have assumed it was just symbolic if I were there myself.*

Things at the church began much the same as they had the previous week. Michael found the singing to be very uplifting. *That's one thing they sure do better than Catholics*, he decided.

After many hymns it was time for his uncle to preach.

"Brothers and sisters, as you know, we'll be convening on Wednesday of this week, in the evening, to look into the biblical instruction that might help us shed light on whether or not a Christian should be growing tobacco for his livelihood. I bring this up to suggest to you that this is not a 'problem' that we are facing."

Michael thought he heard some stirring in the congregation. He wondered if it was the growers or those against growing who were finding it more difficult to sit still.

"No, not at all." His uncle's tone was deliberate and calm. "Rather, I see it as more evidence that the Lord has called our little tiny church into existence. You see, brethren, I've seen how other churches handle such issues that might arise. The leadership convenes, it is discussed behind closed doors, they consider how it might affect how much is taken in the tithing basket, and they render a decision."

Michael had not heard such cutting remarks from his uncle before.

"Well, that is not how the early Christians did it. I had the pleasure of discussing this very issue with my young nephew just last night."

Michael could feel the eyeballs zeroing in on the back and sides of his head.

"We went to Acts chapter fifteen to find out how such issues were resolved."

*I didn't realize it was a collaborative effort*, Michael mused.

Les repeated to the assembly — more exhaustively and with greater animation — what he had gone over with Michael the night before. Michael noticed that his uncle again stopped reading Acts 15 just before the part in which Peter rose to address the early Christians. At that point his uncle simply explained how the whole thing turned out, how Scripture made it clear what the appropriate decision had to be.

He summed up his sermon message with... "They consulted the Word, friends." Les held the Bible up over his head. "It's all right here. It was given to us as a gift so that we might know Christ, that we might be directed in doing what pleases him. If we endeavor to search his Word, he'll guide us to all truth and we'll come to a decision. That's what we're going to do this week. Let us then be thankful that a few leaders can't just decide arbitrarily — like they do in some of the big, prestigious denominations — what is the right thing. If you don't trust the very Word of God to guide us then you're better off just leaving now." Les paused.

It didn't surprise Michael that no one left. *Did his uncle really expect anyone to?*

"And since you didn't leave, I'll not ask you to leave if you happen to disagree with how we are led by Scripture. You'll not be shunned, as the plain people practice. You'll not be excommunicated by Rome."

This reference caught Michael's attention.

"No, I can't separate you from Christ. No man has the authority to do that as long as you persevere in the faith. We recognize Christ as the Head of the Church. I am not the head of any church with the power to cast out believers that I don't agree with. I don't assume the authority that the local Amish bishop wields or that any bishop sitting in Rome exercises. We don't follow some tradition of man that teaches that Peter was somehow left in charge to make all the decisions for everyone when Christ died and that whoever sits in his office, even until today, still has that power."

Now Michael was sure that the first reference to Rome and excommunication was a strike at the Catholic Church.

Les McGuffey had decided to preach with abandon, to be ever bolder in his effort to sway his sister's family through Michael. Michael was the first domino in the family.

For his part, Michael wondered about the implications of his uncle's words. *We'll search Scripture to determine what the truth is... but if we can't all agree in the end, then so be it...*

Back at the farmstead, Tammy sat on a rock by the side of the creek. Dante and Tim were playing upstream and Kate toddled on the grass at her mother's feet. Thinking of Michael she decided to pray. She offered up a short prayer to the Blessed Mother in thanksgiving for the glorious day and all they had received. She prayed for the soul of her husband and for spiritual protection for her son. She asked the Queen of Heaven to present her petitions to her Son, the King.

*What he's saying makes the Catholic Church seem pretty bad,* thought Michael, *but even worse is <u>how</u> he's saying it.*

Les continued with the Bible held aloft over his head. "Then as a fellow believer in God the Father, Christ the Son, and the Holy Word contained in this book, I encourage and exhort you not to become discouraged because some issues seem to come between the brethren. In a sincere search for the truth, the Holy Spirit will guide our steps. Our part is to persevere in our walk with Christ." With that, Les backed away and sat down.

*He is enjoyable to listen to,* Michael realized yet again, *but somehow not so convincing this week. Would the Holy Spirit lead some to be proponents of tobacco and others to stand against it? Does the Holy Spirit concern himself with tobacco at all?*

Unlike the concept of mediation between God and man — that Jesus was the only mediator — this message was not as clearly presented from the Scripture that his uncle used. He didn't present the whole picture when he interpreted Acts 15, decided Michael. It was just the *leadership* of the early Church who met in Jerusalem. Also, it seemed that the matter did not just become evident over time as they continued to address it, as Uncle Les had suggested. Rather it was Peter who, after all the discussion, took the floor and spoke to the entire assembly to explain and then seal the decision.

Michael also questioned some of the other things his uncle had said. *Why don't non-Catholics believe Peter was the leader of the Apostles?*

*For that matter, why do we think he was?* He knew his father had taught him about the special role that Peter had had, but he couldn't remember anything specifically about it except that Peter was the first Pope.

After the service they all walked home along the creek.

"Uncle Les," Michael began, "do you know how in the Gospel of Matthew Jesus got angry with a fig tree and cursed it?"

"Yeah, I'm familiar with it," Les responded. He was glad his nephew seemed to be striking up a conversation. He was beginning to get concerned that he had insulted him deeply with his barbs about Rome and papal authority.

"Why did he do that? I mean, besides the fact that he was hungry and the tree had no fruit."

"That's a good question, Michael," Les nodded. "Let's take a look at that. In fact, we can stop here by the creek. Pam, you go on ahead home with the rest of the children. I know we've got company this afternoon. Elijah, Michael, and I are just going to set by the creek awhile and figure this one out."

"All right, but mind the time," Pam said, before continuing on.

Michael and Les found suitable rocks to sit on. Elijah sat on a fallen tree trunk.

"That's Matthew twenty-one, right?" Les already had his Bible open to the passage.

"That's right," Michael responded. Elijah had his Bible open, too.

"I'm not surprised that it's a bit confusing to you," Les began. "First we've got to understand some things about Matthew's Gospel and then consider it in the context of where Christ was at this point of his mission. Now, the first Gospel was directed at the Jews. That is, that's who the audience was. We can understand that by looking at how it was written and what kind of terms are used, namely in a way and using language that would be especially appropriate for a Jewish audience. Do you follow?"

"Give me an example," Michael asked. He could feel his confidence growing in dealing with his uncle. A week ago he would have just nodded yes.

"Okay, the term 'Messiah,' used in Matthew, is a term peculiarly familiar to the Israelites. In the very beginning of the Gospel, the author gives us this very long, drawn-out family record or genealogy of Jesus: Abraham was the father of Isaac, Isaac was the father of Jacob, Jacob of Judah, on down through Joseph the carpenter.

"For any other people, this drawn-out genealogy would be painfully boring, but not for the Jews. They understood from Scripture — what we now call the Old Testament — that God made a covenant with Abraham. This covenant included the promise of a kingdom, that the tribe of Judah would be the source of its kings and one day, the Messiah. Matthew cites Scripture to explain things to his audience, again the Old Testament... Remember, what we call the New Testament was not compiled until long after Christ was crucified," Les said parenthetically.

"All this wouldn't make sense if he were writing to non-Jews. Now to the fig tree... You're gettin' more than you bargained for, aren't you?" Les joked.

"Not a problem," Michael responded, "all of what you've explained is news to me." Michael was wondering why Father Bucham wouldn't, or maybe couldn't (he didn't know which was worse), answer his question this well.

"Now, just before the 'fig tree' what happens? Jesus comes into Jerusalem riding an ass and the crowds love him, layin' cloaks and branches on the ground before his humble little animal. And what was Jerusalem? The center of the world, if you were Jewish. The site of the foundation rock, upon which the Temple stood. The learned, the influential, and the powerful controlled Jerusalem and were responsible for the Temple. You remember the Levites and Aaronites from last week?"

Michael nodded.

"Jerusalem was New York, Chicago, and L.A. all rolled into one. So we have the entire Temple 'establishment' on the one hand, and this rabble-rousing, young upstart, who is exciting the crowds, on the other. Now the establishment knew of this Jesus character who had likely been in Jerusalem before during his ministry. But this time was going to be the showdown, so to speak. So what does Christ do when he gets to the Temple? Does he lay low to show the powers that be that he isn't contesting their 'turf'? Does he extend the hand of peace to them that are plotting to destroy him? Does he gently encourage the elite to take up their crosses daily and follow him? *Not on your life!*" Les bellowed with great animation. "He went into the Temple and cleaned house!" He was still animated. "Threw out the money changers — all those buying and selling. He came to the great city in these last few days of his life to point his proverbial finger at the Pharisees, Sadducees, and scribes — the entire establishment — in bitter rebuke. This is all happening right before the fig tree is cursed the next day."

Michael was soaking it all in. It had never been presented to him in such a way to make it simple, interesting, and exciting. He was beginning to see a Jesus he never knew — a radical, anti-establishment type. This radical, though, extended his hand to the blind and lame right after cleaning out the Temple. He didn't seek to consolidate power by forming an alliance with those who could have helped him in a temporal sense. He had all the power and popularity at that time to launch an armed rebellion, but that was not why he had come.

Michael suddenly understood it all better. He thought of some of the teenagers back home who hung out together on Ridge Avenue at night. They wouldn't be caught dead at St. John's, even though that's where they had been baptized, made their first Holy Communion, and been confirmed. They thought of the people who went to Church as a bunch of hypocrites and phonies. *Maybe they're right to some extent,* he thought, *but they've missed the whole point of Jesus' message. They were never introduced to*

<u>this</u> *Jesus, the one who was not afraid to "rock the boat," who tossed out the "respectable" and invited in the pathetic; the one who was flogged, crowned with thorns, and nailed to a cross for their sake.*

"The fig tree," continued Les, "represents Jerusalem. They, the learned establishment, the ones who studied Scripture, who followed the Mosaic Law, couldn't recognize the Messiah. They couldn't see the forest for the trees. So concerned were they with social position, material goods, and being viewed as righteous by others that they railroaded their Savior. It was spelled out for them in Scripture, but they were too sophisticated. Conversely, the simple and lowly recognized and accepted him.

"Let's look at Matthew twenty-one, startin' with verse forty-two:

> Jesus said to them, "Did you never read in the scriptures: 'The stone that the builders rejected has become the cornerstone; by the Lord has this been done, and it is wonderful in our eyes'? Therefore, I say to you, the kingdom of God will be taken away from you and given to a people that will produce its fruit.

"When Jesus returned to Jerusalem, he dealt with the chief priests and elders cleverly, then went on to tell three parables in a row: the two sons, the tenants, and the wedding banquet. They knew those parables were directed at them and that he had to be dealt with before he destroyed their credibility completely. I'll let you read through the next couple of chapters in Matthew. Check out the beginning of chapter twenty-three especially — that's where he really let's 'em have it." Les wanted his nephew to read and understand the point he was making, but also knew that Michael would come across the "Do not call anyone on earth your father" verse in Chapter 23.

"We'd better get a move on, Pop," Elijah interjected at the pause.

"Right Eli, let's go before your mother starts to howl."

Back at the McGuffeys', the company had already arrived. There were lots of children running about. It was so pleasant outside that everyone gathered on the porch while they awaited the meal. There was a porch swing, a glider, and Eli came out with some folding chairs.

Michael recognized Les's guest as one of the men from his uncle's church.

"I'm gonna get going, Uncle Les," Michael began. He wanted to slip out before Les got involved with his company.

"If you could just wait one minute." Les got hold of the father of the family. "Michael, this here is Luther Moore," Les said as he led Luther over to Michael.

"Michael O'Shea," Michael responded, as he shook the man's hand.

Luther already knew all about Michael, but had not been formally introduced. Luther seemed short, standing there next to Les. He wore a beard and had intense but animated eyes.

"Pleasure to meet you." The man seemed polite and pleasant. "You're new down at the church?" He asked, though he knew that already.

"Yes, sir, just down from Philadelphia visitin' my uncle for the summer."

"Do you attend a church back home where you live?" Luther wasted no time in zeroing in.

"Yes, we go to a church right in our neighborhood." Michael was purposely ambiguous about belonging to the Catholic Church, especially after today's sermon.

"Uh huh," the man nodded, "what's the name of that Church, or is it a particular denomination?" Luther couldn't be so easily deflected. He was in bloodhound mode and was already picking up a scent. He knew beforehand that Michael was a Catholic.

"St. John the Baptist." Michael didn't bother offering that he was a Catholic after naming his parish. It seemed obvious enough, especially with a last name like O'Shea.

"That's a Catholic Church?"

"Yes."

Luther's accent seemed more pronounced than anyone he had ever met from the South. Suddenly Michael realized it was that "backwoods preacher talk" that his Dad used to joke with his mother about. *It's for real.*

Luther was on the trail! Les had since moved inside the house. He knew Luther would start in with the big guns, which was partly why he had been invited. Les thought it best to make himself scarce. It was almost painful to watch Luther "at work."

"What did you think of the sermon today?" Luther began in again.

"I enjoyed it," Michael answered politely. Luther nodded his headed as he considered his next charge.

"Well, the reason I ask is, I imagine that it must have been challenging for someone like yourself coming from a Catholic background." Luther noticed Michael's look of slight confusion. "I mean, the way I understand it is that you'all have to obey a church hierarchy, that they more or less tell you what to believe and what not to believe."

Michael didn't know how to respond. He guessed there was some truth to what the man asserted, as far as he understood, but would not have expressed it like that.

"Well, we have the Pope and other bishops and then priests at the local parish level," Michael began, knowing it wasn't really an answer.

"Yeah, well that's what I mean. Now don't get me wrong. I hope you don't feel that I am somehow doubting you or questioning what you believe."

Luther was very expressive and animated.

"See, I come from kind of a similar background as you. I was raised a Baptist."

*That's a similar background?* Michael asked himself.

"I was married in the Baptist church and even became an elder in my church."

As he related this, his projection of empathy and support was apparent. He had shifted from straight interrogation to an "I was once like you" approach.

"But to make a long story short, what we believed or at least what we said we believed was not always what was in this book." He held out his Bible, which he had had in his hand since they had begun talking.

*Not the best position to be in, arguing religion with a guy who carries a Bible even while socializing,* Michael thought. He realized Luther was implying that he had "figured it out" and saved himself. Now, he felt responsible to rescue others.

"Now, the Baptists aren't exactly like the Catholics. They don't follow some king in another country, light candles, and worship the dead and many other things that Catholics do, but they still practice all kinds of unbiblical traditions. They would insist they don't, but once you start showing them from the Word, they have to admit they do. Of course, then, unfortunately, they'd sooner throw you out of their church than embrace the Word. I am truly concerned about the souls of people who, as Scripture says, 'worship God with their lips but their hearts are far from Him.' That includes many people in my own blood family."

"That's unfortunate," Michael began, not knowing quite how to handle the situation or how to counter some of the comments Luther had made. "We all should be open to hearing from others and not disregard what they say just because we don't agree immediately."

"Well, I'm glad to hear you say that," Luther jumped right back in. As far as he was concerned, this was giving him the green light to point out the errors of the Catholic Church. "So like I was saying, that sermon today must have been quite a challenge for your ears." It was not a question, rather a statement that demanded a response.

"How do you mean?" Michael asked. He thought he knew roughly what Luther was getting at, but didn't want to start talking and spouting errors. He was by this time quite intimidated by this powerful-looking, intent little man.

"Well, you'all have this Pope who lives in Rome and at least, from what I understand, you believe he doesn't make mistakes, that he's infallible." He said it politely, but it was nonetheless clear that he viewed such a belief as incomprehensible.

"We do believe the Pope is infallible," Michael struggled to answer. He did not offer an explanation as to what infallibility meant, though, because he was too nervous and a bit unclear about it himself. He knew, however, that it *didn't* mean that the Pope never made any mistakes.

"Well, y'see, that's unscriptural." Luther was hot on the trail. He would have this prey tree'd in no time. "Paul says in Romans chapter three, verse nine that all men have sinned. Now sin is a mistake. All men are sinners." He was in full preaching mode now. "That means I'm a sinner, you're a sinner, and anyone sittin' in Rome, even if he thinks he's infallible or the whole rest of the world thinks he is, he is a sinner." He paused. Getting no reaction from Michael, he continued, "Where in the Bible does Jesus tell someone to be the leader of the church? Y'know, the word 'church' is hardly even in the Bible."

"Well, we believe that Peter was the leader of the early Church," Michael offered with no confidence that this would satisfy his questioner.

"Now I've heard that that was what Catholics believe. I just don't know how to account for it, because that is so contrary to what the Bible actually says. We've got all these people runnin' around out here teachin' deceptions, and bunches more just acceptin' 'em without question. Why? We got God's Holy Word right here. What does it say about Peter?" He began flipping through the Bible.

"Peter's the one who insists that he'll be loyal to Jesus, it's right here in Mark fourteen. I can appreciate his spirit and intentions, but let's see what happens. Peter takes the sword to one of the guards who comes to arrest Jesus. Jesus rebukes him for doing that. Y'see, Peter still didn't understand that Jesus had to go through this. But later, when Peter didn't have a big sword to swing around, he denied our Lord three times. Later, after Christ died and rose, Peter still stumbled. Now don't get me wrong. Peter was one of the twelve chosen. I believe Jesus picked these men who displayed their weaknesses at times to show us that we need to rely on Him, that *Jesus* was to be the leader and the head — and the only head — of the Church."

Michael nodded; he didn't know what else to do.

"Over here in Galatians," Luther paged forward in his Bible, "now this is Paul writing about Peter, beginning at Galatians two, verse eleven:

> Now when Peter had come to Antioch, I withstood him to his face, because he was to be blamed; for before certain men came from James, he would eat with the Gentiles; but when they came, he withdrew and separated himself, fearing those who were of the circumcision.

"We don't need to go into what this was all about. It has to do with the relationship between the Jews and Gentiles, the purpose of the law, and so on, but we see Paul insisting that Peter was in the wrong and he rebuked him in the presence of all." Luther paused to consider his words. "It's just amazing to me how a group of people could be deceived into believing in the Pope based on the understanding that Peter was the first one. All the Scriptural evidence is against that. They just don't read the Bible. They can't be reading it or else they'd know better. Paul warns us constantly about false teachers, deceivers, myths, fables and gossip. And he said that many will be deceived."

Luther remained silent for just a moment, then continued in a compassionate and caring voice. "It's going to be hard for you, Michael. All those people you grew up with are going to say you're wrong and cast you out. It happened to me with my old Baptist friends. But you know enough of the truth to let your eyes be opened. Start reading the Bible and don't let other folks tell you what it means — you can know what it means for yourself. You don't need some priest to tell you what you can read and under-

103

stand yourself."

"What about when Jesus called Peter the 'rock'?" Michael asked. He had remembered that just as Luther was finishing up.

Luther flipped back in his Bible a bit impatiently. He searched for the text. "You're talkin' about Matthew sixteen?"

"I guess that's it, I don't have a Bible." Michael wouldn't have known where to find the passage anyway.

"All right. I've heard that Catholics believe that this was when Christ made Peter the leader," Luther began. It frustrated him a little, but a short explanation was a small price to pay for being able to snatch a soul from Satan. "I already showed you how Peter was not infallible, that he made mistakes. In this passage, verse eighteen" (he tilted the Bible over so that Michael could read along), "he calls Peter 'rock,' and then says, 'on this rock I will build My church.' The first time he is calling Peter the rock, but the second time he says rock, he's talking about what Peter just said before this, back up in verse sixteen. Peter is the one who says 'you are the Christ.' So the second 'rock' refers directly back to what is called Peter's confession. And that's right, the church is built on the acceptance that Christ is our Savior."

Michael had been listening with one ear but had continued reading down Chapter 16 where Christ was still addressing Peter:

> "And I will give you the keys of the kingdom, and whatever you bind on earth will be bound in heaven, and whatever you loose on earth will be loosed in heaven."

"You made an interesting point when you told me not to let anyone else tell me what the Bible says or how to understand it," Michael said matter-of-factly.

Luther nodded, hopeful that the young man was truly considering what he had said. Just then Les made his way over.

"Luther was one of the first members of our church, Michael," Les began, "we're thankful to have him in the congregation."

"That's great." Michael didn't know what else to say.

"Luther has some concerns about how appropriate it is for Christians to be growing tobacco."

"Oh, so you're the one who brought the issue up at church," Michael said as he realized the connection.

"Yes, I am. Scripture makes it clear that Christians shouldn't be engaged in such business activity," Luther replied.

Michael couldn't decide if Luther was maybe a bit defensive in tone. *Where is Scripture clear with regard to tobacco growing?* Michael wondered, but he dared not ask.

"Listen, I've got to be gettin' home now, Uncle Les," Michael said, thinking this would be a good time to break away — before Luther began a long tobacco growing discourse. The Bible has nothing to say directly about growing tobacco, Michael was sure, and he wasn't about to hang around and learn from Luther how Scripture could be clear on such an issue.

The rest of that lazy Sunday, Michael read the Bible and sought out commentary on various points from the books in his father's collection. He was fascinated. What impressed him most was the depth and breadth of scholarship available in this small sampling of books. None of the authors merely told you what the Bible said in any given area, much less insisted on the simplicity of it. Rather, commentary was built on centuries of biblical scholarship, many times going back many years before Christ to examine how the Israelites interpreted something.

He was especially drawn to a book entitled *Where We Got The Bible,* with the subtitle *Our Debt to the Catholic Church,* by Henry G.

Graham. Michael held the book and considered the title. *Why do all these people down here even believe in the Bible? Who wrote or compiled the writings of the Bible? Who said that this was all that should be included in the Bible and no more?* He considered his situation. *Could Les answer any of these questions? How about Luther?... This book might help me answer them,* he decided, as he put it aside to read it.

He located another book — *Our Father's Plan*, by Scott Hahn and Jeff Cavins — that went through the 14 historical books of the Bible in order to develop a basis for understanding the story of salvation. It was a book to be read in conjunction with the Bible. In his conversations with his Uncle Les and Luther Moore, Michael had felt so abysmally inferior with regard to knowledge of and familiarity with the Bible. His uncle's command of it and Luther's passion for it intimidated him. *Who was Melchizedek? Who was Isaac? Ishmael? Nebuchadnezzar or Hezekiah? Why were they important? Why did God want his people circumcised? What was the beast of Revelation — the dragon?*

He was lost when asked to give a response to something. He couldn't ask his father now. *Well, no place to start like the beginning,* he mused, *or even before the beginning,* as he considered the book about the Bible's origin.

As Michael read about the Bible, he was overwhelmed with new information. His confidence grew. *You can't possibly begin to comprehend the Scriptures,* he realized, *without an understanding of how and why they were compiled in the first place.* The content of the New Testament — called the canon — was not settled until the councils of Hippo and Carthage, which took place in the latter part of the fourth century and early fifth century. Before that time there existed roughly fifty Gospels. Various books circulated among Christians, including a Gospel of James, a Gospel of Thomas, Acts of Pilate, Acts of Paul, and many other epistles.

After much prayer, consideration, and discussion, the councils decided which books were definitely inspired and which were spurious. They sent their decision to Rome for confirmation, for no council (meeting of bishops of the Catholic Church for the settlement of some point of doctrine) was ever to be considered authoritative or binding unless it was approved and confirmed by the bishop of Rome, the Pope. In that way it would become binding for all members of the Church.

Michael learned that the translation of the Bible was the work of one man, a monk named Jerome. He translated the entire New Testament from its original Greek to Latin and the Old Testament, not from the Greek Septuagint that was used at the time of Christ, but from the original Hebrew. Jerome even sought the help of Jewish scholars when the Hebrew was particularly difficult.

Michael read that the books of the Bible are nowhere listed in the Bible, rather that the "canon" of the Bible was established by Rome. The Church never considered the Bible to be a catechism, but rather a collection of writings about the ministry of Christ and various letters and epistles. They were read by the early Christians to inspire, to encourage thought and contemplation, and to give all Christians a window into the ways of Christ. Most importantly, he learned that the Church insisted that she and she alone had the right to render authoritative interpretation of Scripture. After all, it was her collection of books.

Bolstered with this new insight, Michael determined to learn what her interpretation was, to become a patient and diligent student. He may not know as much about what was in the Bible as his uncle or Luther or any of the people he had met, but he was beginning to perceive that their view could be lacking.

Tammy took note that her oldest son kept busy reading the Bible and some other books almost the entire day. She wasn't sure whether that was a good sign or not. She knew first-hand how Bible Christians could challenge and try to discredit the Catholic faith. *You don't realize how strong the tide is until you stand against it.*

Tammy made an attempt to talk with Michael after the others were in bed. She didn't seek to defend the Catholic faith or condemn the arguments against the Church, rather she just wanted to relax with her son and make sure he wasn't losing his balance with all the reading and study.

Michael appreciated her company. They sat at the wooden table and talked by the light of the oil lamp. Michael found it so soothing. They sipped decaf coffee. *Sunday is easy to keep sacred on the farm,* Michael thought. *Everything from the Saturday night bath to the special breakfast to the break from hard physical work helped keep the day sacred.*

After an easy conversation they both made their way to bed.

Michael eased into bed like he was climbing onto a big, fluffy cloud. Momentarily he fell to sleep.

Tammy sank into bed, too, and began praying the Rosary.

Before long, Michael found himself back in the dungeon. He recognized it immediately — the parapet, the barred window, the dark and damp. Though it was more familiar this time, he was still unnerved to find himself there. There was light coming in from the window just like last time, but the light seemed to move.

Michael focused his attention on the window and strained to listen. It wasn't so much that the light was moving, but that the intensity of it rose and fell, creating an impression that the light was dancing into the dungeon. Michael was able to hear some faint noise but couldn't make out what it was. It didn't seem to be of human origin.

Then the door opened onto the parapet and the sound that Michael heard suddenly grew in intensity. It was the roar of flames! They crept inside the dungeon from the opened door. The robed figure emerged, seemingly from the midst of the fire, and closed the door behind him. The sound of fire was dampened for an instant, then the flames started reaching in through the barred windows just behind the figure. It was as if the flames had followed him and sought his company.

The man stood there peering down at Michael who stood below. Again Michael could not make out the man's face. All the light was behind him. He stood there in silence, oblivious to the flames. Michael felt the anxiety rising inside him and coursing through his blood.

"Your father was killed in a fire, wasn't he?" the figure asked.

Michael couldn't decide if his voice was sympathetic or taunting. Besides that, how did he know?

"Yes, he was," Michael finally answered, "he saved a man's life, though." *That's an important point*, thought Michael. *My Dad was a hero.*

"Yes, a drug user, right?" the man responded. "What a pity. Hardly seems right that he died and the other man lived."

It had never seemed quite fair to Michael either, but he had struggled to get beyond that judgment. He remembered the priest's sermon at the funeral... *It wasn't fair that Christ was crucified.*

"Well, that's how it happened," answered Michael, defiant now that he had decided that the man was indeed taunting him.

"You can be protected from fire."

"Excuse me?" said Michael, surprised by such a statement. He had heard it but wanted an explanation.

"There is no need for someone like you to die senselessly in a fire. You can live a long life and achieve great things."

Michael was hurt by the implication that his father died senselessly, even though he had yet to make complete sense out of it himself.

"What kinds of great things?" Michael queried despite himself. He didn't bother asking how this figure could ensure his life, rather he was curious about the possibility of his doing "great things."

"You speak well. You have a good appearance. Your Uncle Mathias has already told you that you could be a crack trial attorney. That's pretty good. Or, you could use your gifts to bring the Bible to the people. You'd help some people by defending them in court, but you'd help the masses by speaking about the Bible."

*He's right*, thought Michael. His confidence was boosted by such recognition.

"There would be no need to scratch out a meager living for your family like your father had to do. Your ministry could be large and prosperous. Using television and radio you could expand into larger markets and even become a nationally recognized evangelist. It would only make sense to reach out to the most people."

It seemed to make sense to Michael, though before this he had never thought there was anything wrong with the humble life his father had led in Philadelphia.

"You have good teachers here," the man continued, "endeavor to learn from them."

"Yeah, they're nice people," Michael responded, "but I'm not so sure they're right about everything."

"You need to be born again, Michael."

"Born again?"

Without opening the Bible that he held under his arm, he proceeded... "John's Gospel, chapter three... 'Most assuredly, I say to you, unless one is born of water and the Spirit, he cannot enter the kingdom of God.' You need to be born again, Michael," the figure repeated.

Michael hesitated to respond. He had heard of "born-again" Christians but it was not a term that was used around his house or among any Catholics that he knew.

"Are you born again, Michael?"

"I don't know." *Maybe I am and we just call it by a different name,* he thought, justifying his answer.

"Have you accepted Christ as your personal Lord and Savior?"

*Maybe I have, but we don't use that terminology*, he thought.

"I believe Jesus Christ is the Son of God and that He came to save us," Michael answered.

"But do you have a personal relationship with Jesus?"

*Where is that in the Bible?* Michael asked himself.

"I believe in God and am trying to live the way his Son taught us," he answered again, hoping that it would satisfy the figure.

"Live the way he taught us?"

"I'm trying to be a good person. I try not to sin. I try to do what I can for anyone I might be able to help... all of that kind of stuff."

"Trying to work your way into heaven, are you?"

"There's work involved."

"We are saved by faith alone, Michael — Romans three twenty-eight — not works."

Michael didn't respond. He didn't know how. That's not what he'd been taught.

"Will you accept Jesus as your personal Lord and Savior? Will you be born again?"

"I don't know." He was too confused to give a definitive answer. Was the figure asking him to leave the Church? If he was, the answer was no, he thought.


Tammy finished the Rosary, gave her child Michael to Mary, the Blessed Mother of Jesus, for spiritual protection, and drifted off to sleep.


"You could be a great leader of Christians, Michael."

The reminder interrupted Michael's thought. He saw himself respected and admired, his talents well used and productive. Was God calling him to do great things? He was endowed with great ability. God would be pleased if he used it. He thought about the evangelists of the day. They reached throngs of people. They had business empires that did good work. Their name recognition was high. Some dabbled in politics, others were quite influential in other spheres of life. Presidential candidates called on them. He couldn't think of any Catholic religious figures that held such sway over business, politics, and entertainment. Were there any Catholics out there? Anyone with great fame and power, teaching and leading the people? Aren't they even in the game?

As Michael stood there on the floor of the dungeon querying himself and growing increasingly anxious for lack of answers he felt something happen within him. It was as if something were poured inside of him that quickly coursed through his body and brought peace. A power came over him. Then in his mind's eye he saw a faded image of a shrunken-looking, old woman. As he considered her he forgot about the questions he had been asking himself and his inability to answer them. The woman wore a long garment and a striped head covering. She was looking down upon a dirty back alley that teemed with humanity. Old people lay on the side of the alley. Children ran about half clothed. The sun beat down mercilessly and the stench of raw sewage was overpowering. A handful of young women, clad in long white habits and striped head coverings just like the older woman, made their way down the alley. Their movement was quiet and unobtrusive.

They were Missionaries of Charity, Michael realized with excitement. He had read about their work among the people of India and how it had spread throughout the world. They strove to serve the poorest of the poor. He knew they had some convents near Philadelphia. One served people dying of AIDS.

The young nuns in his vision went about greeting the various families who made their homes right alongside this alley. Their warmth was infectious and the people brightened when they approached. The nuns were concerned with the health and comfort of these lowly people. The people talked with them about the old woman known to them simply as "Mother." They expressed their great sadness now that they she was no longer with them. "She is with God," was the simple response, given with a smile.

It became apparent to Michael that these young women were somehow "daughters" of the older nun and were carrying on the work assigned to her. By all appearances it was thankless, humbling, and filthy work. Yet the young nuns seemed full of joy, peace, and good cheer. They had genuine love for these lowly people. It was as if they were thankful for the opportunity to be of service. *How can that be?* Michael wondered. *What is their secret? What makes them do this? Where do they get such energy and enthusiasm?*

He could not answer these questions readily.

The scene then changed. He saw throngs of these nuns going about their various chores at their convent in the early morning. It was like watching bees in a hive. He observed them as they gathered in a large chapel. They sat in silence. On the altar Michael noticed the Eucharist, the Most Blessed Sacrament. The sisters continued to sit together in silence with Jesus present in this unleavened bread. They sat and were spiritually replenished.

Michael again saw the faded image of the older nun. Could that be Mother Teresa? He stared momentarily at her face. She was an ugly, wrinkled old woman on the surface, but there was a great depth to her being. Her face drew one immediately beyond the surface and into a beauty of substance. As he considered her beauty, he felt as though she spoke to him, although her lips never moved. *Is she an answer to my question? A Catholic hero? She is that without a doubt, yet so unlike the type of hero I had been imagining.*

He thought of Mrs. Clancy, who lived down the street back home. She had been caring for her ailing mother for five years. Michael's parents had been so moved by her commitment and love. There was Anne Clark over on Pechin Street whose husband had just died of cancer. She had lived with that and shared his burden for six years. There was Mr. Monroe, who was in charge of taking communion to the "shut-ins" in the parish. He thought of the Carpers, the young couple who struggled to raise their severely retarded son. He saw them always at the 10:15 mass. *They're all heroic in their way, picking up their crosses daily.*

He continued to gaze at the fading image of Mother Teresa. Again she seemed to speak to him, without opening her mouth...

*How many are going to bed hungry or sick every night, not only hungry for bread but starving for a simple word of encouragement, sick because they have no love, because nobody is kind to them?... So many are needy. They need love and compassion. Are the people I meet everyday in need, and am I unable to see their need? Perhaps they are sick from loneliness, from anxiety, from feeling helpless or worthless. Is this one an elderly person who feels unloved? A mother who is unappreciated? Is that one a teenager who feels lost, afraid, and misunderstood? Is he a husband who feels weak, inadequate because he doesn't earn enough money for his family?*

*What can I do? Who is lonely in my family? Whose burden can I share? Am I a good son? A loving brother? A thoughtful neighbor? Am I blind to those in need who cross my path every day? Can I feed this one with a kind word? That one with a helping hand? The work is great but the laborers are few. Ask the harvest master to send more laborers.*

"Work with me, Michael, and we can achieve greatness together." The voice brought him back to the dungeon. He sounded sincere, sympathetic, and caring, but not in the way that the young sisters had.

Then Michael said something without even thinking. He did not even know where it came from.

"Maybe we are not called to do great things. Maybe we are just called to do small things with great love." There was a long pause.

"You need to reconsider," the man said.

Michael thought the man's voice was shaking. *With frustration? Anger?*

"Don't be foolish. Don't waste your life." With that he turned to leave and made his way out the door. The sound of the flames could be heard as the door opened. It closed behind him and Michael was again alone in the dungeon. Before he could think about what to do or how to get out, small arrows of flame shot through the barred window. They landed to his left and right. The stone floor of the dungeon became engulfed in flames. It was as if the floor were covered with gasoline-drenched rags. The fire grew from practically nothing to an inferno in seconds.

Michael remained standing, petrified where he was. He stood in a small circle that was not on fire, but the heat was intense. He felt his skin burning from the heat of the flames. *Am I really burning?* The flames were so thick he couldn't see through them, so high that he couldn't see over them. He looked up, only darkness. *I'm going to die here,* he realized, and panic seized him.

Michael woke with a pounding heart in the darkness of his cottage room on his Uncle Les's farmstead. He was drenched in sweat. He was thankful to be delivered from the dungeon.

*Martin de Porres Kennedy*

# 6

Hours later he was glad to wake in the pre-dawn blackness, dress by oil lamp, and get out to help Elijah with chores. The activity of the day would put the dream behind him, at least for now. There were many tasks to be accomplished that week. Eli and Michael were going to disk the field one more time and then harrow it to prepare for planting. It was to be sown in a mix of pasture grasses for the grazing animals. There were also things to fix, supplies to buy in town, sheep starting to lamb, and people to visit.

"It'll just be another typical week on the farm," answered Eli when Michael asked him about what would be going on. "I think Dad's a bit pre-occupied with Wednesday night, though," he continued.

Michael had to stop and think. *What's going on Wednesday night? Did I forget something?*

"Oh, that's the church meeting about tobacco with Luther," he finally recalled. "Why? What's the big problem about the meeting?" Michael assumed that this was all pretty much just routine church business.

"There'll be fireworks all right," answered Eli, "nothing's ever routine when Luther's involved. And talkin' about not growin' tobacca' to some of these people..." Eli rolled his eyes. "You may as well be talkin' to the Amish folk about how they should farm with tractors and combines."

Michael picked up immediately on Eli's change of posture. *He's talking to me like a friend now, and not just a friendly cousin. He's giving me the real story instead of just the facts.*

Michael found himself interested in the real story about what might happen at the little church. *I can't miss this one*, thought Michael. It was becoming like "the big fight" on pay-per-view that the promoters did their best to hype. Or would it resemble more the scene from Acts 15? Things seemed to have proceeded rather smoothly from the decision in that council. Eli seemed less confident of the outcome in this dispute.

"What's the big deal?" asked Michael. "Why don't the farmers just grow something else?"

"You've got to understand, Michael," laughed Eli. Anyone who didn't know the "big deal" about tobacco in Kentucky really didn't understand. "Farmers have been growin' tobacco for generations down here. It's a good small farm cash crop and it's become part of the culture. It's a way of life." Eli was trying his best to convey what tobacco meant to farmers in the region. It was probably impossible to relate entirely to an outsider.

"But Luther says the Bible is against it." Michael didn't know where Luther saw that in the Bible, but he wanted to see how Eli would respond.

"Well, we're sure gonna see about all that," Eli responded, as they continued on and finished up their chores.

Michael was again thankful for his cousin's company. He sensed that Eli would not have spoken so freely had his father been there.

"See ya after breakfast," Eli called, as they began to go their separate ways.

"So, what do *you* think?" Michael called.

"Pardon?"

"About growin' tobacca." Michael's accent was adapting to Kentucky.

Eli stopped and considered it. He obviously didn't have a ready answer.

"I really don't know, Michael," he began, "I'm kinda interested in what's goin' to be said this week myself." He proceeded on toward home.

Michael went his way and thought about tobacco growing. He wondered what Uncle Les thought.

◆ ◆ ◆

Farm work that week went well. Michael continued to enjoy it and learned by doing. On Wednesday, before the big church meeting, they planned to go to the feed mill. Michael didn't know where it was, but assumed they'd be taking the truck. It surprised him when Les told him and Eli to get the horses hitched up.

"We're takin' the buggy to town?" Michael asked, thinking about driving along that busy road in a buggy.

"No, the feed mill's just less than a mile away, at Levi Schroeder's," Eli answered with a smile. "We'll take the wagon, but first we gotta fill it up with some corn."

Now Michael was really confused. Why would we want to bring feed to the feed mill? Eli noted the expression on Michael's face.

"We load the corn from the corn crib, it's dry but still on the cob, into these old feed sacks. Levi grinds corn on Wednesdays for all the Amish farmers. He's Amish himself," Eli added, trying not to assume anything. "We feed the animals ground corn, the chickens and pigs especially. For the horses we mix in some grains. Animals eat most of the corn grown in this country. Did you know that?"

"No." Michael had never really thought about it. Eli got busy filling the feed sacks.

"About eighty-five percent or so is fed to cattle, hogs, and poultry. Sweet corn — what humans eat — makes up only about ten to fifteen percent of the crop. That's why the price of corn is a big thing to the big factory farmers. It's a major cost of their production."

"What's a factory farm?"

"Oh, that's just an expression we use to describe the really big farms. Basically the trend, over the past half-century especially, has been to lower costs through large volume production. Now we have fewer farmers, but just as much production. There's been a move toward more specialization, too. Really it's the big producers of cattle, hogs, and poultry that are most affected by corn prices."

They got the horses harnessed, backed them up to the wagon, then pulled the wagon out toward the road. Les came from whatever he was doing and jumped aboard.

"Why don't you give Michael the reins," Les said to Eli. Eli handed them over. The sun was moving higher in the sky and warming everything up. It was going to be a beautiful spring day.

"Geeeet up," Michael bellowed, and the horses stepped forward.

"Yeah, corn is everywhere," continued Eli as they made their way down past the house and out toward the gravel road. "If you drive through Indiana, Illinois, Iowa, Nebraska anytime in the summer, it's all corn."

"Soybeans, wheat, and oats are some of the other major crops in this country," Les said, joining the conversation. "Produce is still an area where a smaller farmer can make a little money because it's more labor intensive. Combines can't harvest melons like they can harvest soybeans. But there's no gettin' rich doin' it." Les sounded tired and a bit worn out as he said that. "It's about embracin' a way of life more than a way to make a livin'."

Les considered what he had just said and his mind began wander. He found himself falling into the same thoughts that had visited him from time to time when he felt the burden. *I've had to convince myself of that — that it's about embracing a way of life — too often through the years,* thought Les. How many times when the "wolf was at the door" had he rationalized their way of life? At times he wondered if he wasn't just kidding himself. Was he just being self-centered and cheating his family out of what he could have provided if he had worked at an outside job like a regular guy? *I'm a married man with children and responsibility. I have no business pursuing this ridiculous dream. It's selfish.*

Discouragement visited him with various faces and names. One year it took the form of a bacteria wilt that killed half his tomatoes and melons. Another year it was an unethical wholesaler who knew he had them over a barrel and managed to nickel and dime the profits away. Then there were the unexpected bills, so frequent that they shouldn't really have been thought of as "unexpected." One year it was too much rain, the next not enough. *The weather I have to leave up to God,* he sighed...

> Cursed is the ground for your sake;
> In toil you shall eat of it
> All the days of your life.
> Both thorns and thistles it shall bring forth for you,
> And you shall eat the herb of the field.
> In the sweat of your face you shall eat bread
> Till you return to the ground,
> For out of it you were taken;
> For dust you are,
> And to dust you shall return.

As the years went by he realized that he was limited, even if he did decide to quit the farmstead. He knew he was smart and a good speaker, could learn quickly, and was responsible, but he could just imagine the job interview! It would take place somewhere in downtown Nashville, in a high-rise office building.

"So tell me about yourself. What have you been doing the past ten years or so? What kind of experience do you have?"

"Well, I've been a subsistence farmer most of my working career. It has really provided me with an extremely varied set of skills and quite unique challenges…"

If the interviewer didn't excuse himself at that point to go and reprimand whoever let this nutball in, he'd continue…

"I pursued this 'way of life' so that I could do the best possible job raising my family and because I felt called to it. I wanted to be there for my wife to help her with the children. I wanted to be near my children, to work with them, instruct them, play with them. I tried to follow what the Bible said, that I should 'train up my children in the ways they should go,' that I should be there as they wake in the morning and when they lay down at night…"

At this point the well-dressed man, had he restrained himself thus far, would have pressed the red button underneath his desk, the one that signals his secretary to save him from whoever is in his office. But say the man did continue the interview — perhaps he was enjoying the practical joke and wanted to play along to be a good sport. He'd ask, "What makes you want to leave your present, ah, 'way of life?' And why our company?"

"Your company? Well, it really doesn't make any difference to me whether I work for you or your competitor as long as I am paid for the work I do. You're five minutes closer to where I get off the Interstate, though. And what was the other question? Oh yeah, about why I'd want to leave my life as a subsistence farmer? Basically because I'm real discouraged with it. We're always broke. We have no savings, no health insurance, and unlike my Amish neighbors, no one even to share the burden with. I'm tired of being a freak. I just want to have a regular job like a regular guy and start living a regular life."

"Are you against the trend toward the bigger farms, Uncle Les?" Michael asked. He had noticed that his uncle was lost in his thoughts and had seen the forlorn look on his face. It was the look of an athlete whose team is losing late in the game and there just aren't enough ticks left on the clock to mount a comeback. That time when emotion changes from excited intensity to acceptance and reservation, when one has to dig deep to finish strong, with honor, yet is aware of the futility of it all.

"It's not a matter of being for or against, Mick, it's a reality that you come to grips with."

There was a pause. It was the first time anyone had called him Mick, his father's nickname. They were out into the heart of the Amish community now. The humble, gray farmhouses stood about fifty yards back from the road. The young Amish children could be seen running around near the houses, their mothers busy hanging their wash to dry or in the kitchen gardens hoeing, preparing their farms for planting. They rolled on past, waving to those who looked up — everyone waved back and smiled. All in the community knew the McGuffeys. Near one of the barns a teenage boy was starting to drive down the path that led to the road. He stopped the wagon and his father hopped up with him. Two younger sons were in the back. They were all in black or gray. The women wore their heads covered.

The hills rolled beyond their houses in a patchwork of frozen waves of various shades of green and brown. There was still plenty of wooded area as well. It was not spectacular beauty, Michael decided. It was not so much magnificent landscape alone, but the people at work and play against the landscape. It was an intense beauty in its own way, a simple beauty perhaps.

"The big farms are not all bad," Les continued his answer. "More people eat more things, at any time of the year, at a lower price than ever before in the history of the world. Like all other areas we can enjoy more wealth in a material sense than our forefathers ever dreamed of. Walk into the local supermarket. Pick up some lettuce from Northern California. Choose from the various types they offer. Get some bananas from Central

America, some grapes — even in the dead of winter — from Chile. The apples are from the Northwest usually. It's all moved in refrigerated trucks along our interstate highway system. We're a well-fed people, by and large. Basic nutrition is not really an issue for the vast majority of us."

Michael reflected on his uncle's words. He had never given much thought to where food comes from, how it gets where it goes, who produces it, and the relative lack of variety even fifty years ago. He just took it all for granted. *How could anyone be against the trend toward the big farms, then, if they are responsible for all this bounty?* The wagon continued to roll past the humble farms, the children at play, the men at work.

"There is a cost, though." Les began the "but" side of his discourse. "Small vibrant family farms used to lay outside the cities and towns they served. Their produce fed the people, and in return they patronized the hardware store, the feed mill, the local drugstore. Old Jim, the produce manager at Kroeger's, used to have his own market. It was his, it had his personality, his personal service, and his sons worked with him. He bought from the local farmers. Kroeger's, on the other hand, has the personality that some consultant said the members of her focus group liked best. They buy produce from another state, from a big farmer who grew it on contract using migrant workers to harvest it, instead of dealing with ten or twenty local farmers. It's more efficient that way. Jim wasn't the most efficient all the time.

"Then the local farmer went off to work somewhere. His family had to start buying their food, plus new clothes and more reliable transportation. His wife got a job, too, to help pay for the extras. The kids went to school and didn't have the farm chores to help with. Grandma was moved into a retirement community when she was too old to care for herself and too much of a burden to be cared for by the rest of the family. Everyone got his or her own little compartment.

The kids grew up and moved into the towns or just commuted to factory jobs. They drive pretty nice trucks now, have more extra income than before, but I don't think they're richer. There's been a lot of what they call economic growth in these rural communities and the local mayors and town councils can brag about how much growth there's been. The men running for president of the country know that the people are most concerned about economic growth. It's funny, no one dares question the desirability of "growth" or what kind of growth, just give us growth, show us the economy is expanding. Of course growth is good!"

Michael stood listening to his uncle, the scenes of activity in the "plain" community continuing to roll past as if it were a movie backdrop with Les as Jimmy Stewart in *It's a Wonderful Life* or Henry Fonda in *The Grapes of Wrath*. He was rambling, but there was truth to what he was saying. He was spelling out his philosophy with his observations and comments. He was standing against the tide of human history and development, armed with nothing but his sincere beliefs and simple way.

"When the industrial park or stadium needs to hire more security folks to protect some citizens from other citizens, that's included in growth. When a young mother goes back to work after her maternity leave is up, they — the ones who determine growth — say she is contributing again...to growth. In fact, because she has to pay for childcare, even her new baby is contributing to the economy. The extra clothes she needs for work, the new car or bus fare, the prepared foods her whole family relies on now, it's all good for growth."

They were nearing the feed mill now. There were other wagons, also loaded, making their way toward the mill that joined them on the road. "Every Wednesday it's like this," Eli explained, as he noticed Michael marveling at all the wagon traffic.

Michael thought that taking the corn to be ground was an errand; he didn't realize it was an event. *That's the way it is with the plain people, though*, he was beginning to understand. Their community is one body. They cut themselves off from much of the world, but bind themselves to one another.

Les had long ago observed that the plain people act as a sort of mirror for conventional society. People have become increasingly connected to the rest of the world through technology — television, faxes, cellular phones, e-mail, the Internet — but never more isolated from their neighbors. In a three-minute news story one knows more about the current situation in the Middle East, than about what has been happening with the neighbor's grandmother, who has been sick for a week. A short profile of some sports star can give people a better understanding of that person than they have of the parents of their children's schoolmates. People have become experts on celebrities and events, while being ignorant of much that is happening right around them. The global village has emerged at the expense of the local village. The town square is the network news or CNN, the local market replaced by the mall, or worse, the home shopping channel.

They pulled up to the feed mill. There must have been ten wagons already there and another ten or fifteen on the way. Men and older sons milled about talking in groups of twos, threes, and fives, checking a horse's teeth over there, a hoof over here.

The horse-powered mill was up and grinding, the huge Belgian draft horses leaning into their work. The sun warmed Les's shoulders. His nostrils filled with the smell of horses and freshly ground feed. The sky was blue. Eli was already out in front securing the horses to the post. Les soaked it all in, and didn't even notice that he had stopped wondering why he subjected himself to such a life.

"... But if a woman makes a nice home-made meal for her husband and family, well that's not registered by the accountants," he continued. He wanted to finish his point before he got occupied in another conversation. "Changing her baby's diaper and talking to her child just doesn't show up anywhere as 'growth,' 'development,' or 'progress.' Y'know, the Scriptures don't tell us to 'seek ye first the kingdom of heaven, and efficiency in production.' Jesus didn't say 'Go therefore and make disciples of all nations and spread your technological ways.' I think it was the Russian writer Alexander Solzhenitsyn who said that 'Growth for the sake of growth is the ideology of the cancer cell.'"

Then Les looked up at Michael and smiled. He wondered if the poor boy was overwhelmed with all the philosophy that was just unloaded on him. "Oh well, end of discourse," he said, still smiling, and walked off to visit with some of the Amish.

They waited their turn at the feed mill. There was plenty of time for visiting, farm talk, and to otherwise catch up on events in the plain community. Michael kept his mouth shut as he stood next to Eli. He was content to listen to his cousin chat with the young Amish men. It was as if he were privy to the casual conversation of a mysterious secret society and any noise he might make would serve to alert the members to an outsider's eavesdropping, at which point they'd disperse. They'd look over, notice that you weren't dressed the same — no straw hat, no black suspenders — and they'd quiet down and drift away.

They spoke with Eli freely, but when they called to another outside the circle or even when they mentioned things just to each other, a different language came out of their mouths. Michael remembered learning about the Amish in Lancaster County, Pennsylvania — that they still spoke a dialect of German with one another. He remembered reading about the first Germans in America. Thirteen Mennonite families sailed from Krefeld to Philadelphia in 1683. They were well received by William Penn and settled in a section that to this day is called the Germantown section of Philadelphia. Soon the Amish and Mennonites settled farther west in Lancaster County. From there they continued to spread.

Forty-five minutes later they were on their way, freshly ground corn in their sacks. Michael noticed that his uncle seemed more upbeat and lively.

"What d'ya think about those people?" Les asked his nephew.

The question caught Michael a bit off guard. It was rather a general question and he didn't know any of them personally.

"I don't know. They're interesting," he answered ambiguously. He couldn't miss with that response. If people didn't find them interesting, then Lancaster County wouldn't be such a tourist attraction. He didn't understand, though, why they lived the way they did or why his uncle imitated their way of life to the extent he did.

"Well, considering what we were talking about before, they are kind of interesting. They don't just adopt the latest gizmo or gadget just because it's available or increases productivity." The wagon rolled back onto the road. The scene hadn't changed much. The little farmhouses were still peaceful beehives of activity. "Their first concern is with how technology will affect their community. Tractors enable men to farm much more acreage. That means bigger farms... and that means living farther away from your neighbor. Then cars become necessary so that you can get around in the larger community. But why would you need to get around? With a big fancy tractor your neighbor won't need your help so much anymore. So they don't use tractors."

"Well, that's no good for economic growth," Michael joked.

"Now yer gettin' the idea," Les shot back smiling. "Progress and efficiency are not even questioned in our day. If you can do it faster, bigger, and stronger then it must be done that way, by golly! And it is. Then you have these strange people, dressed in black, white, and gray, who speak a funny language, who do question it. They question it quietly and make no fuss about the way others choose to go. They just go their way and they make it work. They are living proof that you can still make it on a small farm. You don't even need mechanized equipment. They're doing it now and have been doing it for generations."

Michael thought about what his uncle was saying. He looked out across the Amish fields, onto the patchwork of greens and browns. *Are his uncle's observations and conclusions accurate? Are they fair? Is the car a bad invention? What about modern surgical techniques? Aren't the Amish just being slaves to their ideology? Or are the rest of us slaves to ever more sophisticated technology, to the pursuit of "progress" and material wealth?*

"I don't know, Uncle Les," Michael started with doubt in his voice, "is that how we all should live?"

"No, I don't think so, Michael. Not everyone is called to be a farmer or tradesman, but it is worthwhile to consider things, to see what genius they may have in their ways." They rode on for a ways farther. "They're not perfect people, Michael, but they're doing some things right. They don't have the tragedies in their communities like the ones you'll find everywhere else. You don't see marriages end in divorce, or children neglected or abused. I've never seen problems with alcoholism or drug abuse in this community. Young boys don't have idle time on their hands, the kind that leads to trouble. Women aren't exploited. They don't work as waitresses with skimpy outfits or as dancers in go-go bars. The older folks live out their lives in dignity, contributing to the family 'til the end."

"Have you ever thought about joining their community? Or do you have to be born into it?" Michael asked. He hoped it was not too presumptuous of him to ask, but his uncle seemed to admire them and promote them so.

"No," he answered with a laugh, "I mean you can join and go through a trial period with them, but no, we never asked or seriously thought about becoming part of their church community. Too many things I can't accept about what they believe — their doctrines. We'll have to discuss it sometime. It is interesting." Les realized that much of what he rejected about the Amish was similar to his criticism of the Roman Church, and that discussing it with Michael would give him a good opportunity to open his nephew's eyes.

It was turning out to be another good day on the farm, as far as Michael was concerned. They didn't tackle any major jobs, but worked their way through a couple projects that needed doing. He was learning the basics from Eli about how to fix and patch everything from plumbing to chicken pens. He learned the most from observing Eli's approach to a problem. He was patient and analytical. He came up with a plan before starting in with a hammer, saw, or screwdriver. Michael thought of his Uncle Matty, so brilliant in the courtroom but notoriously inept with any kind of handy work. It's not that he was somehow genetically handicapped in the area, but rather lacking in patience. He had long since been able to pay people to do that kind of stuff for him.

◆ ◆ ◆

Michael and Eli walked to the church that night and arrived just before the council started at 7:30. Serious, solemn, and thoroughly adult on the outside, they were giddy as two boys sneaking into the circus on the inside. They entered the church and sat in the back pew. Les, sitting in a wooden chair up front, did not turn around at all to watch as the people came streaming in.

Les had not even mentioned the event the entire day except to ask Eli if he were going. Eli did his best to sound nonchalant about it when he said, "Yeah, I guess so."

Les's relative silence was his way of downplaying the whole affair. He wished in a way that he had never brought it up with his nephew. He had tried his best last week to get a feel for how deeply Luther felt about the whole thing, how passionately he would argue. Luther, he had decided, was going to be Luther. He already knew about the other fellows, the ones who grew tobacco. They were not unreasonable men, not at all. They were decent, fair, hardworking, even flexible to a degree. Whether or not to grow tobacco, however, was not a negotiable point.

Les looked down at his watch, then turned around to gauge the assembled crowd. The church was full, people were standing in the back, people he had seen before but did not know, people from other local churches. It was meant to be a church affair, meaning that it would involve just the members of this church. *I guess that was never spelled out to the congregation*, thought Les. Looking out at the crowd, he would have guessed that someone had sold tickets and promised there'd be dinner followed by coffee and pie afterwards.

He swung back around. He looked to his right and locked eyes with Luther, who was seated at a long cafeteria-style table facing the congregation. He had his Bible in front of him. He looked to his left. There sat four men at another table, with their Bibles in front of them. *The storm clouds are approaching*, he couldn't help thinking, *and all these people have come to see the storm. Are they really interested in the question at hand here or are they like spectators in Atlantic City with ringside seats, hoping to get their money's worth, to see a good fight? Or could this be how the Lord is sending more people to join our church? They'll see how we open the Bible and truly seek His will and be impressed with our way, the Christian way... I hope it works.*

As he sat there just before he began the council, he began to empathize with the other pastors, the ones who simply rendered a decision when a disagreement in the church came up. He bowed his head and prayed silently. The entire congregation was hushed in anticipation. Then he spoke a prayer aloud: "Lord, you show us with your Sacred Word how we are to come together and discuss the issues that divide us. If this is what you mean... if this is how we should be handling things in the church, then show us. Guide us to all truth... and lead us."

He raised his head.

*Pretty short for a Protestant prayer*, thought Michael.

131

Les swung around in his chair so that he faced the crowd. "Brothers and sisters, we are gathered here in the middle of the week not for worship, or at least not for worship as we normally view it, but because members, or a member rather, of the brethren has raised an issue and there is disagreement on the issue." His voice was casual, as if he didn't expect any heated and passionate exchanges to ensue, but rather biblical arguments presented dispassionately. Or perhaps he did not really anticipate calm and reasoned discourse at all, but wanted to encourage it by setting the tone himself.

"I'll act as mediator, but not arbitrator. That is, I will try to ensure that all are heard who want to be heard, but it is not my job to listen and then split the difference. As Christians we are seekers of truth, not compromisers for the sake of peace."

He then turned to address the men seated at their respective tables, like a referee reminding them of the three commands in the ring: box, break, and stop. "Don't interrupt one another. I may interrupt you if I think it would help if you explained a point. Let's seek the truth rather than just push our own arguments."

*"Now let's have a good clean fight," is how the ring announcer would finish his instructions,"* remembered Michael. He used to watch boxing with his father sometimes.

"Luther, why don't you tell us how you see it first," invited Les.

"Thanks, Les," he began politely. "I don't have any fancy arguments. Matter a' fact, I don't have any argument at all." He was looking and talking to the entire congregation with ease and grace, quietly and reasonably. "The Bible that we all read and believe in makes all the argument I need." He lifted his Bible as he said this. Heads nodded. "It's a simple book really." He paged through it. "Oh, I know lots a' folks make it all pretty complicated, try to bend what it says, come up with all kinds of weird philosophy and interpretations, but we know there can't be private interpretations. Peter says so. In second Peter three sixteen we're warned that the Bible contains certain passages that are hard to understand...

> ... which untaught and unstable people twist to their own destruction, as they do also the rest of the Scriptures. You, therefore, beloved, since you know this beforehand, beware lest you also fall from your own steadfastness, being led away with the error of the wicked.

"Now we see that happen all the time when—"

"Luther, you ain't talkin' nothin' 'bout tobacca. You the one startin' to give us high brow philosophy—"

Les: "All right, Jimmy, let Luther finish his point. Luther, you get to the point now. You'll get plenty of time to make your case."

Jimmy: (*voice louder*) "He's startin' right in to callin' us ignorant and unstable, Les. If we came here to talk tobacca, let's talk tobacca."

Les: "Luther, go on."

*Let's not have a free for all*, Les prayed.

*Who needs TV?* thought Michael.

Luther: (*calmly*) "That's what I came here to do, Jimmy, and I'm gonna do it. I'm not callin' anybody unstable and ignorant. I love you as a brother, Jimmy, and that goes for George, Arnold, and Monroe, too," (*the others sitting at the table*) "and that's why ah'm even botherin' to bring this to your attention, because I believe you're in danger and that grieves me. I think it would be remiss, even un-Christian of me to say nothin'."

Michael glanced at the four men who were sitting patiently while Luther lectured. They were stonefaced, but there was hostility beneath their stoic surface.

Luther: "What ah'm sayin' is that tobacca growin' is a kind a' farmin' that Christians oughtta stay out of—"

Jimmy: (*volume up, with passion*) "I ain't interested in what *you* gotta say, Luther. We are Christians, same as you. We wanta see where it says that *in the Bible.* If ya cain't just show us that, then let's all just go on home and forget this whole thing..."

Les: "You're going to get your chance to speak, Jimmy. Let's let Luther finish up his point. Luther, we're all Christians here. We all believe that the Bible is the inspired Word of God. I think what Jimmy is concerned about is that we could be here for weeks and not solve anything if we just talk about what we think, but by considering what the Bible says the Lord's will should be made known to us. That said, is it your intention to start using the Bible to state your case?"

His uncle's ability to mediate and keep the peace impressed Michael.

Luther: (*acting slightly hurt*) "Yes, it is, Les. I'll do that right now, but again I want t' emphasize that this is not my case. I didn't write it. God wrote it using men to do the actual work."

Les: (*with a hint of frustration*) "Make the case you believe God makes in Scripture, Luther."

Luther: "Well, if we go to Exodus twenty," (*Bibles open and pages are turned by nearly everyone in the church*) "we see the Lord giving the Ten Commandments. Verse thirteen tells us that we shall not murder—"

Jimmy, George, and Arnold: "Hold on just a minute! That's enough, Luther Moore! Whose side are you on, Luther?" (*Jimmy had risen out of his seat.*)

Les: "Let 'im finish, boys." (*Calmly but firmly*) "Jimmy, sit down and let Luther continue."

Jimmy: "But growin' tobacca ain't murderin' people, Luther, except to those pointy-headed busybodies in Washington who are tryin' to put tobacca farmers out a' business."

Luther: "No, it's not killin' people maybe like shootin' with a gun is or runnin' 'em down with your truck is, and I ain't no pointy-headed busybody tryin' to hurt the small farmer. You all know that. I didn't come here tryin' ta tell ya what ya gotta do. I'm not makin' any laws. I'm tryin' t' do my Christian duty to point out the laws we've been given by God."

Jimmy: "Whose killin' anyone, Luther?"

Luther: "We've got to be concerned with more than just the obvious ways of killin' people, Jimmy. I considered what Jesus had to say about the Ten Commandments in Matthew five." The sound of ruffling pages filled the room. "I'll read it, startin' at verse twenty-one..."

> "You have heard that it was said to those of old, 'You shall not murder, and whoever murders will be in danger of the judgment.' But I say to you that whoever is angry with his brother without a cause shall be in danger of the judgment."

Luther: "We can see that Christ set a higher standard for us."

*Good point*, thought Michael.

George: "Yeah, but he wasn't dealing with things we eat or drink, Luther. Christ meant that not only shouldn't we kill out of anger, but that we shouldn't even stay angry at all with our brother. If I give 'im a cigarette, I ain't doin' it because I'm angry with 'im, but because I like 'im".

Luther: "But we know now that the cigarette is goin' to kill him, not directly maybe, but over time, slowly. Can't you give something else to your brother to show 'im you like 'im?"

Michael was fascinated now that the debate had begun. It was not unlike the court room scenes with his Uncle Mathias, except more informal, and there was none of the "who's telling the truth" element involved. The words of the Bible, which everyone believed, were right there in black and white. It was a difference about what they meant, whose interpretation was right.

135

George: "Each day kills us in the sense that it brings us closer to the end of our life. Is it a great matter to God if we die after seventy-five years instead of after seventy-eight or eighty or even ninety years? Isn't the point of Christianity to speak to *how* we live and not so much to how long?"

*That makes sense, too*, thought Michael. He had felt that way about the tobacco issue from the beginning, but could not have articulated it so. *That guy would be a good lawyer,* thought Michael.

Luther: "There's a temptation to try and comfort ourselves with that kind a' thinkin', George, but Scripture makes it clear what is good and wholesome and what is to be avoided. In the book of Sirach, check out chapter eighteen, verses thirty to thirty-three."

George: "Now hold on, Luther. What is this book of Sirach? That's not in my Bible, or Jimmy's, or Monroe's, or anyone's."

Les: "It's in the Apocrypha, George."

George: "Yeah, I heard a' that, but that ain't the Bible. He cain't use that like it was part a' Scripture."

Luther: "Now, not everything in the Apocrypha is wrong. Most of it is good. A lot of people include it in their Scripture——"

George: "Like who!?"

Luther: "The Catholics do."

George: "Since when are we takin' lessons from them?"

Les: "Luther, do you have a lot of Scripture from Sirach or any of the other books of the Apocrypha?"

Luther: "No. Just these couple of verses."

Les: "Let him read it, George."

George: "He can read it, but that's not the Bible, Les."

Les: (*impatiently*) "I know what it is and what it's not, thank you." (*Turning to Luther*) "Now go on, Luther."

Michael leaned over and whispered to Eli, "What's the Apocrypha?"

"I don't know," Eli shrugged.

Luther: "Starting with verse thirty of chapter eighteen...

Do not follow your base desires, but restrain your appetites. If you allow your soul to take pleasure in base desire, it will make you the laughingstock of your enemies. Do not revel in great luxury, lest you become impoverished by its expense. Do not become a beggar by feasting with borrowed money, when you have nothing in your purse.

"Then in Titus chapter two, verses eleven and twelve, Paul writes that...

... the grace of God that brings salvation has appeared to all men, teaching us that, denying ungodliness and worldly lusts, we should live soberly, right-eously, and godly in the present age.

"Now what we see here in the Word of God is the importance of temperance, not livin' for the moment and feedin' our appetites, or becomin' a slave to them. That's why the covenant agreement for our church, that hangs right on the back wall, forbids any member from usin' or sellin' alcohol."

Michael turned around and noticed a framed document hanging on the wall. *But Christ changed water into wine for the people at a wedding for his first miracle,* he thought. *He couldn't have been against the use of alcohol.*

Monroe: "So far, Luther, you might be able to make a case against smokin' or chewin' tobacco, but we came here to talk about *growin'* it. Now I'd be happy to listen to why you think I shouldn't smoke, but we're due to set out our tobacca plants next month, and unless I can be shown somethin' in the Bible about tobacca *growin'*, my plants are goin' in."

Luther: "Now if we're goin' t' be honest with ourselves about how the Bible speaks to us, then we have to see that warnin's against smokin' should send an even louder message to those who make it. That's even more dangerous in a spiritual sense. For this we can look to Luke chapter seventeen. Verse one states... 'It is impossible that no offenses should come, but woe to him *through whom* they do come.' It's really worse, ya see, much worse t' *grow* tobacca than just ta use it."

The four seated at the table were struck silent. Michael sat dumbfounded in his seat. *This Luther seems to have an answer for everything, and he's always convincing.*

Luther: "I didn't come here t' make life difficult for you. I've thought a lot about this question since my father died a' cancer a few years back. I searched the Bible, and the Lord really spoke to me. I believe strongly that I am bein' called to warn my brothers who are in sin."

George: "We ain't established that anybody's in sin yet, Luther. I've listened t' what you said an' it seems to me that yer bendin' some of the Scripture to mean what you want it t' mean."

Luther: "I've just read it the way it's laid out and cain't come up with a way of lookin' at it any differently, George. This ain't a personal rebuke. For years I didn't realize that Scripture even addressed the whole tobacca question, but it does."

George: "I don't know if it does the way you say it does, Luther. You *think* it does. I believe that."

Luther: (*irritated*) "Well, you show me where it says somethin' different than what I jus' said."

George: "Well, I guess t' start I'd jus' point to Paul's letter to the Colossians, chapter two. Beginning in verse sixteen he wrote...

> So let no one judge you in food or in drink, or regarding a festival or a new moon or sabbaths.

"Then continuin' down on to verse twenty:

> Therefore, if you died with Christ from the basic principles of the world, why, as though living in the world, do you subject yourselves to regulations – "Do not touch, do not taste, do not handle"…

*Powerful stuff,* thought Michael. *How's Luther gonna answer that?*

George: "Luther, yer gettin' caught up in the things of this world by spendin' so much time figurin' out how the Bible says that we shouldn't be growin' tobacca. You interpret the Scriptures to fit what you believe, instead of lettin' Scripture *teach* you what t' believe—"

Luther: "Scripture says what it says, George, and if you want to ignore it then I really cain't do nothin' about that. I just have t' hope and pray that the Lord moves you t' be honest with yerself."

George: (*losing patience*) "What about what I just read? Why do you continue to pass judgment on me for growin' and smokin' tobacca? Who gave you the authority to do that?"

Luther: "It's not my authority. It's the authority of Scripture. It's your—"

Jimmy: "But it ain't the authority of Scripture. It's what *you* think!"

Luther: "It's not what I think. It says what it—"

George: "It's what *you* think, Luther!"

Luther: "Anytime y' don't agree with somethin' you can just say you don't happen to agree with that interpretation and go on yer merry way. At some point, George, there cain't be any further debate about what somethin' says. It's that basic sometimes."

Monroe: "Nothin' you said was that basic, Luther. The Scriptures don't mention tobacca directly. Any prohibition from Scripture has got t' be the result of someone's interpretation."

Luther: "So yer goin' t' go on your merry way, too, Monroe? That's how we all ended up formin' this here church. We came together because the other churches stopped worryin' about what Scripture says. They follow tradition, or what the pastor says, or what will cause the least amount a' trouble."

Jimmy: "Maybe you should just go on *your* 'merry way,' Luther. Form your own church."

Luther: "If ah'm the only one followin' Scripture, then that's what I'll have t' do."

Jimmy: "Yer *not* the only one followin' Scripture, Luther! You come in here sayin' tobacca growin' is unchristian, callin' my Daddy unchristian, my Daddy's Daddy, and on past that." (*With pointed finger*) "Now, I've been patient with you long enough, Luther—"

Luther: "I've been patient with you, too, boys. I've spoken to each one a' you about this issue privately just like the Bible says that I should—"

George: "And I told you then that you had no right to cast judgment on a man for what he might grow to earn his livelihood."

Luther: "What if a man was growin' something illegal, some kind of drug? Should you say something then?"

Jimmy: "We're not growin' anythin' illegal, Luther, and you know it!"

Luther: "Is that the only reason it's okay to grow? I mean the stuff don't do anythin' good for a person—"

George: "You don't know that, Luther. You can't say it don't have any benefits."

Luther: "Well, now we're getting way off the Bible..."

Jimmy: "You're the one who got us off the Bible, Luther! This is too much, Les."

Les: "We've got to try and stay on the Bible and discern what the Lord wants. Luther, what do you have to say about the passage George brought up, about not heedin' rules made by men — the 'do not handle, do not taste, do not touch' rules? On what grounds can you make a judgment with regard to what these fellows are growin'?"

Luther: "I don't believe the apostle Paul meant that we couldn't cast judgment on things which are unhealthy. He was talkin' about arbitrary social laws and customs. The whole idea was that after Christ there was no Jew nor Greek, slave nor free. He didn't want people lookin' down their noses at others, or feelin' bad when others looked down at them, because their ways were different. They were being called to rise above all that, but it really wasn't dealin' with things that were bad for your fellow man and that played on his weakness."

Les: "What about you, George? Why don't you feel swayed by what Scripture says with regard to temperance and not feedin' men's appetites?"

George: "Because Scripture's talkin' about things like leadin' men to excess, things like too much liquor, carousin' at night, gamblin', greed, deception in business dealings. These are the areas that are dangerous to your very salvation, not if you have a smokin' habit. Luther shares this blindness that many of the unbelievers have. They go runnin' around worryin' about cigarettes and second-hand smoke and all the evil it does while families continue to fall apart, while every level of gover'-ment continues to tax everythin' we eat, make, and buy so as to pay for studies about cow farts. If all this tobacca talk ain't rearrangin' the deck furniture while the ship goes down, I don't know what is!"

The meeting continued for another hour. Les had to restore order a couple of times, but it seemed that the discussion did not progress beyond what had been established in the first hour. Michael continued to listen and marvel at the whole situation. The entire scene was so foreign to him that he couldn't compare it to anything he had ever seen or heard at his parish.

Finally, Les rose to speak to those assembled in the church. "We've been at it for awhile now, and I think it best to stop the council for tonight so that we all can get home at a good hour. Of course nothing is settled for the moment, but we're going to continue addressing this issue until the truth is made clear. I want to thank Luther, Jimmy, George, Arnold, and Monroe and encourage you to continue dealin' with one another with patience, love, kindness, and forbearance throughout these discussions. To some of the folks who've never been here before we certainly welcome you to join us for Sunday worship."

"It's got to be more exciting and interesting than any other church around here," Michael said to Eli about his uncle's invitation to Sunday worship, as they rose to leave. Eli just smiled back. They made their way out of the church and proceeded to walk home along the creek in the dark.

"What'd *you* think, Eli?"

"I don't know, Michael."

"Is growing tobacco wrong?"

"I don't know. I never thought it was before."

"What's your Dad think?"

"I don't know. He hasn't said anythin' to me. I think he's most worried there could be a split in the church over it."

"Really! Over growing tobacco?" They continued walking along. "What exactly do you mean by a 'split' in the church?"

"Some people will leave and go to another church if they don't like the result, or they'll start up a brand new church."

"Wow," Michael exclaimed quietly. He didn't appreciate how much was at stake for his uncle's little church, over tobacco growing of all things.

"What would your church do?" Eli asked.

"I don't know," answered Michael. "Nobody grows tobacco in Philadelphia." *Besides,* Michael thought, *Father Carney's a smoker.* "We don't really get into arguments like that. Mostly disagreements are over who gets to use the gym which night of the week... you know, scheduling things, not doctrine."

Eli nodded, not quite understanding. "You got a gym at your church?"

# 7

O ver the next couple days, Les didn't talk about the mid-week coun-cil meeting, but Michael and Eli discussed it often as they worked together. Michael continued to study the Bible and read the books from his father's collection. The commentaries on the Bible helped him make sense of it all and assimilate the material. His understanding brought him closer to his father. After all, it was the shared faith that bound them in an eternal sense, not only to one another but to the generations that pre-ceded and the ones yet to come. There was a richness, depth, and conti-nuity to the Faith that he couldn't imagine existed at any of these little independent churches.

He began to develop answers to the questions raised by his uncle. Things that seemed to be contrary to Scripture on the surface made sense once understood in their fullness. *They know the Bible so well,* Michael had thought, but now realized that knowing the Bible meant more than being able to quote verses by heart.

On Saturday, Michael and Eli began to muck out the barn so that they could spread the manure on the fields. With pitchforks they loaded it into a wheelbarrow. When it was full, one of them would wheel it out of the barn to the horse-drawn manure spreader, then together they'd lift the wheelbarrow full of manure and dump it in the spreader. The manure was well mixed with straw that had been used for bedding in the horse stalls. The straw served to soak up the moisture in the manure and urine in the stall and also balanced the nitrogen-rich animal refuse with carbon. That made it a far more effective fertilizer. To Michael the odor was pungent but not foul. He actually liked the smell of a barn. Understanding the value of the manure helped him to appreciate it. They weren't just shoveling "horse poop," they were collecting brown gold for future produce production.

The spreader itself was a simple-looking wagon with conveyor belt type chains on the floor that carried the manure to the rear of the wagon. There, rotating blades would chop it up and spit it out the back as the wagon moved forward.

Eli invited Michael to drive the spreader. Michael took it out to the field they were preparing. It was still green with a cover crop. The manure would first be spread, then plowed under with the winter rye. Upon reaching the field, Michael engaged the chains that helped move the manure toward the rear of the wagon. Eli stood atop the manure heap with a pitchfork to help it along toward the blades in the back. He also wanted to be near in case Michael needed any help. It didn't take long for the first wagon load of manure to be spread. They headed back to the barn for more.

"We'll just spread this until the barn is cleaned out," Eli informed him. "Maybe after lunch we'll start plowing the field... You're goin' to church with your family tonight, right?"

"I don't know," Michael responded. "My mom was mentioning something about going to Mass tomorrow in Nashville. I'll find out at lunch... I mean dinner." Michael still hadn't got the hang of calling the noon meal dinner, as was the custom.

"Well, dependin' on what you're doin', this field can wait 'til Monday if need be." Like his father, Eli got a lot done in a day but maintained a "never-hurry" attitude.

"So folks in the Catholic Church don't argue about doctrine?" Eli asked, recalling the conversation they had had after the council meeting that week. He was sincerely curious.

"No. There's really no room to," Michael answered.

"Whatta ya mean?" Not battling over doctrine and other points of Scripture was a foreign concept to Eli's experience.

Michael paused a moment to think about all that he had learned so recently. How to sum it up concisely and accurately?

"Well, Christ founded His Church. The Bible tells us that Christians are to be united in the faith. Catholics believe that the Church is led to all truth with guidance from the Holy Spirit. We say that the Church renders authoritative interpretation of Scripture. Teaching authority rests with what we call the Magisterium." Michael was articulating all of this for the first time and he wasn't sure how much sense it made to his cousin. He had learned it from his Dad but had read about it himself only since arriving in Kentucky.

"Now doctrine can be rejected and people can and have left the Church, but there really isn't any room for debate on a doctrinal issue." Without quite realizing it, Michael had just made the claims about the Catholic Church that Bible Christians found so unfathomable and infuriating — that it is the one, true Church that Christ founded, that the Holy Spirit guides the Church through the bishops, and that their teaching authority in union with the Pope is binding, and in matters of doctrine, infallible.

"That's it!? The leadership just decides things and you've got to agree to it or get out?"

"Sounds bad when you say it like that, doesn't it?" Michael laughed. "It's not, though, if you think about it. It was only the leadership of the Church that was involved in the Council of Jerusalem in the Book of Acts. It never mentions rank and file Christians being there, much less included in the discussion."

Eli considered that. It was an accurate observation.

"The Church in the New Testament had a structure and hierarchy. There were bishops, deacons, and other positions mentioned. Doctrine was determined and developed together by the bishops."

"I thought the Pope had all the authority," Eli queried, "and there's no Pope in the Bible."

"I think there is, but that's another matter. The Pope is the Bishop of Rome and that office does have special authority and responsibility. Doctrine, though, should not be confused with rules of worship, customs, and—"

"The Pope is in the Bible!?" Eli asked, more startled than anything. He didn't think even a Catholic would make a claim that was so obviously untrue.

"The word 'pope' isn't, but the office is. Peter was the first Pope. Christ said in Matthew sixteen that Peter was the rock upon which the Church would be built."

Eli understood that Catholics thought Peter was the first Pope and that he was infallible, but it was so utterly preposterous he couldn't imagine people actually believing it. He was dumbstruck. It was true, then, what he had heard about Catholics.

"And so you believe from that verse that Peter was the leader of the apostles and was infallible?" Eli tried to be polite with his question, but he couldn't help feeling a bit like a nurse in a psychiatric ward who conducted initial interviews: *"So you believe everyone who wears blue pants and sun glasses is a CIA operative and that they are carrying out a plan to undermine the international financial markets?"*

"Yes."

"But after Jesus was arrested, Peter was the apostle who denied he even knew him," Eli pointed out, with a bit of sympathy in his voice. *This poor guy doesn't know anything about the Bible.* "He was the one who cut off the guard's ear when Jesus was being arrested, and Jesus rebuked him for his violence. Even Paul had to correct him in front of the

Galatians for inappropriate behavior." Elijah didn't fancy himself a preacher like his father, but his cousin was in such a state of profound misunderstanding.

"I know, but he was the one chosen by Christ." Michael felt it was a feeble response, but he didn't have a better answer or any great confidence in his ability to explain it. *Better to learn more before I go any further with this one*, he decided.

◆ ◆ ◆

As usual, Michael filled himself well at dinner. There was fresh lettuce from Pam's garden, green beans, venison that had been canned from the fall hunt, homemade bread, and tapioca pudding to top it all off.

"What do you have planned for tonight, Mom?" Michael asked, as he finished up the last of his pudding, "Are we going to Mass tonight or tomorrow?"

"Well, I'd still like to go down to Nashville for Mass tomorrow at the convent," his mother began to answer, "but maybe we could go tonight too for Vespers."

"Vespers?" Michael asked. He wasn't sure if his mom was asking if he'd like to go.

"Evening prayers with all the sisters of the convent," Tammy answered. "It's part of the Liturgy of the Hours, a tradition of prayer still practiced especially by those living in religious community."

Tammy O'Shea had been praying for her son's spiritual protection and also that she might be led to ways to guide and direct her son's interest and yearning for understanding. She had read about the St. Cecilia Convent in *Sursum Corda* (Lift up Your Hearts), a Catholic magazine that was one of her favorites. The convent was the home of the Dominicans of St. Cecilia, a community formed about the time of the Civil War. Their community was vital and growing. Unlike so many of the religious orders, the Dominican sisters were having no problem attracting young women for religious vocations. Moreover, bishops from around the country had extended open invitations to the order to run schools in their dioceses.

The director of vocations attributed their success to their fidelity to the original mission of St. Dominic, the thirteenth century apologist who founded the order. Like St. Dominic, they were committed to contemplative prayer, but were also active. Dominicans, according to the article, prayed to be filled with sacred truth and that it might overflow to sanctify those around them.

What caught Tammy's eye were the beautiful, full-length, white habits and black veils that they still wore. They were walking anachronisms. To Tammy — a convert — it didn't call to mind 1950's-style Catholicism, for that was not part of her background and cultural experience, but it did impress her as evidence of the radical nature of Catholicism.

During her conversion she remembered being intrigued by the whole concept of the religious life led by the priests, brothers, and sisters throughout the world. Forgoing marriage and the conventional family life had been something totally foreign to her, but the more she considered it the more it had made sense to her. Some men and women, she realized, were called to that life. The Catholic interpretation of Scripture made it clear. When Peter had reminded Christ that they, the apostles, had put aside everything to follow him, Christ replied unambiguously...

> "I give you my word, there is no one who has given up home, brothers or sisters, mother or father, children or property, for me and for the Gospel who will not receive in this present age a hundred times as many homes, brothers and sisters, mothers, children and property — and persecution besides — and in the age to come, everlasting life."

And after addressing the Pharisees on the question of divorce he said to his disciples...

"For there are eunuchs who were born thus from their mother's womb, and there are eunuchs who were made eunuchs by men, and there are eunuchs who have made themselves eunuchs for the kingdom of heaven's sake."

Some men are indeed incapable of procreation from birth by virtue of a naturally occurring condition. And in ancient times, men would castrate other men, their captured enemies, so that they could have them guard and otherwise attend to their women, especially the royal harem, without posing the wrong kind of threat. The third category, though, men making themselves eunuchs, was mysterious. *What could Christ have been referring to?* It only made sense when understood in light of other Scripture. Jesus used the image of the bridegroom and the bride to illustrate the nature of the relationship between Him and his Church. It follows, then, that those who "make themselves eunuchs" for the sake of the kingdom are the men, the priests, who are charged with attending to or shepherding the flock — the Bride of Christ — here on earth.

Tammy O'Shea saw these committed women pictured in the magazine, these beautiful brides of Christ, and decided to plan a visit. It was only an hour away. The sister with whom she spoke was very accommodating. She not only passed on the time for Mass — which was open to the public — but invited them down for Vespers.

"Okay, Mom," Michael responded, "I'll have to go down to Uncle Les's and let them know I'll be knocking off early this afternoon."

"Remind him about the truck. We'll be leaving here late this afternoon and again for Mass tomorrow morning."

◆ ◆ ◆

"Vespers, huh?" Les commented or asked, it was hard to tell which.

The McGuffeys were finished with noontime dinner and were still seated around the dining room table.

"Yes. They're traditional prayers that some religious communities still say," Michael answered, parroting his mother. He hoped his uncle wouldn't ask more about it. He once again felt embarrassed by his lack of knowledge. It was still somewhat intimidating, he decided, to enter into any discussions about religion with his uncle or people like him who seemed to know the Bible so well.

"Well, we'll sure miss you tomorrow, Michael. In fact, I thought you might be particularly interested in the sermon." Les McGuffey wondered about his sister's plan to visit a convent in Nashville. Was she trying to keep his nephew out of his church?

"What's it going to be about?" Michael asked. He sensed his uncle wanted him to ask.

"Well, I was a bit concerned after the council meeting a couple of days ago. Y'know, some people get the wrong idea when there's a little bit of contentious discussion amongst the brethren, so I wanted to talk to them about how the Roman Church has handled dissension and doctrinal challenges throughout history."

Not being sure what his uncle was driving at, Michael didn't respond. He wasn't even positive that his uncle meant the Catholic Church when he said "Roman" Church.

Les looked at Michael as if to gauge his response. Seeing there wasn't one, he continued.

"Well, I plan to discuss a bit about the horrors of the Inquisition." Still no reaction from his nephew. "Are you familiar with what the Inquisition is?" *I don't figure they teach that in the Catholic schools,* Les speculated.

"I've heard of it..." Michael responded. He knew it had something to do with a time when persecution took place. *Was it Spain? Or the Church? And who persecuted whom?* "...But I don't know too much about it," he said, admitting once again his deficit of knowledge in an area with which he probably should have been familiar.

"That's all right, we can talk about it next week as we start planting," Les assured him. "Maybe you can read up on it over the weekend."

"I'll try," said Michael. *That's exactly what I'll do,* he thought, *and next week I won't be so intimidated when he starts to talk about it.*

"Do you have any information about the Inquisition?" Les doubted that there were any Catholic books that would even address the subject.

"I really don't know, Uncle Les. I can look through what we have at home."

"Let me go grab some literature I might have on it." *By all means, Michael, read about how your great Church tortured and killed millions.*

Les left momentarily to retrieve his literature, which was close at hand because he was preparing a sermon on the topic.

"Why don't you take the rest of the afternoon off, Michael," Eli offered. "I can finish up whatever needs doing. We'll plow on Monday."

"That's a good idea," Les agreed as he came back into the dining room. "Help your mom out with things this afternoon. If she doesn't have anything for you, then you can start your reading assignment now." Les handed him a couple of tracts.

"Thanks, Uncle Les," Michael said as he took the literature.

◆ ◆ ◆

It was a lazy afternoon for Michael. He played with his brothers for awhile, and then talked with his mom before cleaning up and getting ready for the trip to the convent. Sitting on his bed he picked up one of the tracts his uncle had handed him. The sketches caught his attention immediately. They portrayed horrific acts of persecution and torture. He scanned the text... "Tens of millions crushed by the Church of Rome." *There was that phrase "Roman Church" Uncle Les had used.* "Torture and persecution ordered by the Pope, carried out under the direction of the bishops and priests"... "Throngs of the faithful martyred"...

Michael continued reading. The tract described the Inquisition as a reign of terror conducted by the Roman Catholic Church against those who sought to reform the excesses and unbiblical practices that had crept into the Church through the centuries. The reformers had insisted on access to the Holy Scriptures and the freedom of all Christians to read the Bible. They wanted the "superstitious ritual" taken out of the worship services. They struggled for the freedom to live their lives out from under the "heavy yoke" of Rome. They wanted to be rid of the greedy and corrupt clergy and to have accountability restored.

For these goals, brave men and women were oppressed and persecuted. According to the tract, they were burned at the stake, had their tongues cut out, were hacked to death, and were subjected to various other atrocities. The reformers succeeded, though, in finally getting the Bible out to the people, thereby freeing them to learn the faith themselves without having to rely on the clergy. The tract concluded by mentioning that although the violence of the Inquisition took place centuries ago, that the Catholic Church even today continued to engage in unbiblical and superstitious rituals, and that hundreds of millions were still being deceived and discouraged from reading the Bible.

Michael sat on the bed and considered all the various claims made by the tract. *This can't be true,* he thought. *No way! If it is accurate history, why isn't it common knowledge? Why haven't I ever heard or read anything else that made these claims? But if it isn't true, how can they print it and promote it? Why would my uncle give it to me to read? He wouldn't give me something that wasn't true.* The images shocked Michael. They made an indelible mark on his conscience. *If it's accurate, then the Church was wrong and evil. How could that be if it is the True Church? Why was I never taught this in history?*

Michael was in a state of solitary panic as he wondered about his very understanding of the basics that his father had taught him growing up. His mother's voice from the foot of the stairs snapped him out of his thoughts and he finished getting ready for the trip to Nashville.

On the hour-long drive down I-65 to the convent, Michael remained deep in his thoughts as he tried to assimilate the information in the tracts. It was like being given a new set of directions while you were engrossed in a project that changed its whole nature. He didn't think even for a moment what the convent would be like, how Vespers were done, or who the Dominicans were. All of that was merely a distraction. He had bigger things to figure out. *Could a sincere Christian resist the truth that his uncle had been presenting him? Was it the truth? Whose truth is the truth?*

He had just begun to feel more confident about the faith that his father had taught him, the one into which he had been baptized. He was learning and appreciating more and more about the Church, what he thought to be the one, true, holy, catholic and apostolic Church. *Could it be a huge deception? Could my father have been just one more who had been duped, and then my mother caught up in it, too?*

Tammy pulled the truck off I-65, and in just a few minutes was driving through the huge iron gate that led to St. Cecilia's Motherhouse. The convent was massive. It was set up on the high ground and the drive-way wound around, bringing one up to the front doors. There were tree-lined walking paths on the grounds that stretched for more than a football field out front. The trees were just coming into bloom.

As they pulled up, they could see many of the sisters coming in from the walking paths up the front steps. It reminded Michael of a trip to the Naval Academy that he had made with his dad — all the uniformed figures hustling off to get wherever they needed to be on time. The sisters, though, were different even from a distance. They didn't move with purpose, like the midshipmen, so much as with grace. They wore the long, flowing habits, the same ones that Tammy had seen in the picture. They were even more striking in person than in the magazine.

Michael and his family entered the convent. Many of the sisters smiled and greeted them as they moved to assemble in the chapel on the wing to the left. To Michael it was all a bit otherworldly. He had been taught by the Sisters of the Immaculate Heart of Mary at St. John the Baptist, so he was not totally bewildered, but this was something he had never experienced.

Beautiful paintings and tapestries hung on the walls. It was like being taken to see a king. And, as Michael entered the chapel he noticed the red flame behind the altar, indicating that Jesus the King was indeed present in the tabernacle. As the family walked among the Dominican sisters, he felt as though they were being escorted by angels. There was a long flowing habit on each side of them, each overflowing with divine beauty guiding them as a family into the chapel.

The sisters genuflected reverently and peeled off away from the O'Sheas. They remained anonymous, delivered the souls charged to their care, then retreated to the periphery. The O'Sheas settled into a pew. Long black and white habits settled in around them, again forming what felt to Michael like a sort of spiritually protective shield. All thoughts of the tracts, the horrors of the Inquisition, his uncle, and his uncle's little white church fled from his mind.

Then the sisters commenced to sing Vespers. *It doesn't sound like human voices,* he marveled. *It's almost angelic.* He felt his spirit being lifted gently and with care, not for its own sake, but that he might experience God. He had been provided a pamphlet so that he might sing, too, but he was lost, as if in young love, in the moment.

Michael then looked at the altarpiece. It was a relief of the crucifixion. Christ hung in forlorn triumph on the cross. His Mother was at the foot of the cross with John, the apostle whom Jesus loved. She was grief stricken. Standing next to them was Mary Magdalene. The precious blood was dripping from the wounds of Christ and winged angels were catching his blood in golden chalices.

Michael stared in awe at the work and meditated on the drama presented before him in paint and stone. He tried to imagine being present for the crucifixion. He could hear the Roman centurions talking among themselves, the ones who were actually part of the detail that day. They had just arrived at the place where they'd hang the three men to die. There was one, a sergeant, who seemed to be directing the procedure. Many of the people who had walked with Jesus were weeping. Most seemed to be women. He envisioned the cross being laid flat and Jesus being laid upon it. He heard the metal on metal clank of the spikes being hammered through flesh and into the wood. They raised the cross and slid it into the hole that would support it. There his beaten and bloody body hung, the Savior of the world, the one Michael had been taught to worship and imitate.

*It's incredible,* he thought, not so much doubting the truth of the crucifixion as the reason for it. *We worship a Savior who was beaten and executed as a criminal two thousand years ago*, he thought to himself in disbelief. *I wish I could have been there so that I could make my own evaluation of this man whom so many claim to be the Son of God. I'd like to talk to someone who witnessed the crucifixion. Did the sky darken like the Bible says? Did the soldiers tear his garments? Did they cast lots for his tunic? Was there an eclipse of the sun and did the curtain of the sanctuary really tear in two?* Michael sat and reflected on all this as he gazed at the image of the crucifixion before him.

Then he felt himself moving through time, being transported not physically but in a mystical sense. He became aware that he *hadn't* missed it. This great and profound event, the sacrifice of God's own Son, the Paschal Lamb, that took place two thousand years ago, was in a state of perpetual re-run. It was truly "the greatest show on earth" and free for the asking. In the re-runs, though, Christ was no longer suffering. He had finished with his suffering when hanging on the cross. He had said, "It is finished" and had given up his spirit. The last words of Christ echoed in Michael's head... *"It is finished."*

Then he saw the hands of a priest coming down upon the Eucharist to consecrate it. He couldn't see the priest, just his hands. Then he saw it again. Then again and again... the hands now coming down to transform the bread and wine repeatedly, rapid fire. They were not the same hands, though. There were black hands, white hands, and all shades of brown coming down over the Eucharist. Some had long thin fingers, others short and thick... Some with pronounced knuckles, some rough and weathered, others smooth and manicured. It was happening over and over again and never the same pair of hands. It was the re-run! Then the hands lifted the host, the Bread of Life. This, too, was done repeatedly by different priests and Michael viewed it from the rear of the altar so that as the priest raised the host the assembly came into view.

Then the chalice was raised. *The same golden chalice held by the winged angels in the altar piece?* It seemed to Michael to be the very same one. The assemblies were large and small, this time mostly white, the next, mostly black, then all brown — all combinations of peoples were represented. Their dress varied. Many represented cultures with which Michael was not familiar. The event, though, was the same. It transcended time and place. It was the same event repeated last week and last century, and five centuries ago, and all the way back to the first century. It was re-enacted in modern, high-tech countries and countries whose economies consisted of subsistence agriculture. The background was a huge cathedral, then a humble adobe structure, then in the secrecy of someone's basement, then a modern-looking church, next an old stone church with stained glass windows that were breathtakingly beautiful... but the event was the same. He soaked it all in, the myriad structures, the varied people, the different cultures.

Then Michael saw the people approaching the altar. They were coming to eat his flesh and drink his blood, the blood of the New Covenant. They were young and innocent, well groomed and fashionably dressed. They were well weathered and wise, some not so fashionable or representing fashions that Michael didn't recognize. Others were old and decrepit, some homely, some beautiful. Some were there alone, others in families large and small. They were all approaching, and no two individuals were the same throughout the entire history of mankind.

The first had begun to reach the altar rail to partake as Michael looked on with anticipation. He was seeing more deeply and was anxious to observe as the Eucharist was consumed. Suddenly, though, as when a movie projector goes down, the images stopped and Michael found himself back in the pew at St. Cecilia's Motherhouse.

The nuns were still singing and the sound was still tenderly massaging Michael's bruised spirit. Then he saw in his mind's eye his uncle's church, the little white building with pews and a podium on a slightly raised platform. On the podium was the Bible. He felt a sense of pity, not due to the austere and simple nature of the tiny white church, but because it so well represented their concept of God, such a limited concept. It was as if they worshipped a small God, one not capable of reaching out through time and matter.

Many of the Catholic church structures in his vision were humble and even ramshackle, yet each was adorned with statues of the Blessed Mother, St. Joseph, and often other saints as well. Each displayed a large crucifix, an altar, and holy water fonts. Most significant was that each had an occupied tabernacle. Christ was truly present there.

The statues, the holy water, the crucifix... these and other aids to worshipping God had been eschewed by the people who went to the tiny white church, as well as the millions who went to various other churches representing so many different denominations or no denomination. For them, God's Word was limited to that Bible that sat upon the podium. The devout man needed nothing else. In fact, the statues represented idolatry pure and simple, the holy water, a remnant of some superstitious medieval wives' tale, and the tabernacle, a blasphemy.

*Could they be right about any of this?* he still wondered to himself.

After Vespers they drove back home. It had been, as Tammy had hoped, a moving experience for Michael. Up in his bedroom he began to settle in for the night. The tracts were lying on his nightstand. *Both can't be true,* he decided as he looked at the tracts. He picked one up and laid himself down on his bed... *Tens of millions killed... terror directed from Rome, supervised by bishops, and carried out by priests and those loyal to Rome... mock trials... tongues cut out... burnings at the stake...*

He tried to reconcile what he read with what he had just experienced at the convent. *It's all a great deception?! Do people really believe that? Could it possibly be true?* He drifted off to sleep with all these questions still rattling around in his mind.

Tammy O'Shea readied the baby for bed, then went to check on her younger boys. She had felt terribly lonely that day, and as night arrived it only seemed to intensify her grief. She summoned the strength to carry on by offering up her loneliness to procure grace for those who might need it most. Though she had never even considered it, such offerings helped her to reach out beyond herself, reach out to God in an attempt to imitate his Son. She prayed especially that those suffering for the Faith might be comforted. In doing this she was granted the grace herself to carry on. Dwelling on her own suffering would only have exacerbated the lonely torment.

Entering her bedroom she reminded herself that she would ask the Blessed Mother to petition her Son to send angels to guard and protect her son from spiritual danger.

As soon as Michael fell asleep, he was back in the dungeon. This time he wasn't so anxious — he remembered it, and was confident that no one there could physically destroy him. They sought only to frighten, deceive, and distort. This time the robed figure was already on the parapet. Again the sun shone through the barred window directly into Michael's eyes and made it difficult for him to look up at the figure and impossible to see his face.

"Who are you?" Michael asked directly, gaining courage.

"I will ask the questions!" the man roared back at Michael, furious that Michael was no longer cowering in his presence.

"Can't I just know who you are?"

"No!" he said, trying to project his might. At first the man was beside himself with fury at the boy's audacity, but finally settled himself and decided to switch strategies.

"No. I mean it is simply not possible, for I am far too many and therefore you can not really know me."

This succeeded in confusing Michael and making him think before he ventured another question, but before he could the figure continued.

"But I have much to show you and tell you, much that I want you to learn for your own good." This succeeded in diverting Michael's attention away from concern about the figure's identity.

"Would you like to see what lies beyond these walls?" he asked. Michael thought anything would be an improvement over the dark dungeon.

"Anything you might want to see lies beyond these walls." He threw down a rope ladder to Michael. Michael stepped forward and began climbing up toward the parapet.

"You want to see some of the years of the Inquisition?" the man asked. Michael nodded "yes" as he reached the balcony. He wondered how the figure could know his thoughts.

"Come with me, then, through this door." Even up close Michael could not get a look at the figure's face. The hood on the robe kept it in the shadows.

They left the dungeon and found themselves just outside a village. There were people gathered around four posts. The posts were twelve feet tall and at the base of each one was piled brush.

"Where are we?" Michael asked.

"Spain," the man answered.

"What's going on here?" Michael asked hesitantly. He was afraid of the answer.

"Watch."

An entourage appeared coming from the village. Three men and one woman, hands secured behind their backs, were being led toward the posts.

*Oh, no!* Michael thought, as he anticipated the horror. He felt as though he had been kicked in the stomach.

The prisoners were led on top of the brush and fastened to their respective posts. Michael took a few steps forward, thinking of some way he could intervene.

"You can't stop it. You have only the power to observe," the robed figure informed him.

"What are they guilty of?" asked Michael, with desperation in his voice. Perhaps they had committed some atrocity.

"The Inquisitor didn't believe that they were sincere converts to the Church," the figure answered matter-of-factly. "They're Jews or Muslims, I'm not sure which."

A man was reading the order to execute. Michael only heard the phrase "by authority of the Inquisitor." Then torches were lit from a small fire that had been burning nearby. The prisoners at the stake started to beg and cry for mercy. It wasn't like in a movie when the heroes accepted their fate with determined looks on their faces. It was too much for Michael to handle. The tears flowed freely down his cheeks. The dried brush began to burn. The pathetic figures, caught there like bugs, writhed in terror trying to loose themselves. The screams continued even as the smoke became so thick that he couldn't see the victims. Soon the smoke overcame them and the screams stopped, but the fire was left to burn up their bodies.

Michael was literally sick with grief. He remembered the night of the fire and how his dad had been overcome with smoke. He was acutely aware of the upset in his stomach and was fighting to keep from throwing up.

*I guess it's true*, he realized with devastation in his heart. *The tracts were not a complete lie, anyway.* It seemed as if it were a grand illusion, this Holy Catholic Church, that they had all been following. *Where might my dad be now?* he wondered. He stood there, zombie-like, drained of emotion. He felt an almost overwhelming sense of despair.

"Why so grief stricken, Michael?" the figure asked plainly.

"This is *my* Church, the true Church... or what I'd been taught was the true Church."

"Worry not, Michael. 'Wherever two or three are gathered in my name' is where the church is. The church isn't a formal organization."

Somehow this revelation only intensified Michael's grief.

"May I see the crucifixion?" he asked quietly. *Is any of it — Christianity — true? Was there even a man called Jesus?* He looked over to his escort as if to beg not to be told that it had never happened.

Instead he heard a sound that seemed to be coming from the figure. It started out sounding sort of like the squeal of a small animal in distress. He still could not see any face on the figure. The squeal continued and grew in strength. It still did not sound human. As Michael stood there watching, the squeal became a very low and ferocious sounding growl, the kind a canine would make baring its teeth. He became uneasy. The growl continued as if the figure didn't even need to take a breath. It became a gruesome, horrific howl. It was menacing, diabolical, and otherworldly, and it grew louder. By this time Michael was shaken. The demon began to approach Michael, his howling loud enough to block out any other sound. Michael, now terrified, finally turned to run.

Then suddenly he found himself flailing about on his bed, back in the guest cottage on his uncle's farm. He stopped running when he realized the demon was gone, and lay still for a few minutes. It was dark except for the bit of natural light from the quarter moon coming in the window. When he had finally caught his breath he reached out and felt around for the matches that were on his nightstand. He located them and lit his oil lamp. The soft glow filled most of the room, but it wasn't strong enough to chase the darkness from the corners. He checked his watch. It was 2:30, the middle of the night, and he was wide awake.

Michael climbed out of bed and stepped over to the collection of books he had assembled from his father's collection. He was hoping that at least one of them would discuss the Inquisition. He knew his uncle would ask, and decided not to rely on what a couple of tracts had to say on the matter. It was important for him to have an answer for his uncle on Monday. He brought the lamp over to the small wooden desk and began his study.

# 8

The O'Sheas drove down to the convent in the early morning. There were a few lay people in the chapel for Mass. Like the previous night, there was a beauty of worship that just wasn't present at his uncle's church. The music was richer than the simple Christian hymns he had heard on previous Sundays, the atmosphere more serious, more reverent.

As he approached to receive the Eucharist, Michael suddenly remembered the mystical insight he had had the previous night. It had ended right at that point, when people were just starting to come forward to eat and drink. He remembered as he had looked on with great anticipation that the images stopped as the climax was approaching. The "projector" went down just before the best part. He watched now as people received the Eucharist and then drank from the chalice. One after the other, the sisters received.

*This is what binds them,* he realized. *The habit makes them look the same, but that's only a physical manifestation of what is going on now. People are in the same family when they share the same flesh and blood. They are all receiving the same flesh and blood now, Christ's. We* — he corrected his thinking — *share the same supernatural flesh and blood. Though my mother doesn't wear a habit, she is receiving now, she is part of the same family as the sisters, she has the same flesh and blood. We're all sharing His flesh and blood,* Michael thought with tremendous excitement as he looked up at the crucifix. He remembered the images yesterday, the many hands coming down over the Eucharist to consecrate it, the myriad assemblies of people gathered as the Holy Spirit came upon the bread and wine to transform it. *We're all in the same family,* he thought, as he recalled Christ's words to his apostles...

> "All of you must drink from it," he said, "for this is my blood, the blood of the new covenant..."

He considered all those through the ages who had received the same flesh and blood as he was now stepping up to receive. Once again he was one with them, part of the same family, part of the same body. This time, though, he felt the exhilaration of truly realizing it.

To Michael's surprise, his uncle did not mention the Inquisition on Monday or that whole week. They stayed busy with farm chores and conversation did not turn to matters of faith at all. This situation continued through the months of April and May. Michael and his family went to Mass on Sundays at the Dominican convent instead of the Saturday night vigil Mass, which meant that Michael was unable to attend services at his uncle's church. Michael persevered in his studying and reading of the Bible and the books his father had left.

Les McGuffey had decided not to press his nephew on the tracts about the Inquisition. He thought it better to present the evidence in the literature and let the young man make up his own mind. He wasn't surprised that Michael did not bring up the topic the first day after getting the tracts. It was so much for a young man to assimilate and come to terms with — what he believed, the emotions connected with how his father had taught him, and the utter confusion he would feel at first. Les was surprised, though, that his nephew did not broach the subject at all that first week and went to Mass without batting an eye the following week and every week after that. Through many weeks, Les persisted with his original strategy of not being the one to start asking about the tracts, but his curiosity grew.

To be sure, he was preoccupied with the fissure in his own church over the tobacco issue. The men who grew tobacco had set their plants for that year, but agreed to continue discussions. Luther was not happy with what he considered to be the compromising of God's Word, and Luther was not one to let a matter rest for very long.

Eventually, though, Les's curiosity gave way to concern. He had been so confident that Michael was on the road to conversion and accepting Christ as his personal Lord and Savior. The literature, he thought, would provide the gentle push that Michael needed to begin leaving the church of his boyhood on his own.

Finally he decided that his nephew must be in a state of denial. The cultural and family attachment to their church was so strong that he was incapable of seeing things clearly and evaluating issues honestly. Les realized too, with the passing of April and May, that he couldn't afford to have things progress at such a slow rate. Very soon it would be time to probe, challenge, and educate.

By the first week of June strawberries were at their peak. The asparagus was just past its prime, but there was still plenty to eat at every dinner and enough left over for market. Every morning there was a strawberry-picking detail. The younger O'Shea boys were fascinated with the idea that both asparagus and strawberries were perennials. They came back every year in the same spot to be harvested and enjoyed. Michael could have never imagined how many berries a quarter acre could produce.  Sometimes Michael and Eli helped harvest, as did Pam, Tammy, and Les, but the bulk of the strawberry harvest was accomplished by the younger children.

Lori, Eli's thirteen-year old sister, generally supervised the effort.  She inspected everyone's small bucket or basket and graded the harvest.  The big, red, unblemished ones went in small pint containers to bring to market to sell.  Small and/or slightly scarred ones were tossed in a five-gallon bucket earmarked for home jam production.  The marginal ones were consumed daily at breakfast, dinner, supper, and even for snacks before bedtime.  Tammy was impressed that Lori was made responsible for what constituted a part of the farm income and that she easily rose to the occasion.  Tammy's younger boys enjoyed their cheerful cousin.  Tammy also thoroughly enjoyed canning the strawberry jam with Pam and Lori.  Michael and his brothers would always remember eating more delicious strawberries in more ways than they had ever thought possible.

One Friday night in early June, Michael headed down to the McGuffeys to pick up some strawberry syrup that Pam, Lori, and his mom had been making earlier in the day.  When he arrived, Pam and Lori were just pouring the syrup into bottles.  Some of the McGuffeys were snacking on strawberries and cream.  Lori insisted Michael have some while they finished the syrup.

Michael joined his uncle and Eli out on the porch.  They chatted briefly about the various projects they had been working on now that most of the planting was done.  Then Les changed the subject.

"Say, Michael, did you ever get a chance to look over that literature I lent to you?" he asked as casually as possible, "I think it was about the Inquisition."

Michael felt the butterflies begin to awaken in his stomach.  He had prepared himself for this very question two months ago, but was rather relieved when it seemed that his uncle would not bring it up.

"Yeah, I did," Michael answered a bit nervously. "I'm sorry. I should have gotten it back to you."

"Oh no, don't worry about that," Les assured him, "I was just kind of curious what you thought, what your reaction was. Remember I gave a sermon about the Inquisition, but that's one you didn't get to hear. I guess that's why we never got around to discussing it."

"Yeah, well I guess Eli and I talked about it a little bit." Michael wasn't very sure of himself, about how or where to begin. Les was surprised at first that he and Eli had discussed it and wasn't quite sure how he felt about that. He considered how much time the two had spent working together day after day and realized it was natural that they would discuss various things during the day.

"What conclusions did you two come to?" he asked with a smile.

"I'm not sure we came to any conclusions—" Michael answered while looking at Eli. Then he thought that this would be as good a starting point as any.

Eli was relieved Michael had answered. Michael had asked some questions and provided some insight that Eli still hadn't fully considered.

"I guess I feel that sincere Christians can only look at that period with a strange mix of emotions," Michael began.

"What about Catholics?" Les asked directly, sitting forward in his seat.

"Well, that's who I meant when I said 'sincere Christians,'" he answered, barely restraining a smile. "Anyway, the first problem is that much of what has been written about that time seems to be bad history, written by people with an obvious bias."

His uncle nodded tentatively. He had never heard that and was not prepared to refute it immediately.

"Records were not well kept during those times and many of the original sources themselves were questionable," Michael continued, "and the numbers have tended toward exaggeration.

"Then there is the nature of the whole thing itself — could anyone truly and comprehensively understand it all even if an accurate history were available?" His uncle couldn't quite see what he was driving at but listened patiently as he settled back down in his chair. It was a pleasant June evening.

"I mean, what people call the 'Inquisition' took place over about six centuries and across half a continent." This was almost verbatim from one of his father's books. Again Les did not comment. He didn't actually know that much about the Inquisition himself. He certainly didn't know those facts.

"Unfortunately, it has been used by many people to promote confusion about various events in Church history and even hostility toward the Church itself," Michael continued.

"Well, isn't it true that many people were put to death for what the Church called heresy at that time?" Les challenged. *After all, even if many things were not completely and accurately preserved, the whole thing wasn't a lie.*

"Many people were executed," Michael agreed. "That's really not in question. I guess what has caused the most misunderstanding is the distorted perspective held by many in considering the Inquisition. Then there have been others who have drawn the wrong conclusions from what happened in that period. That's probably been more of a problem." Michael paused to weigh his uncle's reaction. His uncle nodded slightly as if to express his interest — if not necessarily his agreement — and to assure him that it was okay to continue.

"The thinking and practices in those times are rather hard for people living today to appreciate. There has always been tension within the Church, even from the beginning. In St. Paul's letters to Timothy, to the Colossians, and elsewhere, he warned of false teachers and unsound doctrine. Peter also cautioned against false teachers. The histories that have been preserved show that the Church struggled against different gospel messages right from the beginning. There have always been debates and dissension in the Church among men of good will. Paul rebuked Peter for instance when Peter displayed poor judgment, and that's recorded in the Bible. So we shouldn't be surprised at all to see passionate debate and even temporary disagreement in the body. You've said as much about Luther and the tobacco debate going on in your own church."

"That's right," Les agreed, anxious to hear more from his nephew. This was the longest thought the boy had expressed since coming to Kentucky, and Les was impressed that he obviously had given a lot of consideration to what the tracts had said. For Les, this was a good sign. *If he's willing to discuss and reflect on things, he'll come around sooner or later. Once engaged in discussion he'll be easier to reason with and teach,* thought Les.

"Now, centuries later the Church was still experiencing the same growing pains. There were movements among lay groups in the late Middle Ages who were extremely critical of the 'establishment' in the Church." Michael made quotation marks with his fingers when he said establishment. "Many of the clerics were lazy, greedy, ignorant, and politically comfortable. The lay people who rose up against this situation were often radical, evangelistic, and sometimes unruly men and women. Apparently many of the heretics of the thirteenth century came out of these lay movements. Those were many of the ones executed I'm sure. It is troublesome to think that men and women were killed for their beliefs or only because they were critical of the local cleric, who may very well have been corrupt.

"Others were executed in part for encouraging violence or civil unrest, but the excesses of the Inquisition shouldn't be wished away by any devout Catholic. No, as a Catholic you've got to come to grips with the reality of that part of history."

Les was so intrigued at this point that he had successfully blocked everything else out, even the ubiquitous night sounds of crickets and other nocturnal creatures, Pam and Lori's singing in the kitchen, and the passing of time itself.

"And how have you come to grips with it?" he asked. He had never heard a Catholic discuss the Inquisition before, despite referring to it himself as a means of tearing the proverbial mask off the face of the Roman Church many times. He had always assumed that Catholics just ignored or denied it. *How could one come to grips with such evil?*

"Well, I think the first thing is to realize that the true estimates of how many were executed were more in the five to twenty thousand range, over a number of centuries, instead of the 'tens of millions' that some people have claimed. That's important, of course, but it still would leave you arguing about numbers and missing the more important issues involved."

Michael was proud of his own recall. It had been more than two months since he had looked into it, but he had studied hard, and now it was all coming back to him as he spoke. It was so clear in his mind that it left him with all his powers of concentration to focus on presenting it.

"It's important to consider this time in context, what was going on in other areas around this same time."

*So this is where he's going,* Les thought at that point, *the old "it really wasn't that many people and lots of other people were killing each other besides." That will be easy enough to counter,* he thought, as he began developing his own arguments and explanations.

"In England, for example, just after the Reformation took hold, there were around eight hundred executions a year. Anyone Catholic was a target. Monasteries and convents were ransacked. The Mass was illegal and persecution of anyone loyal to the Pope was the rule."

This angle confounded Les. He had expected to hear of secular brutality and mistreatment, not religiously motivated violence, least of all perpetrated by those he still considered the brave rebels of the Reformation.

"The same violent actions were widespread among the followers of various reformers, like Luther, Zwingli, and Calvin in the sixteenth century. These people also killed those they considered to be heretics where and when they could. But as gruesome as all of that is, it's really not evidence that they were wrong in what they asserted. The reasons they broke from the Church could, theoretically, have been well founded."

Now Les's objections and arguments began melting away as he considered his young nephew's point. The behavior of some people is not necessarily an indicator of the wisdom or truth of the movement they are promoting.

"Did you know that thirty thousand alleged witches were burned at the stake in England after the Reformation, and in Protestant Germany it was a hundred thousand?" Michael pointed out.

His uncle just shook his head. He had never heard that.

"Yeah, and apparently witch hunting was unheard of in Catholic areas." Michael had been fascinated to learn that fact himself.

"Now, again, that doesn't mean that the Christian ideals in which people believed in many of these witch-hunting countries were wrong, much less that they all took part in the witch hunts. Maybe the point is that the truth is still the truth even if all the followers are not very good at following it, or even if there are no followers at all."

"And a lie is still a lie even if many people might happen to believe it," Eli offered.

"That would be its corollary," smiled Michael. Eli had heard this all before in bits and pieces.

"But all that doesn't show that the Roman Catholic Church is the true church," Les challenged.

"No, it doesn't. I don't think it has to," assured Michael. "But what does the Inquisition prove? That the Catholic Church contains sinners? Guilty as charged." Michael was serious and matter-of-fact in tone. "That some of the sinners were in positions of authority, even high-rank-ing authority, in the Church?  Guilty again.

"Individual Catholics or groups of Catholics fall short, oftentimes far short, of the example Jesus provided.  The Inquisition is an extreme example of that.  Even so, the fact that the Inquisition happened is not inconsistent with the claim that the Church was founded and commissioned by Jesus, that it is the True Church."

Les was impressed at Michael's thinking, or whomever's thinking Michael was now presenting.  He was still pondering, however, the distinction being made.

"It's really very biblical," Michael continued.

Les's ears perked up.

"In Matthew's Gospel, chapter thirteen, Jesus told the parable of the farmer who sowed wheat.  His enemy came in one night and sowed weed seed.  When the plants grew, the farmer instructed his workers not to worry about separating out the wheat from the weeds while they grew; rather at harvest the weeds would all be sorted out.  They would be bundled together and cast into the fire."

These passages were especially exciting for Michael now that he was beginning to have an appreciation for the farming and shepherding analogies so often used in the Bible.

Les thought over Michael's interpretation of the passage, that there would be "weeds" within and throughout the Church.  He thought about his response.  He didn't know enough about the Inquisition to question the factual accuracy of anything Michael said.  He was still reflecting on the basic point Michael had made, namely that the fact of the Inquisition didn't prove anything about the Roman Catholic Church that couldn't be proven without it, and that it did not demonstrate that the Roman Church was an apostate church.

"Even Peter, chosen by Christ to be the first earthly leader of the Church, the prince of the apostles, denied Christ three times as the final hour approached," Michael added as his uncle was still considering everything.

"Now that part about Peter being the first earthly leader I'd have to disagree with, Michael," Les laughed. He was well aware of the Catholic position that Peter was the first Pope, and rejected it outright.

"Maybe that ought to be our next topic of discussion," Michael offered, smiling back at his uncle. He had not been planning to challenge his uncle in a series of theological discussions, but he realized maybe that's how things would turn out.

"We ought to discuss these things on a more regular basis," Les responded quickly. He liked the idea immediately. He saw the opportunity to engage his nephew more often and jumped at the opportunity.

"We'll have Bible study after singing on Saturday nights," Les suggested. "That'll be good for us to get back into. We used to do that a few years back and somehow fell away from it... You don't mind if some of the folks who come for the singing stay and listen, do you?" Les asked.

Just then, the thought occurred to Les that such Bible studies could serve to bring the factions in his own church together. The more he thought about those on each side of the tobacco issue, the more he liked that notion. *They'll appreciate just how much we have in common with one another and won't be so quick to spend time and energy fighting amongst themselves.*

"No, not at all," Michael answered. *What have I gotten myself into?*

"Do you want to talk about Peter next week?" asked Les, "and about the Pope?"

"We can talk about that, I guess," Michael answered, trying to sound as casual as possible. He was already anticipating being the victim of a different sort of Inquisition.

"The syrup's ready," announced Lori as she bounded onto the porch, "take this back for your breakfast tomorrow."

175

"Thanks," Michael said as he began to stand.

"You don't have to leave yet. I was just making sure you didn't walk off without it," Lori assured.

"That's right, Michael, sit down, relax," Les joined in.

"No I'd better be gettin' back. Thanks, though, for everything," Michael insisted. He was already too pre-occupied with what he was going to say next week about Peter the fisherman to enjoy sitting around chatting.

◆ ◆ ◆

In the early part of the following week, new items emerged on the "farm fresh" menu. Peas were beginning to come in and Michael learned how to "rob" potatoes. Eli and Lori showed him how to reach into the potato hills, near the base of the plant and feel around for some young potatoes. If you were gentle, you could grab a few from each plant and then pat the earth back down and let the plant grow some more. The "new" potatoes they harvested were extra tender and flavorful, with no tough skins to peel.

The potatoes and peas, just like the strawberries, asparagus, fresh eggs, and milk, tasted so good. No one in the O'Shea family had any trouble finishing what was on his plate for any meal. Part of the better taste was due to the freshness, but another part was psychological, thought Michael. When you harvest your own food directly from the earth, it's as if some kind of bond develops. Or, maybe the bond is strengthened within your own being, between your work and your reward.

His father had worked hard and even risked his life at times so that they could eat potatoes, yet they were so under-appreciated, he realized now. Simple potatoes — when you cut out all the middlemen — when you planted them yourself, cultivated the patch, hilled them, dug them up, transported them, washed them, then finally prepared them, were wonderful rewards to consume. Then they were appreciated for what they really were — a life-giving staple. You couldn't help but become attached to the soil and the tubers growing under it or the beans hanging over it ready to be harvested. Wasting food became unthinkable! Such an offense was almost blasphemous, a desecration.

Lori harvested peas most every day. They were like tiny green marbles of sweetness snuggled together in their pods. Shelling peas became an evening pastime on the McGuffeys' porch. The O'Sheas would come down after dinner and there'd be storytelling, hymn singing, lemonade drinking and always pea shelling. Sometimes, after a story or a song Uncle Les would bellow, "Who needs television anyway?!"

At night, though, after the fun and laughter had passed and his brothers were in bed, Michael read and studied by oil lamp at the little wooden desk. In his father's books he saw a sentence underlined here or an asterisk there. He felt closer to his Dad when he studied the books and he savored it. *They used to be his books... He paged through them at night just like I'm doing now,* Michael thought. But it went even deeper than that. *This is what my father believed. This is what he embraced and tried to pass on.* It was what the books taught, the beliefs of the faith that bound him to his father more than the books themselves. More precisely, Michael realized gradually, the beliefs did not so much bind Michael to his father as it bound both of them to something much larger than their own family. It bound them in a family that spanned generations and continents, an eternal family of believers.

His father wrote very few notes in the margins or on the tops of pages. He wrote nothing in his Bible.

"He's still young, Les," insisted Pam. "You shouldn't come down on him too hard. It might be too much for a boy his age." She had just been informed of the re-institution of the Saturday evening Bible study and what Les had in mind.

"I won't come down on him too hard," he assured her. He knew he wouldn't have to. People like Luther would, and Les would serve as the mediator who would call off the attack dogs. It was a natural "good cop/bad cop" setup. He would allow things to get tough for Michael, but not too tough, and would let Michael feel the heat, but wouldn't let him get burned too badly. Then, after the biblical battles were over and everyone had left, Michael would come to him, feel drawn to him, and seek his re-assurance, comfort, and instruction. It was not a devious plan, Les had decided, but was just the way things would naturally flow.

"Is it going to be an open Bible study? Do you want all the children there?"

"Yes, of course. I mean, you don't have to be there if something else is pressing, but studying the Bible is good," Les insisted. "It'll be good for everyone. We can all learn something when the Bible is opened."

*Only if one's heart is open, too,* thought Pam. She was dubious of the whole thing. "The Bible shouldn't be used like a sledgehammer," she opined weakly. There was no stopping it and she wasn't really trying to, but she was concerned for her nephew. She was well aware that Bible discussions tended to become passionate. She thought it would be overwhelming for Michael.

"It won't be used as a sledgehammer," Les replied, trying to allay her concerns. "I'll make sure of that."

Pam had seen it plenty of times before, though — zealous Christian men quoting the Bible, delivering their pitches, countering the opinions or interpretations of their "opponents," and in the end driving themselves further apart from one another. The arguments often appeared to be sound, all agreed that the Bible was inspired, the application appropriate, but the result was division. She had seen far more souls become entrenched through argument than moved.

*Martin de Porres Kennedy*

# 9

As always, the singing went well that Saturday evening. Michael had become accustomed to most of the old hymns. Luther was there, as were Jimmy and George, two of the men who had opposed Luther on the tobacco issue.

Michael was amazed at how relaxed he felt. Here he was, about to present a Catholic concept to three men who each had more biblical knowledge in his little finger than Michael possessed in his entire being. And, each disagreed profoundly with what Michael was about to say. It didn't matter. What he had read and brought that evening, especially the book on Church history, would make it clear that the Church had always had a leader, a pope. *It should be a rather quick and amicable discussion,* he thought. He had even indulged in dreams of leading these men into the Church.

After an hour or so of hymns, Tammy stood to say good night.

"You're not staying for the Bible study, Sister?" Les asked.

"Bible study?"

"Didn't Michael tell you we were going to have a Bible study this evening after singing?"

"No. Was he supposed to?" Tammy asked. *Was Les expecting me to stay?* she wondered.

"Les, I'd like to, but the little ones need to get to bed, and so do I. I still have to — "

"No, no, that's all right. You go on. I thought you knew about it, though."

"No, I didn't, but it doesn't matter," she said. "Michael, you're staying, aren't you?"

"Yeah," he answered. He had wanted as few people as possible to know about and watch his presentation.

Tammy might have felt differently had she known her eldest was about to subject himself to the rigorous cross-examination of the assembled men, but she was anxious to get back home and into bed.

"Michael can be the representative from the O'Shea family," Tammy said to her brother, smiling. "If we need to know anything, Michael'll fill us in tomorrow."

*You don't know the half of it, sister,* thought Les. Again, he saw that if he could move Michael to embrace the Bible, the rest of the family would follow suit. They'd embrace Christ and leave that Church that was so rife with ritual and superstition.

"Eli, you and Lori help your Aunt Tammy home with the children," he directed them. "Good night, Sis."

"Good night."

Pam walked her sister-in-law to the door. She was relieved that Tammy was going home. It would be hard on a mother to watch her young son on the hot seat. She'd feel so protective of him. It was better that she go home and get some rest.

Les, too, was thankful that his sister wouldn't be there. This way, he could let the meeting proceed naturally, without worrying so much about controlling it for his sister's sake. He was well aware that Luther and the other men could be pretty intimidating, but his nephew could handle it, and ultimately would be well served by it. *After all,* Les rationalized, *the stakes are high. We are talking about his very soul.*

"Michael, why don't you sit here," Les proposed as he stood up away from his seat at the head of the table. "It probably makes more sense so that everyone can hear and see well."

"All right," said Michael, as he gathered his bag — a soft leather briefcase that had belonged to his father. The satchel contained many of the books Michael had consulted and was planning to cite, and also his father's Bible. He was especially anxious to quote from one of the books he had on Church history, and another that contained essays and commentaries by the early Church Fathers.

Michael began to settle himself in his uncle's place at the table. Luther sat just opposite him, while George and Jimmy were on his left and right. Les McGuffey was content to sit back away from the table, as would Eli and Lori when they returned. Michael took a few of the books out of the satchel and proceeded to stack them to his right.

"Now, I see you with various books there, Michael," Luther began, jumpstarting the meeting, "you ain't plannin' to use any of them to support what you have to say tonight, are you?" He knew very well that that was exactly what Michael intended to do.

Michael was perplexed by the question.

"A few of them, yeah. I was just going to show—"

"Now why would you want to do that?" Luther asked, before Michael could answer the first question.

"Well, some of what the early Christians wrote can—"

"Yeah, but is what these early Christians wrote in the Bible?"

"No," said Michael, still dazed from the first question.

"Then why would you want to consult them when you're tryin' to figure out what the truth is?"

Michael couldn't see what Luther was driving at, and was becoming unnerved by this man with intense eyes who could fire questions faster than he could formulate responses.

"Well, because they wrote about some things, practices and understandings, that aren't really covered in the Bible." *At least he let me finish that sentence*, Michael thought.

"Yeah, but what I'm sayin' is that we can't be sure if they are true, can we?" Luther asked.

Now Michael began to relax a bit. *Luther just wants to make sure I'm not going to start quoting some unknown sources to support what we believe,* he figured. "Oh yeah, everyone in here is a recognized early Christian writer," Michael assured. "I don't think there's any debate among scholars that these are all legitimate writings from early Christianity."

"Well, I'm no scholar, but I have to question whether or not I can rely on such writings," Luther offered. "In fact, I know I can't."

Les, George, and Jimmy all held their tongues while this went on. They knew exactly where Luther was going with all this. Pam saw the Bible study going the way she feared right from the beginning. Just then Eli and Lori came back into the dining room.

"You didn't miss anything," Luther assured them. "We're just tryin' to get started."

It wasn't as if it had been planned, but Luther had assumed total control over the Bible study, Les realized.

"Why can't you rely on them?" Michael asked Luther about the writings of the early Christians.

"Because it's not the Bible," Luther answered directly.

"Isn't it helpful, though, to consult other writings that might shed light on how the first Christians put into practice what they learned from Jesus and the Apostles?"

"We don't know that it is pure and without error," Luther explained in reply. "If you come walkin' into this room thirsty and there's ten glasses of water on the table and I says to you, 'the one in the middle is clean and pure, but I'm not positive about the other ones,' which glass you gonna drink from?"

"The one in the middle," Michael answered, not entirely happy with the analogy.

"Well, then, why should we go consultin' various other books when we know that the Bible is inspired and sufficient for our thirst for knowledge?" Without waiting for a response, Luther continued. "Do you believe in what the Bible says?" This time he waited for the obvious answer.

"Yeah."

"Good, because…

> All Scripture is given by inspiration of God, and is profitable for doctrine, for reproof, for correction, for instruction in righteousness, that the man of God may be complete, thoroughly equipped for every good work.

"That's second Timothy three, verses sixteen to seventeen. A Bible study should use the Bible, and the Bible is sufficient. That's what the Bible says. If any other book or source is used, well, who can be sure of the truth of it? It just serves to confuse things," Luther concluded.

This lecture flustered Michael and made him feel even younger than his seventeen years. He weighed his options. He could debate the simple analogy Luther had used. After all, he would have had to trust Luther's word as to which glass was clean and pure, or how else would he know just by looking? *Forget that,* he decided, thinking that the whole meeting would break down into an argument over whether or not Luther's analogy was fair.

"All right," he acquiesced, "I'll limit my presentation to the Bible, but Catholics don't feel that that's necessary or even a very good idea."

"That's an interesting comment," Les said from his seat against the wall. "It'd be interesting to have a Bible study on that." Les could not pass up that opening. He felt that this very issue was the key to saving his nephew — that Michael begin to put the Bible before Roman Church custom and tradition.

Tammy had just settled herself down into the soft living room chair. The three younger children were in bed. She tried to still her soul and quiet her mind. Then she began the Rosary. She prayed to the Blessed Mother for — among other things — the soul of her husband, and to provide spiritual protection and guidance for her eldest son.

Michael sat for a long while collecting his thoughts and trying to reclaim his composure. *How to proceed?* He could not have foreseen such an obstacle. *Oh well,* he figured, *what does the Bible say?* He looked through the notes he had taken the past week.

Luther, Les, and all the others looked on patiently. Luther had practically declared victory in his own mind.

"Well, I guess the best place to start is John one forty-two," began Michael. Bible pages began turning. Michael waited until everyone had reached that page, then read aloud:

> He brought him to Jesus, who looked at him and said, "You are Simon son
> of John; your name shall be Cephas (which is rendered Peter)."

"So Christ changed Simon's name as soon as he met him," Michael commented. "Then we can—"

"Christ changed other names, too," Luther inserted.

"Yes, he did," agreed Michael quickly. "I guess the important thing to look at is what he changed a name to and why. The meaning of Peter was 'rock.'"

Les knew where Michael was going with this argument. It would lead to Matthew 16.

"Now in the Old Testament God is called a rock. There are other name changes in the Old Testament, too — Abram to Abraham, Jacob to Israel — but no man is *given a name* that means 'rock'," Michael continued.

Les paused. He had never considered that before, but didn't think it momentous by itself.

"Then in the Gospel of Matthew, which was written with the Jews in mind, it—"

"What do you mean it was written for the Jews?" Luther questioned.

"Well, I just meant that it was written for a Jewish audience," Michael began to explain. "Some of the — "

"Does it say that in the Bible?" Luther challenged. Then, not waiting for an answer, "How do you know that, if it's not in the Bible?"

Michael looked over to his uncle, from whom he first heard that Matthew's Gospel was for the Jews. *That's a fair question*, he thought. Seeing that his Uncle Les was not about to offer his explanation, Michael turned back to Luther.

"Some of the terms used in Matthew's Gospel would have been recognizable to Jews and not to Gentiles," he explained. "The title 'Messiah,' for example, or the genealogy in the very beginning of the Gospel." Michael was relying now on much of what he had studied in the last two months and was thankful he had done it. "It didn't matter to Gentiles that Christ was a descendant of David, but it was crucial for the Jews. They needed to see how Old Testament prophecy had been fulfilled, that the Messiah was in fact in David's line, of the tribe of Judah."

"That's interestin'," Luther allowed, "as long as we understand that all of that is not revealed to us explicitly in Matthew's Gospel, that it's not in the Bible. It might be your idea or best guess, but we have to be careful about ideas and guesses."

"Sure," Michael said calmly. *Not revealed explicitly in the Bible*, Michael repeated in his head. *I need to start thinking like my Uncle Matty to handle him.* He was tempted to ask Luther how he even knew who wrote the first Gospel. After all, Matthew never identified himself as the author; rather, that was the name assigned via oral tradition to the first Gospel. But Michael didn't want to get bogged down in that discussion right now.

"Now in the sixteenth chapter of Matthew we have Peter's confession. Eli, do you want to read, starting on verse fifteen down through nineteen?" Michael chose Eli because he felt a bit awkward asking his uncle or one of the other men to read a passage in the Bible, as if he were the teacher and they the pupils.

> "And you," he said to them, "who do you say that I am?"
>
> "You are the Messiah," Simon Peter answered, " the Son of the living God!"
>
> Jesus replied, "Blest are you, Simon son of Jonah! No mere man has revealed this to you, but my heavenly Father. I for my part declare to you, you are 'Rock,' and on this rock I will build my Church, and the jaws of death shall not prevail against it. I will entrust to you the keys of the kingdom of heaven. Whatever you declare bound on earth shall be bound in heaven; whatever you declare loosed on earth shall be loosed in heaven." Then he strictly ordered his disciples not to tell anyone that he was the Messiah.

"Those are two different kinds of rocks referred to there," George said as soon as Eli was finished reading.

Les was glad that George had understood this point. It saved him from having to explain it, and the more he stayed in the background the better.

"The New Testament was written in Greek," George continued, "and the first rock is *petros* meaning small stone or pebble, while the second rock is *petra* which means large immovable boulder. Peter couldn't have been the rock, the foundation upon which the Church was built. He was the small rock, the *petros.*"

George was polite and deliberate with his interpretation, in contrast to the bulldog style of Luther.

"That's an interesting interpretation," said Michael. He was already familiar with it from one of the books he had studied, but wanted to be gracious as he refuted it. "It is true that the New Testament was written in Greek and that the original rendering of rock was with the two different words, *petros* and *petra.* So what you said, if that were simply the case, would make good sense, but..." *Everyone sat forward in his seat, especially Les and George.* "Christ didn't speak Greek. Or, maybe I should say he would not have spoken Greek to fellow Jews."

Les had never considered this, but he had to admit to himself that it was probably true.

Michael continued. "They would have spoken Aramaic to one another, and the word for rock in Aramaic is *kepha.* When it was written in the Greek, though, they ran into a gender problem. *Petra,* a feminine noun, could be used for the second place that the word 'rock' appears, but not for the name of a man. It would have sounded silly to tell Simon that his name was now *Petra,* so they used the masculine form, *Petros.*"

Michael noted that no one nodded in agreement. He assumed that it still wasn't clear.

"If, for example, the word for large rock in Greek was Roberta, then that is what they would have used: 'on this Roberta I will build my Church.' But they would have translated it to read: 'I declare to you that you are Robert and upon this Roberta I will build my Church.' The writer would use the masculine form of the word, because it was a *man* Christ was talking to, and unfortunately the meaning in Greek is not identical. Do you follow what I'm saying?"

"Now hold on just a second," bellowed Luther. The others were still considering it all. "You're tellin' me that I'm not readin' what I'm readin'?"

"What do you read in English?"

"Whadd'ya mean?"

"How does verse eighteen read?"

"They use the word 'rock' both times."

"That's right," concluded Michael, "in English, as in the original Aramaic, you don't have the same translation problem that you do in the Greek."

Les was amazed at his nephew's argument, both that it sounded plausible and that he had that much understanding at all.

"Aside from the whole *petra-petros* thing," began George, "the second 'rock' in verse eighteen is talkin' about Peter's *confession*: 'you are the Messiah,' *not* that Peter is the rock. The Church is built on the belief that Jesus is the Son of God, not that Peter would be the leader. If you just consider for a moment what you're sayin', that Peter was the head of the Church, you'd realize how ridiculous it is." George had never heard the explanation that Michael had just given, but knew that the notion that Christ was singling out Peter was preposterous.

"I've heard that idea, too," began Michael. Actually he had just read recently about it. "It doesn't seem to make sense, though, when you think that Peter's confession, 'you are the Messiah,' was in verse sixteen and the second 'rock' that we're talking about is in verse eighteen. Just reading it naturally you come to the conclusion that the second 'rock' is the same thing as the first 'rock.'"

"You're talkin' about the man who denied Christ three times in his hour a' need!" Luther practically shouted.

"I know that," Michael responded calmly.

"How could that be? Why would Jesus give all this power to someone he knew was goin' to deny him?" Luther was intent and passionate.

"Well, that's a pretty hard question, Luther," Michael answered. "I don't know. Why would the Savior of the world choose to be born in a stable? Maybe he chose Peter to show that God works through weak men."

The others were speechless for the moment, but Luther thrust again.

"So you're tellin' me that all you Catholics believe that Peter was chosen as the leader by Jesus, and that there have been all these popes through the ages because of what you'all think Matthew sixteen says?"

"There's more," Michael said, "even in Matthew sixteen. One thing that is kind of interesting is that in verse seventeen Jesus says, 'Blest are you, Simon son of Jonah,' but back in John one forty-two it says that the father of Simon was named John."

Les and the others had no idea where he was going with this, but did flip their Bible pages to John's Gospel.

"Back in Matthew twelve" — *pages began turning* — "Jesus tells the scribes and Pharisees, who were asking for a sign, that the sign of Jonah would be given them, which was that the Son of Man would be in the bowels of the earth for three days and three nights, just as Jonah was in the belly of the whale. Jonah was a type and shadow of Christ. So when Christ says 'Blest are you, Simon son of Jonah,' he was hinting at the nature of their unique relationship. Of course they were not blood relations, but symbolically at least, Christ was designating Peter as the 'firstborn son,' the one who would inherit the kingdom."

"But Christ said that his kingdom was not of this earth!" Luther protested.

"It isn't of this earth, but that doesn't mean that it can't be *on* the earth. It has no army, no wall around its territory—"

"What are you saying the kingdom is?" Les asked. He was incredulous at what Michael seemed to be suggesting.

"That's just readin' too much into something," said Jimmy. It was the first time he had spoken. "There's a danger to drawin' conclusions about such things that might just be a coincidence. The Bible says that there can be no private interpretation."

"Well, there's something else that may be worth considering earlier in Matthew's Gospel," Michael offered. "Chapter seven" — *pages turned* – "verse twenty-four reads:

> Anyone who hears my words and puts them into practice therefore is like the
> wise man who built his house on rock.

"Who is the wise man of the Old Testament?" Michael asked. The question took them by surprise. Les expected maybe a comment about the reference to the 'rock.'

"Who was *the* wise man, the one recognized by all Jews to be wise?" Michael asked again.

"Solomon," George answered tentatively. It wasn't that he was unsure of the answer — anyone who knew the Old Testament knew that. But, he wasn't sure what the significance of it was.

"That's right," Michael agreed with excitement in his voice. He felt comfortable now discussing the Bible in a way that he would not have imagined a month ago or even an hour ago.

"And what did Solomon do? What was his noteworthy achievement?"

"Built the Temple," George answered again.

"And where did he build it?!" Michael's voice was full of enthusiasm. The others were somber.

"Jerusalem," answered George again.

"Where in Jerusalem? What was the surface of the land like?" Michael dug intently.

There was a pause. George didn't know what Michael was driving at.

"On the threshing floor of a Jebusite," answered Les. He was starting to see where Michael was headed. He knew that the site was unique in that it was actually a massive rock.

"That's right, on rock!" Michael practically shouted. "The same thing that his Church was built on, verse eighteen in the sixteenth chapter."

"That's certainly interestin', and I've never considered that before, but what's it got to do with Peter?" George asked.

"It goes back to the whole question of the relationship between Christ and Peter, Jonah and son of Jonah," said Michael. "David, the first king of Israel, brought the Ark of the Covenant to Jerusalem and there established the capital. He gathered material and funds and even had directions for its construction, but the Temple was actually built under his son, King Solomon. You see, it's not until Acts, after Christ ascends to heaven, that the Church really gets started. The first two chapters of Acts go over how they stayed in Jerusalem, as Christ instructed, and how the Holy Spirit descended on them on the feast of Pentecost. It wasn't 'til all that happened that they then started preaching and teaching and building the Church." He paused to catch his breath, and since there was no quick objection, he summarized.

"David gave instructions for the construction of the Temple. His son, Solomon, carried out the work. Christ gave instructions for the formation of his Church. His spiritual son, Peter, began the work." The men were silent as they considered the parallel.

"Then," Michael added, his voice lower, "it was not long after Pentecost, thirty or forty years, that the Temple was destroyed, just as Christ had prophesied."

"Matthew twenty-four," replied Les, more stating than asking.

"That's right," answered Michael, "it had served its purpose."

"I have a picture of the Wailing Wall, the wall of the Temple that is still standin', in the back of my Bible here," said George. He showed Jimmy the picture, then the others. The stones were massive rectangular blocks.

"That's all that's left of the Temple? There's just nothing there anymore?" asked Jimmy.

"The Dome of the Rock, a mosque," answered Les, "is built there now. Jerusalem is a holy city for the Muslims, too."

"This is all interestin', Michael, and I certainly appreciate you presentin' all this," began Luther, "but it only shows a certain relationship between Peter and Christ. Now, I wouldn't deny that Peter was called out to have a prominent position early on, but I don't believe you can say definitively that Christ was choosin' Peter to be the first undisputed head a' the Church."

"Well, first of all, *I'm* not the one saying it definitively," Michael responded, unruffled. He knew what he was going to say might rankle them. "The Church holds and teaches this interpretation. I didn't just come up with it myself. I can't."

"Why not!?" asked Les. This was a point to which he had a visceral objection.

Michael looked at him, surprised by his question, or rather by the intensity of it. He was thinking about how to answer when Les continued.

"Why can't you read the Bible and determine what it says for yourself? Why can you only accept the 'official' interpretation of the Bible?" Les had long held that this was at the heart of the lie carried out by the Roman Church — the authority they commanded. *If only those caught in the deception questioned the very authority of the Pope and bishops, they would see for themselves!* cried Les deep within himself.

"The former Roman Catholics that I have known," Les continued, trying to remain charitable, "who became Christians, began by asserting their right to understand things for themselves. The Spirit led them to throw off the 'Roman yoke' because it contradicted the Bible."

Les had not intended to get so involved, but the passion of the discussion and what was at stake fueled his intensity. "Now, Michael, I think I can speak for everyone here and say that we're happy to consider what you're saying about Peter or anything else in the Bible with an open mind, but you need to have an open mind, too."

Michael was taken aback. *Is he saying that I'm not being open-minded? But I'm the one giving the presentation! They're the ones free to think about it, to accept or reject it. What am I not being open-minded about?* He was insulted by his uncle's words, but more than that he was hurt.

The other men were relieved by Les's comeback. They were quite at a loss to counter the information Michael was presenting about Peter. They had never heard it before and did not have time to consider the argument, but knew it must be flawed. It was a Catholic interpretation, and Les's response was a good way to cut to the quick.

Michael was silent as he pondered. The room was quiet as everyone waited for him to reply. He wished they could have just stuck to discussing Peter. Now he had to decide whether to answer his uncle. He prayed to the Blessed Mother for guidance.

"Why the Bible?" asked Michael.

"What?" asked Les. The question had surprised all of them.

"Well, why the Bible?" Michael repeated. "Why is the Bible so important to read and understand?" Michael wasn't sure himself where he was headed with this question.

"It's the inspired Word of God," answered Les flatly. "Even Catholics believe that." He sensed his nephew was trying to get at something else and was suspicious already.

"Yes, we do believe that," Michael agreed quickly, still unclear about where he was going, or being led. "Why do *you* believe it?"

"Faith."

"What do you mean, faith?" pressed Michael.

This irritated Les. Now he felt like the school child being drilled in the obvious, but he restrained any sign of impatience. "Faith cometh by hearing, and hearing by the Word of God."

Though he had not heard that before, Michael assumed it was a quote from Scripture. "But that's in the Bible," Michael challenged. "Are you telling me that you believe the Bible's inspired because it says it is?"

Les realized the absurdity of a "yes" answer to that question. After all, any book could make such a claim. "I believe that it is inspired by God because I've read it and meditated on what it contains," Les asserted confidently.

"Could there be other works inspired by God? Have you read everything that's ever been written?"

"What'all are you getting at?" Luther interrupted. "Why do *you* believe the Bible is inspired?"

"Maybe we should get back to the discussion of Peter," Les quickly suggested before Michael could respond.

Eli noticed that his father seemed anxious to re-direct, to get off the road they had started traveling. He was disappointed, though, that he would not hear Michael's answer.

"Well, there are some other things in the Bible which imply that Peter was chosen to lead the Church," Michael began, thinking of what he would say next.

"That's right," Luther blurted, "I'm glad you used that word 'imply.' I'll be the first one to admit, and I think all these fellows would agree with me, that the Bible implies all sorts of various things. You can see all sorts a' things that people do and they try and tell you it's biblical. A guy leaves his wife and will still call himself a Christian, and if you was to dare and challenge him, he'd show you in the Bible where it was okay to up and leave your wife and children under certain conditions. Another'll show you that it's okay to have strong drink, someone else that God forbids the practice of blood transfusions. There's people out there sayin' the Bible says we shouldn't be eatin' animals, that we got to eat like Adam and Eve did in the Garden." Then a slight smile came across Luther's face. "Now if God didn't want us eatin' animals, why'd he go and make 'em outta' meat?"

There were howls of laughter from everyone. It served to relax the tension, for which Les and Michael were especially thankful. Luther, Michael had seen before, could be a very humorous man. Now, however, Michael felt as though he needed to speak to Luther's point. He was frustrated at being distracted again from the original subject — Peter and the papacy.

"The Bible's not a catechism—" Michael began to explain.

"What do you mean?" asked George, dubious of what was coming next. The others were equally skeptical.

Michael was starting to see the fundamental difference between how Catholics and Protestants viewed the Bible. *This is all they've got,* he realized, *and each is left all by his lonesome to figure it out or to find a church where the pastor has it all figured out.* He was beginning to recognize, too, that despite their years of Bible study and sheer knowledge of the words in Scripture, their understanding, their very approach to Scripture was intrinsically flawed. The commentaries from his father helped him to grasp and appreciate what the Bible was, how it was compiled, what role it played in the Church, and how it should be read.

"It's not an instruction book on the principles of Christianity in question-and-answer format. Things are not laid out clearly like simple 'ready-to-follow' instructions. It's a collection of books, and the books need to be examined within context," he explained, as he began to describe the Catholic view of the Bible.

"Are you sayin' they're not really inspired?" Luther asked.

"No, I'm not saying that at all," Michael answered in frustration. *Could he really think that's what I'm trying to say? Or, is he just provoking?* Either way it was wearing Michael down. He decided to forego any discussion of the Bible itself and try to get back to the question of Peter and the papacy.

"Everyone is familiar with Peter's denial of Christ," Michael said, trying to re-focus the discussion. They all nodded attentively. "In most of the Gospels it tells how Peter followed Christ at a distance when he was arrested and led to the high priest, Caiaphas. Then he warmed himself by the fire in the courtyard while they questioned Jesus. That's when — three times — he denied even knowing Jesus. Then, of course, the cock crowed, just as Jesus had prophesied." Even though they were all familiar with the story, Michael retold it in order to set the stage.

"Then in John chapter twenty-one, after the resurrection, we have the scene where the disciples go fishing in the sea of Tiberias." Les, George, Jimmy, and Luther as well as Eli, Lori, and Pam McGuffey all listened and had become genuinely interested in what Michael would say and how he would interpret it. They were curious to hear the Catholic side of the story from a real live Catholic, instead of from a book or from someone secondhand.

"Peter is the one, in John twenty-one three, who announces that he is going out to fish. The others join him of their own free will. And what happens?" Michael knew full well that they knew what happened, but sensed that how he told the story was important. He wanted to capture their imaginations. His rhetorical question worked; he felt the anticipation of his listeners building.

"They didn't catch anything the whole night. It was the same story as when Christ called Peter to follow him, back in Luke chapter five. At that time, when Christ directed Peter where to cast his net, it almost broke from the weight of the fish. He told Peter not to be afraid, that he was going to be catching men from now on.

"In John twenty-one, too, they had been fishing all night. Then the risen Christ directed them to cast their nets off the starboard side. And verse six says that they caught so much that they could not haul the net up onto the boat. When John recognized and announced that it was the Lord, Peter jumped into the water and swam ashore."

Michael continued. "The net symbolizes the Church. By themselves, they could not spread the Gospel, but with guidance from God, in the form of the Holy Spirit, they would catch many men, yet the Church would not break. In Luke's Gospel, Christ chooses Peter's boat. In John's, it is Peter's idea to go fishing. The others followed him."

"I already admitted Peter did have a special place among the apostles," began Luther. "But that doesn't mean—"

"But what comes next is stronger evidence of what that special place really was," interrupted Michael. Michael began to read John twenty-one, beginning with verse fifteen...

When they had eaten their meal, Jesus said to Simon Peter, "Simon, son of John, do you love me more than these?" ("These, meaning the other disciples," Michael inserted).

"Yes Lord," he said, "you know that I love you."

At which Jesus said, "Feed my lambs."

A second time he put his question, "Simon, son of John, do you love me?"

"Yes Lord," Peter said, "you know that I love you."

Jesus replied, "Tend my sheep."

A third time Jesus asked him, "Simon, son of John, do you love me?"

Peter was hurt because he had asked a third time. So he said to him: "Lord, you know everything. You know well that I love you."

Jesus said to him, "Feed my sheep."

Michael paused after reading, and no one else spoke up immediately either. Luther was waiting to hear what Michael had to say.

"There was a charcoal fire there where they had cooked the fish, just as there had been one in the courtyard where Peter's denials took place."

Each man considered, for the first time, the parallel pointed out by Michael. Les especially was amazed with his nephew and didn't know exactly what to think.

"As Peter warmed himself by a fire in the courtyard of the high priest," Michael continued, "he denied Christ three times, and then, after breakfast, by the fire, the risen Christ posed a three-fold question, 'do you love me?'"

Still no one interjected.

"Christ gave Peter a unique assignment — to be the shepherd, to feed and tend the sheep. The flock was not *given* to Peter, just the responsibility to shepherd it. Christ identified the sheep as his own. We all belong to Christ, but the responsibility to shepherd the flock on earth was delegated to a man."

This was so much to think about that even Luther was slowed a bit. Les feared the silence, the possibility that the others were being drawn to consider this whole doctrine of the papacy. He had to break the silence.

"Just like before, though, there is no explicit directive given by Jesus for Peter to be the undisputed leader with full authority. In the end, the case for Peter as some kind of first pope is built on conjecture and a particular interpretation, one that has led to much confusion and abuse." This statement seemed to bolster the others.

*That's it?* a dumbfounded Michael thought. *You can just reject all that out of hand? It doesn't even make you think about the possibility?*

"Men can be very deceptive with the Bible," George offered.

"I'm open to what the Catholics have to say. I want to be humble enough to learn from any man who has wisdom I don't have," Luther insisted. "But as far as this point goes, I think it's a creation of the imagination. People want to believe it, so they go and find the Scripture to back it up."

Jimmy had nothing to say. He seemed deep in thought.

Eli thought about what his father and the other men had said. *They're really not speaking to the Scripture,* he thought. *If they don't agree, why don't they offer their own interpretation?* George's comment about how men can be deceptive with the Bible seemed especially unfair. He was just assuming it was a deception.

"How do you explain the time when Paul rebuked Peter?" Jimmy asked.

It was a question Les had had, too, but he had decided not to ask it. It would have implied to the others that he was seriously considering his nephew's argument.

Michael had to think for a moment. He then recalled reading something about it in one of the commentaries, though he had not looked it up in the Bible. "Yeah, that's an interesting point. Where is that?" he asked as he began thumbing through the Bible.

"Galatians two," Les answered as he flipped through the pages of his Bible. Les began reading at verse eleven:

> Now when Peter had come to Antioch, I withstood him to his face, because he was to be blamed; for before certain men came from James, he would eat with the Gentiles; but when they came, he withdrew and separated himself, fearing those who were of the circumcision.

Les looked up and awaited Michael's response.

"Well, that's definitely an interesting passage," Michael began, "it shows that the Pope is not some kind of dictator who would demand silence from the other leaders in the Church and expect blind obedience."

That was not an explanation the others were expecting.

"But he was in the wrong and you all claim that the Pope is infallible," demanded Luther.

"We do believe that the Pope is infallible in matters of doctrine, but that's another issue. Infallibility really isn't the topic tonight."

Luther was confused.

"Well, was Peter infallible or not?"

"He was," Michael answered. "Paul was rebuking him for his

hypocrisy, for not practicing what he preached. Obviously the Pope is human," he continued, "and humans sin."

"Well, I guess I don't understand infallibility then," Luther offered.

None of the others did either and were baffled, because they had thought they understood it. After all, it was self-explanatory, wasn't it?

"Well, on that confusin' note, I think it might be time for me to start makin' my way home," George said, gathering up his things.

"Yeah, I guess it's about that time," added Les. The whole meeting had not gone at all the way he had expected. He was anxious to call it a night and re-evaluate the plan to reach Michael through Bible study sessions. Les had not been aware that the Catholics had any kind of biblical basis for believing that Peter was chosen as the leader, the first Pope.

Michael stood and began to stretch. In a way he felt relieved to have this done with, but frustrated because he thought he did not get anything across to them.

"There's still a little bit more in the Bible about Peter that I was going to bring up," he said tentatively. He felt compelled to offer an invitation to listen, however meek it was. *Even if I'm not very good at presenting the Catholic view,* he thought, *I'm the only one there is.*

The others just looked at him for a moment.

"I could finish up at the next Bible study," he offered.

"If you want to make a believer outta' me, why don't you try explainin' Mary to me," Luther challenged. "Why you worship her, idolize statues of her, put her right up there next to Jesus."

Les had not been keen on Michael presenting another Bible lesson, but Luther's challenge made him think twice. *Explain the Catholic infatuation with Mary, using just the Bible. Then we could point out the folly and absurdity of this most cherished belief among Catholics.* He remained silent and tried to gauge his nephew's reaction to Luther's suggestion.

"Well, I don't know," began Michael hesitantly, "I mean, I'm not the one running this Saturday night gathering."

"I'm sure your Uncle Les wouldn't mind, would ya, Les?"

"That's up to you all," answered Les. "If you're asking Michael to present a biblical teaching, then I'll leave it up to him as to whether he wants to give it to you or not. As far as doing it here on a Saturday night, that would be fine with me." Les did his best to seem completely neutral and nonchalant about the idea. Inside he was relishing the thought of demolishing the Mary myth, the goddess-queen of the Catholics.

"Well, you gonna explain Mary to us, son?" Luther asked. It sounded like more of a challenge now.

"I'll do my best," Michael answered. Again he had the sick feeling inside his stomach. *What am I getting myself into, again?*

"Next week we'll be takin' care of some church business on Saturday night, but we'll get around to it soon as we can," Les informed them.

Michael was thankful. He knew it would take him awhile to read up on Mary, but at least he had a couple of his father's books with which to start.

Work on the farm was good the next couple of weeks. Through late June, the early mornings were pleasantly cool and especially quiet and peaceful. Michael always enjoyed starting his day off milking with Elijah, and then doing some other routine chores before breakfast. He would arrive at the cottage, already awake for two hours, with the daily take of eggs and milk, while his siblings were just getting ready for the breakfast table. It gave him a sense of well being and confidence, the feeling that he was, in a way, the man of the house.

He had talked with his Uncle Les and cousin Eli about life on the farm for children. To hear them speak, any child who did not have the good fortune to be brought up on a farm was truly under-privileged. The farm kept children and young adults well occupied with meaningful work, with natural and wholesome forms of entertainment.

The plain people and the few "English" who practiced non-mechanized farming tended to have big families. The extra labor offset to some extent their relative production disadvantage due to the absence of sophisticated farm machinery. In the "plain" homes, children began contributing at a young age to the household economy. They pitched in even at four and five years of age doing the chores they were able to do.

The farm work was more available to children in farming families — as contrasted with their mechanized neighbors — because it was safer and more labor-intensive. The plain folk worked with enormous draft horses, most of them Belgians, which were more docile and less skittish than were some of the other breeds. Les said he could not remember any accident involving a work horse in the local Amish community.

The lack of heavy equipment also necessitated community work projects. On their way to the feed mill, the general store, or when he was out bike riding with Elijah, Michael would sometimes see ten to fifteen buggies lined up at one of the Amish farms. He and Elijah would slow down and try to see what kind of a project was going on there. It would be a new greenhouse, a barn, or some kind of workshop they were constructing. Hammers would be flying, wood being carried into place, and measurements being taken up top. They would be working together and visiting with one another as the work shed went up. The host family would provide a sumptuous spread for the noon meal.

This was all part of their unique way, Elijah had explained to Michael. They don't just forsake technology for the sake of doing things the hard way. And, they don't forego all technology. They'll adopt some new technology if a trial period in the community works out okay. Whether they adopt it or not has little to do with whether it makes life easier or production more efficient. It depends mostly on how it affects community life. With big equipment, they wouldn't need so many men to put up a barn. Instead the men would busy themselves somewhere else, often isolated on their own farms.

That was the whole point. Capital equipment would replace, to some extent, manpower. Without the need for manpower, there would not be so many barn raisings, or so many men needed for one. Gone, too, would be "the bearing of one another's burdens" — helping a brother in the church, the fellowship among the men, the opportunity for young folks to learn how to build and repair under the supervision of those more experienced. The women wouldn't come together to prepare a feast. If the women didn't come together, then the small children wouldn't get together as often to play in the hayloft or chase ducks by the pond.

There's a definite mentality and philosophy to their ways, Eli had explained. They work, play, and worship as a community. They are one body. If one farmer suffers, they all suffer with him. If one enjoys success, they all benefit.

Michael reflected on their ways as he milked the cow, shoveled manure, or did any number of the monotonous tasks that needed doing on the farm. Such work occupied his body, but freed up his mind. He found such work relaxing in a way, therapeutic. They got a lot accomplished (he appreciated by now how much there was to do on a diversified, non-mechanized farm), but they didn't seem to be in a hurry, he had observed. Oh, they moved expeditiously enough, but not frantically, not helter skelter. It was as if they had an inborn sense that such frenetic activity was ultimately counter-productive and unhealthy, for the soul as well as the body.

Also their community, because of the restrictions on technology, electricity, and phones, was not artificial. They needed and sincerely appreciated one another. Michael thought how strangely similar it all was to the stories of old South Philadelphia that his grandmother would tell.

205

They worked together, helped each other out, looked out for one another. When someone died, the whole neighborhood knew it. They knew who was pregnant, when she was due, whose son was away in the service, and when he'd be coming home on leave.

Everyone was somehow involved with the parish and its school. They mourned together, welcomed new life together, felt anguish when one of the fathers got laid off, and tried to do what they could to help. They all were part of something larger than themselves, and that challenge and privilege brought out the best in them. They were not just living for themselves, but were responsible to and for each other.

He thought about it all, about where he might go to college, and about his Uncle Mathias back in the Philadelphia area. *He's probably working right now,* thought Michael. His work, though, was not like the work that the folks did around here. He prepares for cases that he argues in the courtroom, or tries to negotiate ways to avoid the courtroom while working out the best deal for his client. It was exciting work in its way.

Michael thought of the intensity of excitement the night of the Bible study. He had been so wound up that it had taken him awhile to fall asleep. Uncle Matty thrived on that same kind of excitement. There was a sort of camaraderie among the attorneys as well. Uncle Matty knew so many other attorneys and all the judges, but it wasn't community in the sense that the "plain people" had it. Michael pondered what the essential difference could be. *Why wasn't it the same?... Well, it wasn't really real,* he finally decided.

*Kind of funny,* he thought. He remembered Uncle Matty talking about the Amish when he heard Michael's family would spend the summer in Kentucky. One of the things he had said was that the Amish led a wholesome and interesting lifestyle, but that it was not a realistic one for people in this day and age. *What did he mean, "not realistic?"* They, the Amish and Old Order Mennonites, were doing it, were living it everyday, and had been for generations. Not only that, but they were growing.

Originally settling in Lancaster County, Pennsylvania, they had branched out into large communities in Ohio, Indiana, Wisconsin, Virginia, Missouri, Tennessee, Kentucky and up in Canada. They were in Belize, Honduras, Paraguay, Bolivia and other places south of the border.

Most of their children persevered in the "plain" way of life and had big families. Their agriculture remained small scale and was never directly subsidized by the government. They experienced practically none of the social pathologies that plague modern societies — broken families, drug and alcohol abuse, or violence. None of their families declared bankruptcy, neither did they display their wealth ostentatiously. And, many of the families were plenty wealthy.

The fathers were intimately involved in daily family life and were present for practically every meal. Day care centers were non-existent. *It is real,* Michael insisted to himself. *I have been living it and observing it now for three months.*

What's more, it's real in a far deeper sense than how Uncle Matty had meant it. That is, it deals with real things, things that are necessities. The soil that they turn each spring is real. The calves, lambs, and kid goats that arrive each spring are real. Cultivating the rows of corn, or harvesting peas, beans, or root crops is work with a very real and direct result — food.

Cooling off down at the swimming hole after a hot day putting up hay is real. The water washes away all the dried up grass and sweat. It caresses your over-heated body as it flows around you on its way to the river.

In the fall, stripping, harvesting, pressing, and boiling down sorghum cane into syrup is a great community enterprise. It is real when everyone comes together to produce a product that will be poured over waffles or spread on biscuits and enjoyed with a glass of milk.

In winter, there's the mending of fences, barns, and buggies. There's logging with a couple of powerful Belgians deep in the woods.

There's sawing and splitting firewood. There's quilting, mending a boy's trousers, and baking a pie for Sunday dinner, all of it real.

Also, there is sitting by the warm cookstove sipping tea. There is the child on a lap listening to her father read a book about baby animals. There is the group of boys, many of them brothers, going into the woods after some venison. There are games like horseshoes, an impromptu tug of war, and the little ones catching lightning bugs.

For a husband and wife, there is time and peace to talk by oil lamp after the children are down. When the evening is pleasant, time to sit out on the porch, swing and talk, love, and live. Sometimes on summer evenings, time to walk over to the grassy hillside that overlooks the valley and plan, reckon, dream. There is plenty of time for just living, time merely to be.

*It's all real.* Ironically, Michael realized, there is nothing artificial about the simple life they lead. In a time when various groups and people are busy organizing themselves, asserting their right to do whatever, be whatever, or think whatever, these strange people who dress in black and white and gray, who drive little black buggies on country roads, and who work the land, just go about doing.

Michael was getting a tremendous education on the workings of a small, diversified farm. Les appreciated his nephew's help. He was an enthusiastic learner. Although inexperienced, he contributed from the first day. His help enabled Les to be more of a supervisor and thereby oversee the operation with a better perspective. In preceding years, it was not uncommon for Les to become so involved with a project at hand that he failed to plan for the next thing that needed to be accomplished. He realized that his actions were not always efficient or his time well managed, but he would inevitably get caught up in the "tyranny of the present"

as he moved from one thing that needed his immediate attention to the next.

He enjoyed working with his son and nephew at times, and then having the freedom to see to other things and know that the task at hand would be completed expeditiously. Consequently, for the two or three weeks since Michael's attempt to discuss Peter at the Saturday night gathering, Michael and Elijah worked more closely together than ever.

As yet, Les had said nothing more about when Michael should present his next Bible study — the Catholic understanding of Mary — and Michael didn't remind him.

Elijah and Michael grew to enjoy each other's company more and more. Elijah observed how Michael looked at each new task, ones that he had never done before, as novelties. The wonder and fascination he could see in his cousin's eyes was infectious. It energized him, in the way a new mother is excited when her toddler points at a furry gray squirrel and squeals with delight. The child doesn't take the animal for granted. Or like a father who re-discovers the wonder of the ocean by watching his children run and tumble in the surf.

The job at hand for the young men on the last Friday in June was to get the hay into the barn. This would be the second time Michael would help with this task. They had cut the alfalfa on Tuesday using a horse-powered sickle bar mower, the same as the Amish. On Thursday they raked it into windrows, which were one- to two-foot wide rows spaced a bit more than a wagon's width apart, that stretched the length of the rectangle-shaped two-acre meadow. Now the hay would be collected in the wagon, transported to the barn, and put in the loft.

This was a fairly labor-intensive project, one of those jobs that brings people together. Lori drove the wagon between the windrows. Les, Michael, and Elijah pitchforked it up into the wagon. The two younger O'Shea boys and Eli's younger brother stayed in the wagon and stomped down the hay so as to maximize the amount that would fit in each load.

When the wagon was fully loaded, only one of the boys would be left in the wagon, riding way up on top of the towering hay mountain. Lori would drive it over to the stable near the farmhouse. Eli or Les would direct her as she pulled up right under the large opening on the second floor of the barn. As Michael blocked the wheels, Eli would unhitch the team. The horse power was needed to lift the loads of loose hay up into the loft.

When Lori had the horses hitched to the pulley line located on the other side of the stable, Michael and Les would station themselves up in the loft. Eli stayed in the hay wagon and manually set the three large, heavy, grappling-like hooks in the hay. He then signaled to Michael, who stood up in the large opening ready to receive the load. Michael gave the thumbs up to his Uncle Les, who stood at the back wall, which was thirty-five feet away.

Uncle Les gave the okay to Lori, who gave the "git up" command. The team leaned into the load, and the huge ball of hay lifted off the wagon and swayed slightly as it ascended to Michael, who guided it into the loft. From there, Les and he would pull it along the cable into the barn and pull back the hooks so that the hay landed safely on the floor. There it would sit out of the weather until mid to late December, when the horses and cows had nothing left to graze on.

Like much of manual farm work, it was not overwhelmingly strenuous for a young man, but rather mildly strenuous over a long period. The repetition was eventually tiring. Each wagon load contained about five or six loads that needed to be lifted into the loft, and the two-acre field had six wagon loads. The pitching of the hay into the wagon was the constant repetitious movement. Michael did well to keep up with Elijah and his uncle. What he lacked in technique he compensated for with youthful energy and enthusiasm.

Pitching hay did not lend itself to contemplation like some of the other chores, as you had to be keenly aware of those around you, but neither was it tedious. You were constantly moving down the windrow, and you could see the small collection of hay in the wagon grow into a small mountain. It was sort of like what Michael remembered watching in a movie about a chain gang. The three of them would be pitching hay side by side into the wagon, then the last man would leap-frog up front as the wagon moved slowly forward.

Putting up hay was something that had to be done after the morning dew had been burned off. It had to be done in the heat of the day, and today the mid-day sun was full strength. As the wagon continued on, the next man, after having pitched all the hay between the last man and the first man, would leapfrog to the front. And so it would go, all the way down the roughly 150-yard long windrow. Before long the beads of perspiration would grow large enough to be pulled by gravity down your forehead and cheeks. In no time, your hat's sweat liner would be saturated (they all wore wide-brimmed Amish style straw hats for this task), and you'd have to wipe away sweat with your bandana and shirt sleeves as you moved up to the head of the line.

The bandana, after a dunking in the rain barrel near the stable, also served as a dust mask when you were up in the loft arranging the hay. Michael imitated Les, who wore his like a bandit to filter out the dust and chaff that filled the air as the hay was tossed about. Your sweaty arms, neck, and face were a magnet for the tiny particles. Like sawdust poured on an oil spill, the hay chaff absorbed the sweat and lay upon your skin like a moist blanket.

By 5:30 they had put up the last of the hay. The sun still shone brightly and there was a great feeling of accomplishment among all who were involved. There was also the security of seeing all that feed stored away for the winter months.

"Why don't you load everyone up and take the team down to the swimming hole, Elijah?" suggested Les.

"We're on our way," smiled Eli. "Ready to go down to the creek for some swimming, Dante?"

Dante and the other boys responded by scrambling into the wagon.

The swimming hole was an oasis of coolness from the scorching heat. Big shade trees on the bank hung over the creek. The water flowed quickly over the rocks, down a two or three-foot fall and into a pool about five feet deep in the middle. Just the sound of the flowing water produced a cooling sensation. It was only twenty feet across at its widest, but that was plenty big enough to splash around and get refreshed.

The boys just stripped down to their waists and waded right in with their long pants. (They always wore long pants on the farm, as did everyone in the area). Lori emerged from behind a nearby thicket, in a short sleeve top and long shorts. It was the first time Michael had seen her not in a dress. Before long, Elijah was playing with the younger boys, and squeals of fear and delight could be heard a hundred yards away, if there had been anyone to hear them. Michael was sitting over by the little waterfall letting the water massage and caress the back of his neck and shoulders. Lori waded over to where he was sitting.

"You did real well with that Bible study a couple weeks back," she drawled with a smile. She always had a smile.

Michael was pleasantly surprised at his cousin's remark. "Y'think so?" he asked.

"Oh yeah, I could tell Daddy and the others were impressed," she replied.

"I didn't think they were impressed at all."

"Oh yeah, they were. I could tell."

"How?"

"I could just tell, that's all," she assured him confidently.

Michael felt more upbeat about the whole thing than he ever had. It was amazing what a small word of encouragement could do.

"What did *you* think?" he ventured.

"I thought it was good what you said." Pause. "I mean, I never heard any of that before, what you said about Peter being singled out to be the leader of the Church. I just never had it really explained before. I heard that Catholics have a leader of their Church, the Pope, but never understood that Peter the fisherman was the first one."

"What else have you learned about Catholicism?"

"Not much." Pause. "You'all worship statues and such?"

"Is that what you think!?"

"I've heard that. And you worship Mary as a goddess and have other goddesses."

"That's not exactly right," Michael responded. He was too taken aback even to begin a well thought out response. Even if he had not been so stunned, he wouldn't have known where to begin. Just then the younger boys started to call Lori and Michael over to join their game in the pool of water.

After more than an hour by the swimming hole, they loaded up in the wagon, so as not to be late for supper. They all felt cooled off and squeaky clean as the wagon made its way toward the stable. Michael stayed back with Eli at the stable to help unhitch the team, put up the harness, and brush the horses down.

"Has your Dad said anything about having that Bible study, the one where I was going to present something?" Michael asked Eli. His brief conversation with Lori had helped him to get over his anxiety of running the biblical gauntlet again. The level of misunderstanding had shocked him. He thought again that if he didn't at least try to explain things, then they'd never get explained at all.

"No, he hasn't to me," answered Eli. "I think he was kind of uncomfortable having you on the hot seat like that a few weeks back. He doesn't want to make you go through that again, is what I think."

Michael considered what his cousin said. It was another reason to trust and admire his uncle. He truly did not want to traumatize his nephew.

"Do you want to have that Bible study on Mary?" Eli asked, after thinking about why his cousin had asked in the first place.

"Yeah, I guess I do," Michael responded. It was not that he really wanted to, but that he now felt compelled to try. "Is it something that interests you?"

"Yeah, I'd like to hear it," Eli answered quickly.

"What did you think of the last one, about Peter?"

"I thought it was interesting. I'd never heard any of that before. I never knew where Catholics got that idea about the Pope."

Again Michael was gratified to hear that it was something that they had never even heard before. *Now at least they can see that there is a biblical basis for what we believe,* he thought.

"You said that night that there was more in the Bible about Peter being the leader," Eli said, as an invitation for Michael to elaborate. He had been wondering since that night what else the Bible could have to say. His curiosity was sincere; he wasn't asking so that he could have the opportunity to set Michael straight.

"There's more than what I got a chance to go over that night," began Michael. He handed Eli one of the brushes for the horses and they commenced to work over the huge chestnut-colored draft horses. "Do you know that when the apostles are listed in any of the Gospels, that Peter always heads the list?"

Eli stopped brushing and thought about that for a moment. "What else?"

Eli's eagerness to hear was enough to get Michael excited about telling all that he had read about Peter.

214

"In Luke chapter twenty-two, right before Christ predicts Peter's denials," continued Michael, barely restraining his enthusiasm, "Jesus says that he has prayed for Peter, that his faith won't fail. I forget which verse, but you can look it up. And in the next line, Jesus tells him that he has to be a support for his brothers, the other apostles and disciples. Christ is talking about after He is put to death and then ascends for good. Peter is going to have to be the one who holds the Church together, the leader in the early days. It'll make more sense to you if you read it yourself.

"Then just read the book of Acts. Peter was the one who spoke to the crowds on Pentecost. He preached right in the Temple area, and was arrested for it. They warned him not to mention Jesus again, but he explained that he had to obey God. I mean this was the guy who denied Jesus right before the crucifixion!

"And another thing, I think it's chapter five of Acts, when they're talking about the growth of the Church, 'how many are being added each day,' it tells about people carrying the sick out into the streets in hopes that Peter's shadow might fall across them as he passed by... You've got to read Acts, Elijah," Michael said, smiling at his own exuberance.

"I will."

"But now I'm gonna' really drop the bomb on you. Ready for this?"

"Lay it on me," smiled Elijah.

The two had stopped brushing now and were looking at each other.

"Remember that whole thing in Matthew sixteen that we argued about that night, about Peter being the rock and the whole *petra-petros* argument?"

"Yeah."

"Well, we didn't get to talk about what Jesus said just after that."

Elijah waited for his cousin to explain. Michael spoke very deliberately.

"In verse nineteen Jesus says, 'I will entrust to you the keys of the kingdom of heaven.' Then he goes on to grant Peter the power to 'bind and loose.' But the most important part is that the keys are only ever given to Peter," Michael continued. "The key is a symbol of authority. Look up 'key' in your concordance and you'll find something in Isaiah about it, and then again in Revelation chapter three in the very beginning of that chapter. It'll get your attention."

"I'll do that," promised Eli. He was impressed with how passionate his cousin was. "You've sure learned a lot about the Bible," he added.

"Well, I've learned much more than I ever imagined I would down here. My Dad had some real good commentaries that I've been studying, too. This one guy, Scott Hahn, gives a good explanation of why the 'keys' are so important. Any kingdom has a king, obviously, but also a cabinet of ministers who handle the various affairs of the state. The *prime* minister, the one entrusted with the key, speaks on behalf of the king, dispenses with obligations, settles misunderstandings, all with the full authority of the king. Christ, of course, is the King, and we believe that the bishops are his earthly ministers. The Pope, the bishop of Rome, is nothing more than his prime minister."

"And nothing less?"

"That's what we believe," replied Michael, after he thought for a moment about Eli's comment.

Just then the farm bell rang at Eli's house.

"That's probably Mom or Lori," Eli announced. "Supper time! Listen, I'll mention something to my Dad about you giving another Bible study," he offered.

"Okay, but don't tell him I was asking for it, just that I wouldn't mind doing it again," Michael said as he started to back away and make his way home.  "Oh...and I think the 'key' is mentioned in Isaiah twenty-two."

    "Fair enough," Eli said as he waved good-bye.

*Martin de Porres Kennedy*

# 10

The following Saturday evening found all of those who had been involved in the previous Bible study again at the McGuffey dining room table. Singing went fairly well that night, but everyone was pre-occupied with what was going to happen afterwards. Jimmy and George had been taken by surprise at the last meeting. They had heard interpretations that night to which they had not been prepared to respond. It had knocked them off balance, and they weren't sure what was in store for them tonight.

For Les, the last meeting did not go according to script and he had hesitated at scheduling a session on the topic of Mary. Originally, he had been excited at the prospect, but had thought better of it later. He couldn't help feeling that it was a bit blasphemous even to provide a forum for such subject matter. He was considering other ways of reaching his nephew, and hoped that everyone would just forget about "Mary" and the Bible study if he just ignored it.

Last weekend though, Lori and Eli, on separate occasions, had asked him about it. He became a bit concerned that some of that stuff about Peter had raised questions in their minds and that they wanted to hear more about what Catholics believe. He had balked at offering a competing interpretation on the Petrine passages. He really didn't have one yet, and needed to study it further.

The best thing to do, he thought, would be to go ahead and let Michael discuss Mary. After all, she was hardly even mentioned in the

Bible, and the worship of Mary was the most obvious display of Catholic idolatry that they practiced. Once Eli and Lori were exposed to that, he thought, they'll no longer have any doubts about Catholicism. His greatest concern was how to restrain Luther once he smelled the "blood in the water."

Luther was loaded for bear. He, also, had been befuddled by Michael with the discussion of Peter. He felt as if he'd not had a good, "open-field" shot at Michael that whole night. It had frustrated him.

"There's so much that it's hard even to know where to begin," Michael began.

"About Mary?" Luther asked. It didn't take him long to start laying his groundwork. All of them, though, had the same reaction.

"Yeah," Michael said matter-of-factly. He had not begun that way in order to elicit such a response and was surprised by it.

"Well, I'm not sure we're even talkin' about the same Bible now, but go on ahead," Luther finished his first interruption.

"Well, God promised Abraham that he'd have many descendants, that they'd have land and a kingdom, that he'd be the father of a host of nations. I think it's Genesis chapter twenty-two, after Abraham proves himself willing to sacrifice his only son, Isaac, that the messenger angel says that through Abraham's descendants all the nations of the earth would find blessing. Isaac grew up and had Esau and Jacob. Jacob got his father's blessing, and later in life the Lord changed his name to Israel. His twelve sons became the heads of the 'twelve tribes,' the twelve tribes of Israel. The descendants of Levi, one of Jacob's sons, became the priests, just like you preached about a couple months back, Uncle Les."

Les McGuffey nodded. *Where was he going with all this background? He seems to have been studying the Bible, though,* thought Les, *and is speaking with such confidence.*

"From the line of Judah, one of the other sons, came the *kings* of

Israel, just as Jacob prophesied before he died. David, the first king, was in the line of Judah, as was Christ, the everlasting King. The practice or custom in the kingdom of Israel was for the *mother* of the king to have a throne of her own next to her son. This—"

"The Bible doesn't say that," said Luther quickly. He was back into "rat terrier" mode. "You're about to do somethin' very dangerous, Michael. You're startin' to combine history, customs, traditions, and superstitions with the Bible to come up with this idolatrous practice of worshippin' Mary. This is exactly what so many people in the church did, and slowly, over time, folks who wanted to be true to the Bible, and the Bible alone, were either forced out or broke away. That's how we got this big mess of so many churches. They all have varying amounts of the old Roman Church ritual. It'll take a long time before everyone just embraces the Word of God, the Bible alone, and cleanses themselves of the ritual and superstition."

Jimmy and George thought pretty much the same way as Luther. They were going to let Michael have his say, but were glad that Luther challenged him.

Les half appreciated Luther's intensity and half cringed when he started in to attack. Deep down, Les knew that Luther's rebukes would spare him having to do such dirty work. It would free him up to be the consoler and reasoned teacher just as he had planned.

"I think the Bible does say that, in so many words," Michael replied calmly. He was ready for Luther this time. He looked down at his notes.

"If you go to Jeremiah thirteen eighteen..." (*pages started flipping*), "it says...

Say to the king and to the queen mother: come down from your throne; from your heads fall your magnificent crowns.

"Now go to first Kings chapter two, verses twelve through twenty-

221

one," Michael instructed immediately after Luther was finished reading. He didn't want Luther to comment on what he just read. Pages started turning again.

"Why don't you read that, Jimmy."

Then Solomon sat on the throne of his father David; and his kingdom was firmly established. Now Adonijah the son of Haggith came to Bathsheba the mother of Solomon.

So she said, "Do you come peaceably?"

And he said, "Peaceably." Moreover he said, "I have something to say to you."

And she said, "Say it."

Then he said, "You know that the kingdom was mine, and all Israel had set their expectations on me, that I should reign. However, the kingdom has been turned over, and has become my brother's; for it was his from the Lord. Now I ask one petition of you; do not deny me."

And she said to him, "Say it."

Then he said, "Please speak to King Solomon, for he will not refuse you, that he may give me Abishag the Shunammite as wife."

So Bathsheba said, "Very well, I will speak for you to the king."

Bathsheba therefore went to King Solomon, to speak to him for Adonijah. And the king rose up to meet her and bowed down to her, and sat down on his throne and had a throne set for the king's mother; so she sat at his right hand. Then she said, "I desire one small petition of you; do not refuse me."

And the king said to her, "Ask it, my mother, for I will not refuse you."

They sat there, a bit stunned, reading it again to themselves.

"So there is fairly good evidence in the Bible that the queen mother also had a throne, next to that of her son, the king of Israel," Michael offered. "The king often had many wives, but naturally just one mother. Therefore, she became the queen. I think in Hebrew she was called the

'Gebirah.'"

"It's interesting to note what happened to Adonijah," Les spoke up, "just after where Jimmy stopped reading." He had read ahead after Jimmy was finished.

"Solomon had Adonijah killed," said Michael matter-of-factly, without even looking at his Bible as the others were now doing.

"It seems to imply that it is a mistake to go to the mother of the king instead of going right to the king with a request," Les answered.

"Does it? Adonijah seemed to take for granted that the king would not refuse his mother. In fact, King Solomon even says," Michael searched his Bible quickly, "verse twenty, that he will grant her request. I think what Adonijah and Solomon say and how they say it tells us more about what the general custom was than the eventual fate of Adonijah."

Les studied the passage again. He realized that his nephew was right and began to feel uncomfortable. Michael sensed this and decided to move on quickly so as to spare his uncle the embarrassment.

"Anyway, it's important to note that the queen mother had no power in her own right; rather she was in a position of honor. Note again verse nineteen, that even her son the king 'bowed down to her.' She could petition the king on behalf of his subjects, that is, she was an 'intercessor.'"

No one jumped in to object, which surprised Michael. He glanced at the notes he had taken to see how to transition to the next point.

Les and the others hesitated to object. He'd have an answer for them and it would seem to make sense. Luther held his tongue, which was quite difficult for him. He'd try and wait until the end to prove that all this Marian stuff was myth and superstition.

"The prophets in the Old Testament prophesied of a king who would re-establish the kingdom of Israel for good," Michael continued. "That's exactly what Jesus did, but not in the way that most of the Jews expected him to. The Church is the new Israel—"

"Jesus said that his kingdom was not of this world!" Luther shouted as he practically jumped out of his seat. "Yer sayin' that your church is the kingdom!?"

"Well, I don't think I'm the first person to say it," responded Michael, trying to defend himself.

"But it's not of this world! Jesus said that."

"It's not," Michael agreed. *How did that book put it?...* "'The kingdom of Israel was a military, political, and economic kingdom. The Church is spiritual, mystical, and sacramental.'"

"That is just pure balderdash," Luther exclaimed, without even thinking about what Michael had said.

"Let's get back onto the topic of Mary," suggested Les. He thought it pure "balderdash" too.

"The queen mother of the old kingdom was temporal. Mary is the queen mother on the spiritual level," Michael concluded.

"This is just too much to take, Les," said George.

"Why?" asked Michael. He was frustrated and more than a bit bewildered at their response. *At the very least it's worthy of some consideration, isn't it? It all makes so much sense to me. It's rich and deep and mystical. They're rejecting it out of hand as if it were obviously ludicrous.*

Eli wondered, too, why George thought it was "just too much." He was implying that it was ridiculous, but didn't explain why.

"Why, George?" Michael asked again. "Wasn't Christ a fulfillment?"

"Christ was *the* fulfillment," George exclaimed.

"What did he fulfill?" Michael had a new strategy. *If they won't listen to me, maybe they'll listen to themselves.*

"He fulfilled all the Old Testament prophecies about his coming."

"What was in the Temple, though? Why was that such a special place for the Jews?"

"The Ark of the Covenant," Les answered.

"What was in the Ark?"

"The Ten Commandments on the tablets of stone, the jar filled with manna, and Aaron's rod," Jimmy answered.

*Most Catholics don't even know what was in the ark,* Michael reminded himself. *No wonder so many of them leave the Church for "Bible churches."*

"Didn't Christ fulfill all that was in it?" No one answered. They could see that Michael was building up to something and didn't want to give him the sword that he might slay them with.

"Aaron's rod symbolized the true priesthood and Christ became the new high priest," Michael began, answering his own question from notes he had taken. "Paul's letter to the Hebrews, chapter two, explains how Christ was the new high priest.

"The tablets were also referred to as the testimony of God, his Word. In the New Testament, the Gospel of John, first chapter, says 'the Word became flesh.' Jesus was the Word of God who became flesh.

"The jar of manna was the bread of life for the Israelites as they wandered around in the desert before arriving to the promised land. Then in the New Testament, John six, Christ calls *Himself* the Bread of Life.

"Didn't Christ, then, fulfill all that was in the Ark of the Covenant? It only makes sense since through him we entered the New Covenant."

Les nodded slowly. He couldn't counter anything that his nephew said, but this was not how it was supposed to go. They were off the script again.

"Okay, then, what about the Ark itself? What was the Ark for?" continued Michael.

"It was kind of a sacred house for everything that belonged inside it," Luther replied. He had no idea where Michael was going with all this. Les realized and cringed as Luther answered.

"Well, if Christ was the fulfillment of the tablets, the manna, and Aaron's rod, then isn't Mary the fulfillment of the Ark itself?"

Luther stopped to think about what Michael meant.

"Mary literally carried the Word, the 'Bread of Life,' and the High Priest around inside of her."

Michael noticed that his audience seemed to be exchanging glances. Each was looking to the others to see what they thought. He paused long enough to field questions or respond to any comments. None were forthcoming.

Pam McGuffey, who had been listening from the kitchen, was amazed at what Michael had been saying. Though she had always been convinced of the folly of the Catholic infatuation with Mary, her imagination had been captured. *What's a kingdom without a queen?*

"Go to second Samuel six—" (*they were relieved that Michael did not wait longer for a response*) "and keep one finger there, then go to Luke, the first chapter."

"In the Old Testament, in Samuel, David is "making merry" before the ark with all his strength, with singing, tambourines, harps, and cymbals. Down in verse fourteen it says that he 'came dancing before the Lord with abandon.' Then, in Luke's Gospel, when Elizabeth hears Mary's greeting, it says 'the baby' — John the Baptist, that is – 'leapt in her womb for joy.'"

*Now that's a stretch,* thought Les, but they all let Michael continue.

"David was so overwhelmed that he asked, and this is verse nine, 'How can the ark of the Lord come to me?'" He flipped back to the New Testament. "What does Elizabeth say? Verse forty-three, 'But who am I that the mother of my Lord should come to me?'"

*Still a stretch,* thought Les. He looked at the others to try and gauge their thoughts.

"Again back in Samuel, verse eleven says that the ark remained in the house of Obededom the Gittite for three months and that the Lord blessed that household. Mary stayed with Elizabeth for three months. That's in Luke, chapter one."

"Son, that's all interestin' to consider, and I'll do that," Luther promised. "I really will. I'll admit that it's fairly new to me and we all should try and be humble enough to learn something from anyone who can teach us. With all that said, though, you haven't shown me how it is that you can worship Mary, put her up on the pedestal with Jesus and still consider yourself a devout Christian."

*How I can think of myself as a Christian? For Pete's sake! What can I say to that!?*

Luther continued in a sympathetic tone, "I won't deny that many of the things you believe in seem to be Christian, but things like the worship of Mary are from the pagan beliefs that lingered for awhile amongst newly Christianized people. They used to have goddesses and many of the missionaries tried to introduce Christianity to them in ways that they'd understand. They couldn't go in there and teach primitive, superstitious, and sometimes violent people that their goddess wasn't real. Instead, they'd teach them to look at this other goddess, Mary. They had to put it — Christianity — in ways that simple people would understand. Do you understand what I'm sayin', son?"

"I think so." Michael understood what he was saying in the literal sense, but didn't agree with his conclusions. *What should I say?*

"She is important," Les began, "but we shouldn't worship her. Jesus would not have us do anything like that." Les was moving into the compassionate teacher mode.

"I don't worship her," objected Michael. "And the Church doesn't teach us to worship her."

"Well, whatever you call it, then," Les said. "The statues in church, the songs to her, feast days, the Assumption, the Immaculate Conception, the whole infatuation with her."

"Well, maybe you could call it an infatuation, but it's not that we worship her. At least no one should. We would say that we are devoted to and honor the Blessed Mother."

"Whatever you want to call it, why would you want to do that?" Luther asked in frustration. *I just got through explaining how all this Mary gobbledygook got into Christianity.*

"The Bible says I should," Michael answered. He knew such an answer would get Luther riled up but couldn't resist it.

"Where!? Show me where it says that."

"One of the Ten Commandments is to honor your father and mother, isn't it?"

"Yeah, but Mary's not *my* mother." Luther's eyes were intense. He was, at this point, a frustrated rat terrier. "Where does it say that she's *my* mother in the Bible?"

"Revelation twelve," Michael answered without hesitating. Everyone flipped quickly to the book of Revelation, the Apocalypse. They all scanned the text quickly.

"Where does it say anything close to that?" George asked.

"Down in verse seventeen it says that the dragon was enraged at her escape and went off to make war on the rest of her offspring," Michael offered. He knew he'd have to provide more explanation but decided to wait for their reaction. He didn't have to wait long.

"That has nothing to do with Mary. She's not even mentioned in the whole chapter. I don't think she's mentioned in the entire book, Michael." George was naturally more laid back than Luther, but even he was beginning to balk.

"The woman in the beginning of the chapter is Mary...

> A great sign appeared in the sky, a woman clothed with the sun, with the moon under her feet, and on her head a crown of twelve stars. Because she was with child, she wailed aloud in pain as she labored to give birth.

Michael continued, "Now the dragon, the devil, tried to get the woman and when he couldn't, he 'went off to make war on the rest of her offspring.' Jesus didn't have any siblings so 'her offspring' must mean her spiritual offspring."

Les was fascinated with the interpretation. He was not aware that they, the Catholics, even bothered to try and justify their beliefs. *They do have a biblical basis for what they believe,* he realized, even though the explanation seemed rather convoluted to him. He thought he'd better jump in and calmly explain before Luther overreacted.

"That part about 'the woman' is not meant to be taken literally," he began. "Rather the woman represents God's people, the Israelites, from whom the Messiah came."

"That's exactly right," piped in Luther. "The Book of Revelation is a book a' visions. It uses symbols and imagery. It's not to be taken literally."

"By the way," George added, "it's very clear in the Bible that Jesus *did* have brothers and sisters."

Michael found himself being lectured to again. He understood that the Book of Revelation was full of symbols and imagery, but the issue was what they meant. As to Jesus having brothers and sisters, that was another problematic area. He thought for a moment about how he should respond to the assembled teachers. *What would Mathias O'Shea say? Mathias O'Shea wouldn't say anything. He'd ask.*

"It says that the woman gives birth to a son — a boy destined to shepherd all nations with an iron rod. Who is that?"

"That's Christ," answered Luther, a little baffled by Michael's asking something so obvious.

Michael nodded in agreement, "Yeah, that makes sense." He paused a moment. "I mean it's obvious."

"Yes, it is," Luther concurred. By now he was more wary of Michael than baffled.

"And you believe that the woman represents the Israelites?" Michael continued.

"That's right," Luther responded.

Les thought he saw where Michael was going.

"Well, that's not quite as obvious, is it?" Then before Luther could formulate a response, "I mean, it's not as obvious as the child representing Jesus, is it?"

"Whadd'ya mean?"

"I mean, the most *obvious* answer is that 'the woman' represents Mary, the woman who actually gave birth to Jesus. 'The woman' could also represent the people of Israel — you know, sort of have a multi-level meaning, but the obvious interpretation is that she is Mary."

"Well, that might seem obvious, but the fact is that she doesn't represent Mary," Luther insisted.

"How do you know?" asked Michael calmly. He noticed Luther look over to Les, a "rescue me" sort of look.

"That's a commonly understood interpretation," began Luther before Les was able to jump in.

"Again, Michael, it's a matter of consistent interpretation of Scripture," explained Les, "considering things in context and determining how they all fit together."

*Isn't that exactly what I'm doing here, trying to paint the whole picture for them?* sighed Michael to himself.

"There is no biblical basis," Les continued, "for believing that Jesus wanted us to think of His mother as our mother or even that He wanted to give her such a prominent position at all in salvation history."

*Now I know how Uncle Matty feels,* thought Michael, as he proceeded to probe and query, "What about what Jesus said from the Cross in the Gospel of John?"

No one responded quickly.

"You know—" He started to flip back to John 19 and the others followed suit. "John nineteen, down in verse... down here beginning with verse twenty-six:

Seeing his mother there with the disciple whom he loved, Jesus said to his

230

mother, "Woman, there is your son."

In turn he said to the disciple, "There is your mother."

"He didn't want John to adopt this image of Mary as his spiritual mother," Les began explaining intently, "but just that he should take care of her as he would his own mother."

"Why didn't he entrust his mother to one of his brothers or sisters instead? You claim he had siblings, right?"

"I don't know," Les answered. "There is still much that we don't know or fully understand about the Scriptures, Michael. There are theories and ideas, no doubt, but I can't say that there is any definitive consensus on that point. I realize that it was customary that a family member be charged with providing for a parent, but we don't have answers on everything contained in the inspired Word." Les realized that this was the first time he had ever articulated such a notion. He had never had to before.

Michael didn't say anything in response. He just thought for a moment. *Who has "theories"?* Michael wondered. *Who hasn't "come to a consensus" yet? Who are the "we" without all the answers yet?*

"Do you follow that, son?" asked Luther.

"Well, yes and no," offered Michael. With that answer, Les began thinking of a way to wrap up the meeting. It had not gone according to the script in Les's head from the beginning, and nothing he could do was steering it that way.

"I think there is at least one consensus about the meaning," Michael continued.

"Well, we're not making any headway here," began Les. "It doesn't appear to me to be profitable to continue at this point."

"You mean the Catholics have come to a consensus?" suggested Jimmy. Apparently he was not listening to Les.

"Well, I don't know if I'd say Catholics have 'come to a consensus.' That's not the way Scripture is interpreted, but there is a consensus in

231

so far as there is an interpretation, an understanding of what was going on in John nineteen."

"And what, according to the Catholics, was going on?" Jimmy asked. Despite his best attempt to conceal it, Michael could sense Jimmy's sincere interest. He wouldn't have asked at all, had he not been interested.

"Jesus was entrusting his Mother to the Church, represented by John, the only apostle who was actually at the crucifixion. He was doing that on the practical level in the sense that the members of the Church were from then on responsible for her well being and support. But, there was a supernatural or mystical meaning as well."

This was what Les was afraid of, but it was too late to stop now.

"Jesus didn't call Mary, 'Mother.' He said '*Woman*, there is your son.'" Michael noticed that Jimmy, George, and Luther were engrossed despite themselves.

"That's also what he called her in the beginning of John's Gospel. In chapter two at the wedding at Cana when Mary tells him they have no more wine, Jesus says 'Woman, what is that between me and you?'"

"Because he was rebuking her for interfering in his ministry," Les interjected.

"I know a lot of people read it that way," said Michael, "but I think there's a better interpretation. Not that it's *my* interpretation," he quickly added. "If he were rebuking her, it's unlikely he would have performed the miracle of changing the water into wine. Also, Mary does not hesitate to instruct the waiters to 'do whatever He tells you.' No, when Jesus says 'Woman, what is this between me and you?' it shows the special relationship that existed between Jesus and his mother. After all, she knew what he was, or maybe I should say, she knew *who* he was."

There was no response from any of the men. They were considering it themselves while Michael was trying to gauge how open they were to all that he said. Pam McGuffey was still listening intently from the kitchen, not even trying to continue with her work.

"We can go all the way back to Genesis three fifteen and find the same 'woman'"— (*again the flipping pages*). "After Adam and Eve ate from the tree of the knowledge of good and evil, God speaks to the serpent. First, he bans him from all the rest of the animals, then in verse fifteen, still speaking to the serpent, he says...

> And I will put enmity between you and the woman, and between your seed and her Seed; He shall crush your head, And you shall crush His heel.

Then in verse sixteen, God begins to chastise Eve.

"The 'woman' in verse fifteen is Eve, isn't it?" asked George. Michael noted that it was a sincere question. He had grown accustomed to barbs and counterattacks to anything he said.

"God is rebuking the serpent or devil here, and tells him that the 'woman's' seed will crush his head. No where else in the Bible is there ever talk of a woman's seed. The man is the one with the seed. All the genealogies are from father to son, like the one in the beginning of the Gospel of Matthew. So the 'woman' who had a seed must be someone who was able to conceive without the seed of a man. God prophesies that this seed will ultimately crush the head of the devil, so we know the seed must be Christ. The 'woman,' then, must be someone who conceived not by man, and who gave birth to Christ. That someone, who conceived by the power of the Holy Spirit, is Mary, the virgin from Nazareth."

Michael waited for any response, objection, or comment. None was forthcoming, so he thought he'd tie it all together.

"The 'woman' of Genesis three fifteen is the same 'woman' of John two four and John nineteen twenty-six, the same 'woman' who is clothed with the sun in Revelation twelve. It's Mary."

"Well, it was interesting to learn why Catholics believe what they do about the mother of Jesus," Les announced. It was a signal that the meeting was over.

233

The other men nodded agreement and began to push themselves away from the table. *That's it!?* thought Michael. *After all that, it's "interesting" to learn why Catholics — and Uncle Les seemed to say 'Catholics' as if he were referring to some strange sect — think that way? There was to be no further comment, no refuting what he said?* Michael was stunned. Suddenly, without even realizing it, he missed the counterattacks and the barbs. Them he could deal with. Now there was nothing, just a polite thank you.

◆ ◆ ◆

Nightfall was always such a relief, after days when the mercury routinely climbed well into the nineties. Michael walked home in the cool darkness of the moonless night. In the blackness he could barely see his hand in front of his face, which was a bit unnerving. He knew, though, that he had only to stay on the pathway to make his way home. The path was lined on both sides with the dark silhouettes of trees. They were like frozen waves, poised to crash down upon him at any moment. The shrubs and undergrowth just off the path provided the ideal cover for any strange and vicious beast that wanted to lie in wait.

He walked quickly. He couldn't see the cottage yet. It seemed farther than he remembered. *Could I have taken a wrong turn somehow?... Relax and stay on the path,* he told himself. *Settle down.* He thought about the Bible study at his uncle's house. It had all made so much sense to him as he was learning it over the last month. But his uncle and the other men seemed completely unimpressed with the whole thing. *Could it, the whole Mary thing, be a myth, as they seem to be convinced? How could you prove anything in the end? Here are all these Christians running around who all agree that the Bible is inspired, but who all believe it means different things. In the end, we're just left there with so many competing interpretations, competing denominations. We're left with a big mess. Why would God just leave us with a book? Wasn't it inevitable that it would turn into a free-for-all about what the book meant?*

Michael pondered this in his frustration. He had been so excited walking down to the house for the singing and Bible study. He was so discouraged as he made his way back to the cottage. *Where am I?* he wondered to himself. *"Stay on the path." Did I just say that to myself?* He didn't hear anything, but the command was unmistakable. *It's so black out here.*

"Are you coming to bed?" Pam asked. Les was still at the desk reading the Bible by oil lamp.

"Yeah, I guess I better."

"Were you preparing your sermon for tomorrow?"

"Yeah, and just checking out some other stuff."

Pam noticed that her husband seemed pensive.

"How do you think the Bible study went?" She had listened to the whole thing from the kitchen but was interested in hearing his perspective.

"Okay, I guess." Then he let out a chuckle, the kind he laughed when something did not go the way he had planned. "Not like I thought it was going to go, but okay anyway, I guess." He began preparing for bed.

"Did you hear any of it?" he asked.

"Yeah, I caught most of it from the kitchen."

"What did you think?" He thought Pam's opinion and insight might help form his.

"It was interesting," she responded. "How 'bout you?"

*That's not much to go on*, he thought. "He said some things worth thinking about, but there're still a lot of unanswered questions."

*His answer was as ambiguous as mine, just longer,* thought Pam. "Is the Bible study healing the rift between Luther, and Jimmy and George?"

Les sat down on his side of the bed. He had to consider that question. He had forgotten that that was one of the ideas behind the whole thing.

He had been confident that they'd unite to stand against a common enemy, the great harlot of Babylon, otherwise known as the Roman Catholic Church. But now, he wasn't so confident that they were united. If they were anything like him, they were struggling to come to terms with all that Michael had explained as well as some of the long-held assumptions about what the Roman Church believes and teaches.

"I'm not sure at this point," he answered. *Whether or not a couple of men could ever come to terms over what the Bible says or doesn't say about tobacco growing was small potatoes compared to what was at stake now... Peter and the papacy, Mary the Queen Mother.*

"I just want to understand the Bible and be true to it," he said as he lay his head down on the pillow. *How far have I come since my days in the Corps?* He remembered having the same unsettled feeling when he started studying the Bible. What he had desired so intently was to know and embrace the truth. The unsettled feeling had come when he began to realize that the Presbyterian Church was not where he was going to find it.

Finally Michael saw the flicker of a light as he rounded a bend in the lane — the lamp in the window of their cottage. Immediately he felt tremendous relief. Of course it had been there all the time, but it was so good to see it at last. Like the beam from a lighthouse, it guided him off the lane, and up to the house.

In short order he was climbing into bed. He was so thankful to be safely home. He thought again of the Bible study and how it had ended. That was what bothered him so much. He didn't know what to make of it. *What were they thinking? Why didn't they object?* Then he realized that maybe they just didn't have anything to say. Perhaps they didn't or couldn't refute what he had said, but needed more time to reflect on it. Maybe their not saying anything was a good sign. He forgot about the frustration and discouragement of the past two hours and fell fast asleep.

# 11

After Mass the next day at the Dominican convent in Nashville, the O'Sheas decided to spend some time exploring the grounds that surrounded the big stone motherhouse. The younger boys had no trouble expending energy by running around the various foot paths there. Tammy O'Shea put little Kateri in the stroller and set off on a stroll. Michael, however, didn't get too far from the main entrance. He was content to look at the gardens, fish ponds, and beautiful statues that abounded. He had truly begun to appreciate Sunday as a day of rest from farm work.

He felt especially relaxed today, because he had decided to give no more Bible study presentations. *If they're truly interested in discussing things about the Church they'll have to do so with someone else.* He felt that he had given his best shot, and was trying to come to terms with the realization that his best wasn't nearly good enough. Various Dominican sisters in their streaming white and black habits glided by, going in and out of the convent. He noted with amusement that many wore running shoes when out for a walk.

He noticed two of them stopped at one of the ponds. One was pointing something out to her walking partner. To Michael they appeared to be enjoying and marveling at the simple beauty of the little pond. He could imagine small children in the same pose pointing things out to one another and reveling in the wonder of creation. One of them noticed Michael looking over at them.

"How do you like our fish ponds?" she asked.

"Oh, I like them, they're real nice," Michael assured her. He had been taken a bit off guard by her question.

"Do you like nature?" she asked.

"Yes, I do."

"Maybe you'll be a scientist?"

"Maybe a farmer," he corrected her. To Michael, scientists analyzed and tested. He enjoyed working with and around natural things.

They approached the bench where Michael was sitting. He stood up. The Sisters of the Immaculate Heart of Mary had taught him enough to know it was not polite for a young man to stay seated when being addressed by an elder.

"I've noticed your family comes down for Sunday Mass."

"Yes," Michael explained, "we drive down from Kentucky."

She introduced herself as Sister Mary Martin. Mary she adopted after Mary Magdalene, the first to preach the Gospel "He is risen," and Martin after St. Martin de Porres, a black Dominican brother from Lima, Peru. She went on to ask him a bit about how they came to live in Kentucky, about what they thought of Mass at the convent, and about his family. Michael didn't feel that she was prying; rather, she seemed sincerely interested in him.

"Do you know much about our order?" she asked.

"You were founded by St. Dominic." It was the only thing that came to mind.

"Do you know much about him?"

"No, not really."

"He was a great teacher and preacher for the Church during the time of the Albigensian heresy in Europe. He was a great apologist, you might say."

"An apologist?"

"An apologist is someone who teaches, explains, and especially defends the faith."

*I guess that makes me an apologist of sorts,* thought Michael. *A retired one*, he corrected himself, *and a lousy one at that.* His curiosity was piqued, however. *What made Dominic great? Why was he effective?*

"Did he convince a lot of people to come back to the Church?" Michael asked.

The sister smiled and said, "No one can *convince* someone to come back to the Church or to embrace the true faith. He did spread the truth, though."

"If a seed falls on fertile soil — someone who is sincerely seeking — then the grace to see will be provided. Our Lady will see to that," the other sister explained. She had not introduced herself.

"Our Lady?" Michael asked.

"She will procure the necessary grace," Sister Mary Martin explained.

There was still so much that Michael did not understand about the faith.

"Just like at Cana," she continued, "Our Lady knows when someone is in need of wine."

"I've been discussing the Bible with some people down here," Michael began to explain, "and it seems impossible to come to any conclusion. It seems right to me — the Church's interpretation, that is — but the other people have a completely different way of interpreting the Bible. It seems there's no way to prove what is true and what is false."

"Why do they study the Bible?" the second sister asked.

It seemed an odd question to Michael. *Wasn't it obvious?*

"They're Christians," he said. "They believe that the Bible is inspired." He didn't mention that he thought they hoped to rescue him from a church they considered to be an apostate church, or rather *the* apostate church.

She appeared to be considering his answer.

*These sisters must be familiar with the fundamentalist Christian types down in these parts,* he thought. *There are far more of them than Catholic Christians around here.*

"That's what I understand," she responded. "That they do, just as we, consider the Bible to be inspired. Why do you suppose, though, that they believe that the Bible is inspired?" she asked.

Michael remembered asking his Uncle Les that very question at the first Bible study. "They have faith that it is," Michael responded, echoing his uncle.

"Maybe you should consider why *we* believe in the Bible. Is it the same reason *they* believe? If it's different, perhaps that would give you insight into why there's such difficulty among non-Catholic Christians in agreeing on what the Bible says and means."

*Luther had asked me why I believed the Bible was inspired,* Michael remembered, *and I wasn't ready to give an answer.*

"How do they think the Church got along for so many years without the New Testament?" Sister Mary Martin asked.

"I don't know." *She'd have made a good attorney*, thought Michael.

"They look to the Bible to learn what they ought to believe and how they ought to live?"

"That's what they claim."

"Well, then how did those poor early Christians do it? What guide did they have? There was no New Testament as such for the first four hundred or so years of the Church, but the faith prospered, even under intense persecution... Anyway, good luck with your discussions," she concluded. "You are being given a tremendous opportunity to spread the faith."

"Thanks." *I'm being given an opportunity?* He didn't tell her that he had just gone into retirement in the past hour.

"Keep in mind, though, that God has endowed all of us with free will. No one is forced to submit to his authority."

"People have a right to believe what they want to believe," Michael commented.

"That's right. You're a fast learner," the second sister smiled. As a teacher she appreciated his attentiveness and insight.

"Always be charitable," Sister Mary Martin added, "and pray for guidance." They turned to walk away and quickly disappeared behind the ornate convent door.

Michael thought about the questions she had posed. *Why the Bible? What did Christians do before the New Testament?* Something told him that the answers to those questions would lead to more questions. He sensed that he was just scratching the surface of an entirely new area. *Maybe it's some new wine being poured out from heaven,* he thought as he reflected on what Sister Mary Martin had said about the Blessed Mother. *Maybe I'm not out of the apologetics business after all.*

Inside the convent, Sister Mary Martin was just entering her room. She had begun a new teaching assignment a few months ago at St. Catherine of Siena, the Dominican academy for girls, and had been struggling with self-doubt. She didn't question her ability to teach chemistry and biology, but was struggling with the whole idea about what larger impact she was making. As a teacher, she could derive satisfaction from imparting knowledge and an appreciation of the natural world. As a consecrated virgin, she yearned to see how her efforts were leading young people to God.

She knelt in her room and offered a prayer of thanksgiving for the exchange she had just had with the young man outside. As she walked away from him she had sensed so strongly that it had made a difference. *Our Lady saw that my wine was running low.*

◆ ◆ ◆

Work on the farm continued to go well for Michael. Through middle July, cantaloupes and watermelons started coming in. "Coming in" was the term everyone used locally to indicate that a crop was ripe and was being harvested for market. Melons had been planted in rows about eight feet apart, using four-foot wide black plastic mulch that ran the length of each row. This kept the weeds at bay when the melons were young. It was easy to cultivate between the rows of plastic mulch using one horse and a simple adjustable cultivator. Before the middle of June, the vines would be creeping off the plastic onto the dirt, and the broad leaves on the vine would be enough to shade the ground and thus keep down the weeds. Every six rows there would be an extra wide space left so that a wagon could be driven down the middle during harvesting.

The harvest was another group effort. They'd begin with Elijah picking the fruit from the farthest row out. He'd toss the melon across a row or two to Michael, who would toss it another couple of rows to Lori. Lori would toss it up to her Dad who was driving the wagon. In this way the wagon would make its way slowly down the field. Les would then turn the wagon around and start back the other way while the second farthest row was harvested. And so it went, back and forth until the six rows on either side of the wagon path were picked clean and the wagon was loaded down under the weight of a mountain of green watermelons or tan cantaloupes.

On one of those days Les noticed an abrasion on the neck of one of the workhorses, right near where the collar rubbed. Michael volunteered to run back to the house to fetch some salve. He arrived at the house and told Pam where Les said the salve would be. She located it quickly and asked about the horse. It was really the first time Pam had ever spoken with Michael without her husband or Elijah being present.

She was relieved that her husband's "conversion through Bible study" plan had been put on hold indefinitely. She had seen firsthand that the Bible study format didn't work, but not because Michael was overwhelmed. On the contrary, it was foiled because he explained the Bible in a way that none of the other men could have anticipated or even imagined. She, too, had been surprised. She had always understood that Catholics didn't even bother with the Bible much. They believed what they did and claimed that it was their tradition even when it went against the Scriptures, or seemed to.

She wanted to talk with her nephew a bit. Much of what he had said at the Bible study sessions intrigued her, as did the way in which he had expressed it. She, too, would cringe sometimes at Luther Moore's sledgehammer style and had been impressed at how Michael handled his attacks time and again. She had been moved at Michael's ability to maintain a level of civility and charity. He was able to stay focused on *explaining* what the Bible meant without necessarily trying to *convince* everyone present to accept his way of seeing it.

All of her previous experiences with serious discussions among non-Catholics on the meaning of various Scripture passages were contrary to this. The emphasis was on persuasion. It was all for nothing if you didn't convince the other side of the truth of your understanding.

Pam had considered this difference over the past few weeks. *Which is God's way?* she wondered. *God allows us to make our own decisions. He doesn't force us to obey His commandments or to strive to imitate His Son. He thinks enough of us to allow us to have free will. After all, if He forced us to be the way He wants us to be, what merit would there be in that? We'd be slaves, not children. Maybe it's best merely to present the truth and then go about the business of living it instead of using so much energy in trying to convince everyone about it.*

"Did Eli tell you about the big auction in the community next Saturday?" Pam asked after handing him the salve. The "community"

243

was what everyone called the Amish area.

"Yes, he did," Michael answered. "Said it was all the rage around these parts."

"Oh, it is. I think you'll surely enjoy it. There'll be Amish folks from various communities around Kentucky, Tennessee, and even Missouri there. There'll be plenty of 'English' too."

"What do they sell?" Michael asked.

"You name it — everything from nuts and bolts, to kitchen utensils, to horses and horse-drawn equipment. They have good Amish-style food at good prices. It's a fun day."

"Well, I'm looking forward to it."

"How have you enjoyed the summer on the farm so far?" No one in the McGuffey family had asked him since the first week.

"Oh, I like it a lot," he beamed. "I like farm life."

"Good. D'ya think you'd want to be a farmer yourself?"

"I don't know," he answered honestly. He thought of his Uncle Mathias back home. "I sure enjoy it well enough now." He could not conceive at this time what vivid memories were being imprinted indelibly in his mind from this summer.

"What about the Bible study sessions? What did you think of them?" she ventured.

"Oh," he chortled at first, "I'm sure I'll remember *them* for a long time. I appreciate Uncle Les giving me a chance to say some things, but I'm not sure I did a real good job."

Pam wasn't sure if he was just trying to be humble or whether he really believed that he had botched the presentations. *It's possible that he actually thinks that,* she concluded. She had been truly impressed with his composure and attitude as well as with his explanations.

"I thought you did well, Michael. Your father would have been proud of you." She realized that her words were perhaps serving to frustrate her husband's plan to work on Michael to convert. She justified herself by reasoning that Michael himself had already foiled her husband's plan because he had been ready with answers when called upon to explain.

Also, she felt pity for the young man because he was fatherless. She could see that their faith was the bond that held them together still. He had been orphaned by fate, by the tragic fire, in a physical sense. If the Bible study plan had succeeded in tearing Michael from his faith, the faith of his father, he would have become an orphan again, this time a spiritual orphan. Pam could hardly believe she was rationalizing like this, but as a woman, she saw things that the men could not see. *If we are living the truth, then Michael will see that and come to the truth eventually,* she concluded. *And, if it's the truth that he spoke...* she stopped her herself from thinking.

"I never heard much about Mary growing up," Pam continued. "I guess because she didn't seem to play such an important role in our salvation. She's not mentioned in the Bible much. It was interesting to hear what you all think about the mother of Jesus." She was trying to be considerate of her nephew and help him to feel at ease. That would be the first step to any process of conversion. He probably regarded them all with suspicion since the Bible studies and the unleashing of Luther.

"No, she's not mentioned much, but she was there at all the important times," Michael responded. He felt comfortable with Pam and his response was not defensive, nor was it an attempt to impress anything particular on her.

"What do you mean?" she inquired. She was just trying to be nice, and his response only seemed to echo what she had just said — that Mary, the mother of Jesus, was not mentioned much in the Bible. When she was, it did not seem particularly noteworthy.

"Well, she was there at the Annunciation, when the angel told her that she would carry and bear the Messiah," began Michael. He held out the thumb when he said this, so as to start counting all the important times

Mary was present in the Bible. "She was there at the birth of our Savior—" *The index finger went out.* "She was there when Jesus was presented at the Temple. She was there with her husband to flee to Egypt to save Jesus from King Herod's slaughter of the innocents when he was too little to save himself." *Michael had three fingers and his thumb out.* "Mary was at the wedding at Cana when Jesus performed his first recorded miracle." *Now his hand was completely opened.*

He put his hand down but continued with the litany. "She was there at the foot of the cross. Mark wasn't there. Matthew wasn't there. Peter wasn't there. She was there at the foot of the cross when her Son entrusted the Church to her and she to the Church. And, she was there in Jerusalem after the Resurrection, with the other disciples on the day of Pentecost when the Holy Spirit was poured out upon them. Some call it the birthday of the Church."

Though Michael had recounted all of it very matter-of-factly, Pam was a bit overwhelmed at all that he said. It was something he had hoped to point out that night around the table but had not had the opportunity.

"All that, of course, is just what's written in the Bible," added Michael. "The Blessed Mother and Joseph the carpenter raised Jesus from a tiny babe up into a man, long before he chose even one apostle." Pam took note of Michael's use of the term *Blessed Mother.*

"Now why do you call her that?" Pam asked.

"The Blessed Mother?"

"Yeah."

"That's in the Bible. After her cousin Elizabeth greeted her, Mary prophesied that "all ages to come shall call me blessed." Michael couldn't help but feel a little strange explaining this to his aunt. Two months ago he could not have imagined teaching any of the McGuffeys anything from the Bible. He saw that Pam looked a bit unsure about whether that meant we should all call Mary the Blessed Mother.

"Don't get hung up on that," Michael told her. "The difference in how Catholics and non-Catholics view Mary has to do with things so much more basic than that." Since the meeting about Mary he had read more. He had come to a far better understanding himself and wished that he'd have approached things a bit differently that night. *This is my make-up test,* he joked to himself as he collected his thoughts before explaining it all to Pam.

"The Bible is the story of our salvation history," he began.

"That much we agree on," she nodded.

"The very first book starts with man's fall from grace. They were kicked out of the garden because Adam disobeyed God and ate from the tree of the knowledge of good and evil. Eve took the apple first, but her sin would not have earned them removal from the garden. She was important because she was the conduit through which Adam sinned. In other words, she disobeyed first, passed the fruit to Adam, and his eating the fruit resulted in the fall."

"Hold on—" Pam said, and went to get her Bible. She didn't know what this had to do with Mary but she wanted to see Genesis for herself.

"We look at Christ as the new Adam just like you, but also Mary as the new Eve which I don't think you consider," Michael said. "Go to Genesis two."

She opened the Bible on the kitchen table so they could both look at it.

Michael paged through to the creation story. "Let's see, Genesis two is where God places Adam in the garden... Here in verse fifteen it says, 'Then the Lord God took the man and put him in the garden of Eden to tend and keep it.' The word in Hebrew translated as *keep* in verse fifteen means *to protect*. Okay, then chapter three is where the Serpent comes in. That's who Adam had to protect the garden from. Down in verse six it reads...

247

> So when the woman saw that the tree was good for food, that it was pleasant to the eyes, and a tree desirable to make one wise, she took of its fruit and ate. She also gave to her husband with her, and he ate.

"Now down in verse twenty-two it says...

Pam's head was spinning. *What does this all have to do with Mary?* she wondered, but she struggled to follow.

> Then the Lord God said, "Behold, the man has become like one of Us, to know good from evil. And now, lest he put out his hand and take also of the tree of life, and eat, and live forever" – therefore the Lord God sent him out of the garden of Eden to till the ground from which he was taken. So He drove out the man; and He placed cherubim at the east of the garden of Eden, and a flaming sword which turned every way, to guard the way to the tree of life.

"So it was Adam's sin that led to the fall while Eve played the supporting role," he summarized. "The Serpent would not have been able to seduce Eve at all if Adam would have stood up to him, had he *kept* the garden. Instead he stood by silently while his wife was tricked and then ate of the fruit himself. Really he was afraid of the Serpent and the struggle that would have ensued if he resisted." Michael had read Genesis and then a commentary from one of the Catholic theologians. The book pointed out that the Serpent in Genesis was the same creature as the Dragon in the Book of Revelation, the same Hebrew word.

"Now let's go to..." Michael started paging through the Bible. "Mark...here in chapter fourteen starting in verse thirty-two:

> Then they came to a place which was named Gethsemane; and He said to His disciples, "Sit here while I pray."
> And he took Peter, James, and John with Him, and He began to be troubled and deeply distressed.

> Then He said to them, "My soul is exceedingly sorrowful, even to death. Stay
> here and watch.
>
> And he went a little farther, and fell on the ground, and prayed that if it were
> possible, the hour might pass from Him.
>
> And he said, "Abba, Father, all things are possible for You. Take this cup away
> from Me; nevertheless, not what I will, but what You will.

Pam waited for Michael to elucidate the connection between all
this and Mary.

"This is the Agony in the Garden. Jesus was put to the test; he
was distressed at what lay before him but said 'not what I will, but what
You will.' Unlike Adam, he trusted and obeyed the Father, and went to
the Cross."

Pam saw the parallel. Adam failed his test in the Garden and all
mankind suffered. Christ passed his test and we all benefited. *But, where
was Mary?* she asked herself.

Michael started flipping through the Bible again. "In Luke chapter one the angel appears to Mary, the young Jewish woman. Beginning
with verse twenty-eight...

> And having come in, the angel said to her, "Rejoice, highly favored one, the
> Lord is with you; blessed are you among women!"
>
> But when she saw him, she was troubled at this saying, and considered what
> manner of greeting this was.

"In some translations the salutation to Mary is rendered, 'Hail,
Full of Grace,'" Michael interjected.

> Then the angel said to her, "Do not be afraid, Mary, for you have found favor
> with God. And, behold, you will conceive in your womb and bring forth a
> Son, and shall call His name Jesus. He will be great, and will be called the

Son of the highest; and the Lord God will give Him the throne of His father David."

"Then down in verse thirty-eight we hear her response...

Then Mary said, "Behold the maidservant of the Lord! Let it be done to me according to your word." And the angel departed from her.

"She didn't have to accept what the angel said," Michael began to explain, "and she had good reason to be troubled. She was betrothed to the carpenter, Joseph. She didn't know that he'd be willing to divorce her quietly. By saying 'yes' to carrying the child, she was exposing herself to the severest form of condemnation. She would have been torn from her people at the least, and could have been stoned."

Pam started making the connection. "Mary parallels Eve."

"Eve was the conduit for the fall, Mary for the redemption," Michael continued. "Eve had to leave the garden with Adam. Mary was told by Simeon when they presented the baby at the Temple that 'your heart too a sword shall pierce.' Mary suffered, too, through the redemption. Most important, though, is that both Eve and Mary, like all of us, were endowed with a free will. Mary didn't have to say yes."

"But God knew she would," commented Pam.

"Yeah, he did, but it's still a mystery. God's plan of salvation was not to be thwarted, but at the same time, he doesn't compromise the gift of free will." The commentary, as Michael remembered, had explained it pretty much like that. "Mary's trust in God did not directly *cause* the Redemption but it enabled the Redeemer to enter the world," Michael summarized.

Pam just nodded as she considered what he said.

"Now we have free access to the tree of life again," Michael said as he closed the Bible and began backing away. *Do I dare?* he asked himself. "And, if we want to live forever we've got to eat from it...

"Well, they'll be sending a search party out for me soon," he said as he moved toward the door with the salve for the horse in his hand. "Thanks for the salve." Michael didn't know if he should wait for his aunt to respond to anything he said.

"You're welcome," Pam finally said. "We'll be seeing you."

Michael hustled back to the cantaloupe field. He felt somehow relieved that he had finally been able to say some things he wished he'd said at the formal Bible study, yet his aunt's response was not very motivating. All that he had learned about Peter and the papacy and the Blessed Mother was so fascinating to him, but he was deeply disappointed at his inability to communicate it effectively. On the one hand, he was excited at all that he had learned from the Bible and his father's books, and on the other, discouraged because of his perceived failure at passing it on.

*Martin de Porres Kennedy*

# 12

Michael and Elijah strolled leisurely through the auction grounds. There was a carnival atmosphere. Auctions were being held at three different locations on the grounds — a regular three-ring circus. One area was dedicated strictly to livestock. The auctioneers began in the morning with pigeons and rabbits and they'd work their way through chickens, goats, sheep, puppies, and on up to huge draft horses by late afternoon. Another area was dedicated to farm machinery and equipment, all of it of the horse-drawn variety. The third auction ring seemed to be anything and everything that did not fit those first two categories. There were wood cookstoves, Amish-made quilts, furniture, butter churns, and much more.

The concession stand, run by the local Amish community, was strategically located in the middle of the grounds. As people drifted away from one auction ring to another they couldn't help but pass right by the stand and be enveloped with the smell of funnel cakes and caramel-covered popcorn. They were forced to look upon the assorted pies that sat upon the shelves behind the Amish women who manned the large concession stand. They passed right by others who were wolfing down hot dogs covered with mustard and sauerkraut or buns filled with chopped beef drenched in homemade barbecue sauce. "Let nobody tell you otherwise," his uncle had laughed to him the night before, "these plain people are marketing geniuses. They make and grow good stuff and know how to move it."

Just as he had been told to expect, there were throngs of plain people there. It was interesting to note the slight differences in dress among the various groups. One group could be easily identified by the hats the men wore — a sort of black derby instead of a straw hat. Various style bonnets could be seen among the women.

Michael had learned that the uniformity of dress was very important within a community of plain people. It was part of the *Ordnung,* the German word for "order." Endeavoring to have *alles in Ordnung* (everything in order) within their particular community was essential. God provided for order when he created the entire universe, and that order was manifested even within the tiniest organism in the universe. Therefore, the body of Christ, their Church, should be strictly ordered.

The bishop of a community exercised far-reaching authority within a community. He was the judge over what was in *Ordnung* and what was not, in everything from dress to a man's financial dealings. Michael knew that this understanding and mentality with regard to the *Ordnung* was something that Les and the other Bible Christians could not endure. They were dubious of any sort of church authority and considered the regulations on dress particularly onerous and completely unbiblical.

Michael, though, had an appreciation for the concept of having things in *Ordnung.* It was not so unlike the Catholic way. The Church, as it is presented in the book of Acts and subsequent books of the Bible, had a very definite structure and means by which authority was exercised. It was a visible Church. (Michael's uncle and the other men seemed to view the Church as an intangible — sort of an invisible blob of believers. It was made up of men and women who confessed that Jesus Christ was their Lord and had accepted him as their "Personal Savior." After that, it was a free for all.) Les was critical of this whole notion of identifying dress for members of a particular church. "It's an apostasy," he had declared, "but then I guess all churches are apostate in some way or another."

Michael and Eli bellied up to the crowd at the livestock auction. It was only ten in the morning, but already the hot July sun had burned all the dew off the grass. They were still selling off the small animals. Young Amish boys were responsible for bringing the various cages of chickens, rabbits, pigeons, and other critters up to the auctioneer, who stood on a slightly raised platform under a canvas canopy to provide shade. The local Amish ran the auction, but they hired out the actual auctioneers for the day. The auctioneer wore a brown cowboy hat, blue jeans, and a red bandana around his neck. He held a cordless microphone. The speaker dangled from the top of the front part of the canopy as if it were put up there as an afterthought with whatever twine was available.

"All right, whatta we got now?" asked the auctioneer. A pre-teen Amish boy brought a cage onto the platform and held it up.

"Looky here," began the auctioneer, "a bunch a' black layin' hens. How many we got in there?" he asked the Amish boy.

"Five layin' hens," he announced, "an' a egg." Indeed, one of the chickens had laid a nice brown egg that was loose in the cage.

"Now how much for these fine lookin' layers? One and five times your bid now, one and five times your bid." Eli explained to Michael that that meant the bidding would be done as if you were buying just one of the birds. So, if you won the bidding at $6 then you'd have actually purchased five birds for $30.

The auctioneer continued... "Five fine chickens here. Whatta ya say, a five dollar bill? Five dollars, fi'e dollar, fi'e dollar, fi'e dollar, fi'e dollar, fi'e dollar, fi'e dollar." He scanned the crowd for hands going up as he recited this mantra. No one moved. "Now three dollars? A three-dollar bill? Anyone at three dollars? Okay then one dollar and let's go!" A couple of hands went up. He pointed at one of them and continued...

"All right, I got one dollar, now two dollars. Two dollars, two dollars. Another hand shot up quickly. Again he acknowledged them by pointing at them and continued... Who'll give me three? Three-dollar bill?" — *another hand* — "Now four dollar, four dollar, four dollar..." — *another hand* — "Five dollars? A five dollar bill." — *He saw a hand.* — "Now six dollars, one and five times your bid at six dollars?... Now I got six..." He looked to the right side of the crowd. "Anyone for six dollars?" — *looking at middle of the crowd* — "Six, six, six..." — *now looking to the left* — "Sold!! At five dollars to number two seventy-one!"

The whole thing had taken less than a minute. Then, with barely a pause, the auctioneer again asked, "Okay now, whatta we got here?" as the next cage was brought up. It went on the same way every time. The auctioneer would start out at six or seven dollars and be forced down to one dollar before anyone would open the bid. Then the bidding would continue up until six or seven dollars or wherever it was that the auctioneer started the bidding. It was as if all those bidding were engaged in a secret conspiracy to force the auctioneer to work as hard as possible to sell each item. The cartel of bidders held together because, like people at auctions everywhere, they were angling for good deals. So even after the thousandth chicken had sold for six dollars, the bidding for the next chicken wouldn't start until it was down to one dollar.

Elijah had taken Michael to get a number when they had first arrived at the auction. You couldn't bid without a number. When you did win the bidding on something, a clerk would write down your number along with a description of what it was you bought. The slip of paper would be sent to the shed that served as the office for the day, with the young Amish boys acting as runners. It seemed to Michael that it all ran smoothly, despite the carnival-like atmosphere. What most impressed him was that the system depended so much on the basic integrity and honesty of those in attendance. It would have been absurdly easy to walk off with merchandise or even small livestock, but apparently that was never a problem at these country auctions.

Michael was reminded of the day he had spent with his father one time in another neighborhood of Philadelphia. They had been helping to fix up a row home into which a Catholic refugee family was preparing to move. For lunch, his dad had taken him to a local fast food eatery. Thick, bullet-proof glass separated the cashier from the customer. Money and food were exchanged by way of a small, transparent revolving door. After they downed their burgers, they stopped in at a corner store for dessert. There, instead of bullet-proof glass, they had a wire fence that extended from the top of the counter to the ceiling. The cashier and all of the merchandise were on the other side of the fence from where Michael and his father stood. You had to tell the cashier what you wanted and she'd fetch it for you. He remembered it feeling stifling and oppressive. Everyone was assumed to be untrustworthy because of the sins of others.

In contrast, there was something uplifting about being in a place among hundreds of people whose characters were being trusted. Michael realized that in some strange way, the conditions of both were self-fulfilling prophecies. A person would be more likely to try to steal where that expectation was understood. Likewise, the possibility of thievery was not even in question at the auction. The culture of trust and honesty, which prevailed at the auction, was a far more powerful shield than the bullet-proof glass back at that burger joint. It was less costly, too.

"Let's get a funnel cake," Eli said as he nudged Michael. "My treat."

Michael, though not very hungry, followed him over to the concession stand and they took their place in line. The sun was high, but a slight breeze managed to keep things cool. Michael noticed a family at one of the picnic tables enjoying barbecue sandwiches, creamy coleslaw, and homemade lemonade. The sights and smells awakened his stomach and suddenly he felt a hunger that he hadn't realized was there. Michael, enjoying the anticipation of his cousin's treat, stood in line watching the Amish women hustle to and fro behind the stand.

"Hey, fellas."

Eli and Michael both swung their heads around and saw Jimmy approaching them.

"Why don't you all come on over to our table and join us," he invited as he pointed out a table where a few men were sitting.

"Be proud to," responded Eli.

Michael still wasn't sure exactly what being "proud," as many locals used it, actually meant. He understood enough, though, to know that it was an acceptance of the invitation.

Jimmy made all the introductions as Eli and Michael took their places. It seemed that Eli was familiar with most of the men. Michael promptly forgot almost all the names and couldn't match any of the names he did remember with a face. One of the men, he thought the oldest man present, was introduced as the pastor of a church, the "True Gospel Church," or was it the "Gospel of the True Tabernacle Church," or maybe the "Full Gospel of God's Holy Tabernacle." At any rate, it was one of the local churches.

The talk around the table was about the goings on at the auction — who got some good buys, who was waiting for something to go on the block and so on. Then there was some talk about the tobacco crop — whose looked good, what the politicians in Washington were trying to do, and how their local congressman was committed to defending the tobacco farmer. Michael looked around to see if he could spot Luther in the crowd. He surely wouldn't pass up an opportunity to share a bit of his anti-tobacco brand of Christianity. *Well, I guess even Luther can take a day off from proselytizing,* Michael noted when he didn't see Luther anywhere.

As Michael contented himself with his share of the funnel cake he watched the people as they passed by. It was interesting to see so many

"English" milling about among the plain people. The contrast varied. Many of the English men wore bib overalls. A couple of weeks ago Eli had classified such men into three groups: farmers, old-timers (who might still be active farmers to some degree), and "wannabees." These men didn't strike such a great contrast with their plain counterparts. Most of them did smoke, however, and they were more likely to be a bit overweight than the plain men their same age, Michael decided. The bib overalls themselves contributed to that perception, Michael thought, but it was also probably due to the difference in farming methods. *Walking behind a plow or cultivator certainly burns up more energy than steering a tractor.*

The English women and children provided for a much starker contrast. With the women it was evident in the dress, the hairstyles, and the make-up. Most of the women wore shorts regardless of age. Those that wore dresses sported either stylish-looking sundresses (probably antique shoppers from the Nashville area) or knee-length jean skirts. Women's hair and make-up was not something Michael typically took note of. Again it was more the contrast that drew his attention to both this day. The English sported varying styles, colors, and lengths, as compared to the Amish, who looked so uniform in their bonnets and long dark dresses.

The young English people wore shorts and brightly colored athletic T-shirts, the kind with team names emblazoned across the front, or some superstar's name across the back. The plain children, on the other hand, were miniatures of their parents.

Michael had learned over time that the "plain" dress reflected both their desire to practice the biblical virtue of modesty and to adhere to the *Ordnung*. *It certainly does set them apart*, Michael thought, *perhaps too much.* Michael considered how the intent of both groups was reversed in a strange way. The vast majority of the English women, with their unique hairstyles and clothing, would blend right in on the streets of

Philadelphia and become rather unremarkable. An Amish woman, though, would stand out because of her dress and draw an inordinate amount of attention to herself.

"So you're the young man that's been giving Bible lessons?"

The question or statement — it was hard to tell which it was — startled Michael. He turned his head and saw that it was the pastor of the local church who had addressed him from about the middle part of the picnic table. At first he wasn't sure what the man was talking about, then understood that he was referring to the sessions over at his Uncle Les's house.

"Well, I'm not sure how much in the way of lessons they were, Reverend... Brown, was it?" Michael responded with self-effacing humor.

"*Pastor* Brown, Pastor Hank Brown," he said. "God's the only one who merits our reverence, son."

"Oh, I'm sorry, Pastor Brown. I didn't realize," began Michael. *I can't even address someone respectfully without offending some sort of religious sensibility*, thought Michael. He was beginning to feel hypersensitive about such things. The trouble was that the rules changed from person to person. He couldn't imagine his uncle — also a pastor — feeling uncomfortable with the title of Reverend.

"That's quite all right, son," Pastor Brown assured magnanimously. "So what were you lecturing about?"

By this time everyone at the table was listening to their conversation.

"Oh, I was just trying to explain some things about the way I understand certain parts of the Bible," Michael explained, trying to satisfy the good pastor's curiosity.

"Uh huh," nodded the pastor. "Did you help them to understand your interpretation?"

The tone of the question put Michael on guard. He sensed that the man was insistent on engaging him for the purpose of setting him straight.

*Oh Mary, Mother of the Church, please guide my thoughts and words,* Michael prayed.

"It wasn't exactly *my* interpretation I was trying to explain," Michael clarified, "and as to whether or not anyone understood it, I don't know... You might ask Jimmy. He was there." Michael suggested this while nodding over at Jimmy.

Unfortunately, the suggestion didn't deflect any attention away from Michael. Pastor Brown didn't even look at Jimmy. *He's like Luther,* Michael decided, *if a tad more tactful.* He wasn't sure which type of persistent personality he preferred.

"Whose interpretation was it that you were trying to explain?"

*Enough with the games,* Michael thought, though he was still reluctant to engage in another big biblical discussion.

"It was the Catholic interpretation," he answered.

"I take it, then, that you are Roman Catholic?"

"Yes, I'm Catholic," Michael responded, avoiding the word "Roman." He had just read recently that the modifier *Roman* only became popular after the Reformation, so as to distinguish between the breakaway Anglican Church and the original Catholic Church. The simple term, Catholic, from the Greek meaning *universal,* was used as early as the turn of the first century. After learning this he had formulated an informal, personal policy of saying just Catholic, not Roman Catholic. He wasn't particularly confident, though, that Pastor Brown would appreciate the subtlety.

"The Catholics, as I understand it, hold their Church above the Bible. Isn't that right?" the pastor asked, holding his meaty right hand out flat about three inches above his flattened left hand.

"Well, it's not quite like that, I wouldn't say, Pastor Brown," Michael responded, trying to be diplomatic.

"Well, when your traditions and rituals come into conflict with Scripture, what happens?" he asked.

Michael was confused about what the pastor was saying or trying to imply. "I'm not sure I understand, Pastor."

"When there's a contradiction between what your Church believes and practices and what the Bible teaches, it's your Church that wins out, so to speak, isn't that right?"

It was obvious to Michael at this point that he wasn't really asking. He was asserting, and merely trying to get Michael to concur.

"No, I wouldn't say that," Michael began, not sure of how to respond. "I'm a bit confused about what you mean by contradictions."

"Well, that's interesting that you don't even perceive any contradictions," the pastor announced. "There's a couple real obvious ones that I can point out real quick." With that he lifted a small brown leather case that had apparently been on the bench next to him and unzipped it.

Michael watched as he removed the Bible from the leather holder and it was all he could do to suppress a guffaw as he thought of the old credit card promotion that his father had been so fond of mimicking ... *Don't leave home without it.* Michael concluded that the pastor seemed very pleased that he'd been given an invitation, or at least perceived that he had been given one, to explain what he meant. No sooner was the Bible out of the case than Pastor Brown began flipping pages. He knew exactly what he was looking for.

Suddenly he stopped short and looked up at Michael. "Now I hope you don't mind me showing you this. I really think it could be to your benefit, son." He set up his close with this line in a way that would have made any salesman proud.

"Please go right ahead," Michael assured him, playing the part of the unsuspecting prospect. It wouldn't have seemed appropriate for Michael to be anything but gracious at this point.

"Now, the one that's always struck me the most..." *Pastor Brown had found the passage he sought, and the Bible lay open in front of him...* "is here in Matthew twenty-three. You can read it if you want to," he offered, indicating with his hands and expression that he'd pass the Bible over to Michael.

"No, that's all right. Why don't you read it out loud so everyone can hear." Michael knew that that's what the pastor wanted. He still didn't know, however, what the passage would be.

"All right, then. This is from Matthew twenty-three verse nine... 'Do not call anyone on earth your father; for One is your Father, He who is in heaven.'"

Pastor Brown simply raised his head from the Bible and looked at Michael. All eyes at the table were on Michael. Michael looked back at the pastor unfazed. His experience over at his uncle's had taught him how to relax while on the hot seat.

"What do you have to say about that teaching from Matthew twenty-three?" the pastor asked.

"Well, I don't have anything in particular to say about it right now," Michael responded innocently. He had decided not to jump in with any defense, for he knew what the pastor was charging now, but rather to wait and listen.

"You do recognize that this directly contradicts the Catholic practice of calling priests *father*?" Pastor Brown said patiently. He was a bit befuddled, as he had heard enough about the young man he was addressing to know that others had been impressed with what he had to say about the Bible. Now it seemed that he wasn't particularly sharp at all.

"No, I don't recognize that," began Michael very politely, "I do recognize how that passage could cause a tremendous amount of confusion and misunderstanding if it's not properly interpreted."

Michael determined how he was to respond, or rather the response had somehow just come to him.

"And how do you interpret it?" The pastor was still patient, if a bit guarded now.

"Maybe it would be better if I didn't go into a long explanation about what we believe Jesus meant. Maybe it would be more helpful if you could explain first why it should be taken literally."

"It should be taken literally, son, because that's what it says... literally." The pastor's voice betrayed his waning patience.

"Simple as that?" Michael asked.

"Simple as that."

"May I see your Bible?" Michael asked, with his hand held open to receive.

The pastor, trying not to look reluctant, handed him the Bible. Now he was the one who had no alternative but to be gracious. It was Michael's turn to flip through the Bible. For those watching, it was only getting more interesting. They, like the pastor, wondered what Michael might have up his sleeve.

"I'm looking at John, chapter six," Michael began. He looked up from the Bible. "Now this is when Jesus multiplies the loaves and fishes and feeds the five thousand, which was right before the feast of the Passover. He fed them and then left. The next day they went looking for Him and found Him. This is what he said to them...

"Do not labor for the food which perishes, but for the food which endures to everlasting life, which the Son of Man will give you, because God the Father has set His seal on Him."

"Then the disciples go on to say to Jesus...

"Our fathers ate the manna in the desert; as it is written, 'He gave them bread from heaven to eat.'"

Then Jesus said to them...

"Most assuredly, I say to you, Moses did not give you the bread from heav-

en, but My Father gives you the true bread from heaven. For the bread of God
is He who comes down from heaven and gives life to the world."
Then they said to Him,
"Lord, give us this bread always."
And Jesus said to them,
"I am the bread of life. He who comes to Me shall never hunger, and he who
believes in Me shall never thirst."

Without looking up, Michael added, "A little bit lower down we
see the reaction of those who heard him." His tone was casual, and he
proceeded in an unrushed manner.

The Jews then complained against Him, because He said...
"I am the bread which came down from heaven."
And they said,
"Is not this Jesus, the son of Joseph, whose father and mother we know? How
is it then that He says, 'I have come down from heaven?'"
Jesus therefore answered and said to them,
"Do not murmur among yourselves. No one can come to Me unless the Father
who sent Me draws him; and I will raise him up at the last day."

"Skipping down to verse forty-seven...

"Most assuredly, I say to you, he who believes in Me has everlasting life. I
am the bread of life. Your fathers ate the manna in the wilderness, and are
dead. This is the bread which comes down from heaven, that one may eat of
it and not die. I am the living bread which came down from heaven. If anyone eats of this bread, he will live forever..."

Then Michael looked up at the pastor briefly before lowering his
head and proceeding, slowly...

"…and the bread that I shall give is My flesh, which I shall give for the life of the world."

The Jews therefore quarreled among themselves, saying, "How can this Man give us His flesh to eat?"

Michael looked up briefly again…

Then Jesus said to them,

"Most assuredly, I say to you, unless you eat the flesh of the Son of Man and drink His blood, you have no life in you. Whoever eats My flesh and drinks My blood has eternal life and I will raise him up at the last day."

Now Michael looked up at the pastor. It was his turn to wait for a response. The others looked on with great anticipation. To a man, each was relieved that he was not the one who was being asked to explain this passage. The pastor, though, appeared unruffled.

"It's obvious that that passage from John is *not* meant to be taken literally," responded the pastor.

Michael looked down at the Bible…

"For My flesh is food indeed, and My blood is drink indeed. He who eats My flesh and drinks My blood abides in Me, and I in him."

"It's a matter of properly understanding Scripture, son," the pastor began. His unfazed manner was dissipating. "These words in John chapter six are isolated in the Bible. They don't build on anything else that went before it. It's dangerous to pull these out of the middle of nowhere and assert that they have to be understood this way or another."

"I didn't assert anything, Pastor Brown," Michael said politely. Frankly, he didn't see how the "call no man your father" passage in

Matthew's Gospel passed the pastor's test of having to "build on something," but thought better than to get bogged down with an argument over that.

"Do you believe it should be taken literally?" the pastor asked, in a way that implied that even suggesting such a thing was absurd beyond comprehension.

"It's not so much that I believe it, but that Jesus said it that's important."

"And what he said should be taken literally?" the pastor persisted with irritation in his voice.

"That's the way it reads to me," Michael answered in an almost apologetic voice. Then he looked down at the Bible... "For My flesh is food indeed, and My blood is drink indeed."

"I know what the Scriptures say, thank you!" the pastor yelled back loudly. Regaining his composure, he tried to explain himself.

"John six cannot be taken literally. Christ did not call us to be cannibals."

Michael looked down at the Bible and waited a moment before saying anything. He saw that the pastor, in his frustration, was having a hard time controlling his temper. He didn't want to provoke the man to anger.

"No, of course he didn't," Michael agreed. "Let me read this one verse, verse sixty-three, and I think that will explain things...

> "It is the Spirit who gives life; the flesh profits nothing. The words that I speak to you are spirit, and they are life."

"So Jesus made it clear that he wasn't desiring cannibalism. His flesh was not to be a source of physical sustenance like the manna in the desert. It was, and is, his Spirit in the flesh that gives spiritual sustenance and eternal life."

267

There was no immediate reply from the pastor nor from anyone else seated at the table. The pause in discussion finally became uncomfortable.

"Aside from what we believe about the Eucharist, I just was trying to show something in the Bible that I figured you didn't take literally," Michael added.

There was another pause.

"The Scriptures say that many will be deceived," Pastor Brown announced. "Many will be deceived."

*What!?* thought Michael. *What's that supposed to mean?*

The pastor started to get up from the table and motioned as to reach for the Bible that was still in front of Michael. Michael quickly handed it to him. The others who had listened began to get up from the table.

"You boys enjoy the rest of the auction today," the pastor threw out as he moved away from the table and off into the throng of people, followed by his entourage.

"What was that all about?" Michael asked Elijah almost apologetically. He feared his cousin's disapproval for his being the source of ill feeling and division.

"I don't know," Eli responded slowly. "Many will be deceived? Well, that's true enough, I guess."

Eli had a pensive look as he spoke. He was pondering the entire exchange between his cousin and Pastor Brown. "At least I think it says that in the Bible. The question is, though,..." *He paused for a long moment...* "*Who* is being deceived? And about what?" He looked up at Michael with a smile. Michael smiled back. He felt such a sense of relief that his cousin wasn't going to condemn him for being a troublemaker. The last thing he wanted to do was make trouble.

"No, that's no way to end a Bible study," Eli continued. "I mean, that's like the kid who quits and takes his ball home so no one else can play with it."

"I wasn't trying to offend him," Michael offered.

"'Course you weren't. I didn't hear you say anything offensive. C'mon, let's go see the equipment auction."

Michael was thankful for Elijah's attitude. He would have brooded about the whole incident for a long time. As it was, it took him a while before he could relax and start to put it behind him.

They enjoyed the auction for a few more hours and then decided to walk the couple of miles back home along the country roads. The shadows were lengthening and the day just starting to cool off. The creek, which ambled alongside the road, beckoned them. Not far from home, Eli pointed out a good swimming hole and they answered the creek's call. They splashed and jumped while the creek carried their sweat, dust, and cares downstream.

"Y'know when you were reading that part from John's Gospel today, I thought you were going someplace different with it," Eli said as he perched himself on a submerged rock and enjoyed the water flowing around and past his body.

"Where?" Michael asked curiously. He had become so at ease with his cousin that he didn't even imagine such a discussion with *him* ending in hostility.

"Well, you were reading early on and the Jews said to Jesus that their fathers ate manna in the desert. When they talked about their ancestors, they said, *our fathers.* Jesus didn't use that opportunity to rebuke them."

"Huh, I didn't even realize that," laughed Michael. He was semi-floating in the middle of the pool of water. "Why didn't you say anything?"

"I ain't tryin' to be no troublemaker either, cuz'," Eli said laughing.

Michael laughed, too, from deep in the belly, and the tension from the experience at lunch continued to ooze out of him.

"But seriously," Eli continued after a couple of minutes of laughter, "later on in the chapter, and you just read right over it, Jesus called their ancestors, *'your fathers.'*"

Michael was truly amused and amazed at the revelation. "Maybe he hadn't made up that 'call no man your father' rule yet, and that's why he said it," he joked.

Eli laughed, then added, "Maybe he made the rule and just forgot."

"Maybe the Bible has a misprint," Michael shot back.

"They'd likely condemn the two of us and string us up if they heard us jokin' like this," Eli speculated after he finished chuckling.

Even hours ago, Eli would not have imagined joking about things in the Bible. He didn't feel guilty. He realized, though he hadn't worked it out in his mind yet, that they weren't laughing at the Bible, but at the posturing, at the behavior of so many who claimed to stand on Scripture. He was laughing good-naturedly at his fellow man, at the human condition.

They were both quiet for a while as they reflected on the day, the events of the summer, and that Michael and his family would be leaving for Philadelphia soon.

"So what do you'all believe about the Lord's Supper anyway?" Elijah asked, breaking the silence.

"Just what it says, really."

"But I mean about it really being the flesh of Jesus." Elijah had heard the Catholic belief discussed by a preacher before. The preacher had condemned and even mocked it — the Catholic belief — in his sermon. *It's easy to mock,* Elijah remembered thinking. *It's so ridiculously outlandish.* "And what about that whole thing Pastor Brown said about it 'standing alone,' that it wasn't supported anywhere else in Scripture?"

"I have no idea what he was talking about," laughed Michael, "do you?"

"No."

"I do know that when Adam and Eve ate from the tree of the knowledge of good and evil, they were kicked out of the garden," Michael began after he finished laughing.

"Yeah," Eli nodded, showing that he was willing to follow the explanation.  He was surprised, though, that it started way back in Genesis.

"That meant that they could no longer reach the Tree of Life — which was also in the garden — and eat from it."

Eli nodded again.

"It meant that they couldn't eat from it and live forever.  It meant that they, and all of their offspring, were going to die.

"Now when Moses was bringing the Israelites out of Egypt, he was given the instructions about how the Passover was to be carried out.  You remember — the angel of death killed all the first-borns in Egypt that night, but passed over the Israelites who did what Moses said.  They killed the unblemished lamb or kid goat which was a substitute for the first-born, sprinkled the blood on the door, ate the unleavened bread and the rest of their meal standing up and all that."

Eli nodded his understanding.  He knew salvation history well.

"Then the Israelites left Egypt, only to wander around in the desert for forty years before being led by Joshua across the Jordan into the Promised Land, the land which was promised in the covenant that God made with Abraham.  But back in the desert, like we just read in John chapter six, they were sent manna from heaven to keep them alive.  In John's Gospel, Jesus is called the Lamb of God.  He was the first-born Son of God."

"Not in the sense that there was more than one Messiah?" Eli commented just to make sure Michael wasn't implying that God sent more sons like Jesus.

"No," Michael assured, "He is called the first-born to emphasize the importance of that position in the family throughout the story of salvation."

"That's right," agreed Eli.

"Jesus was the fulfillment of the unblemished Passover lamb. He had to be sacrificed. Of course, he knew it and went along willingly."

Then Michael stopped and thought about what to say next.

"And you know what had to happen to the Passover lamb?"

"What?" Eli asked, unsure of what his cousin was looking for.

"It had to be eaten." He paused and let that sink in. Then he explained...

"If the Israelites killed the lamb, sprinkled the door posts with blood, and did all the things that Moses instructed, but didn't *eat* the lamb... then it was curtains for the first-born son of the household that night."

Eli didn't respond. He was soaking up everything Michael was saying.

"You had to eat the lamb," Michael repeated. "The Lamb — Jesus Christ — was nailed to a tree. He became the new Tree of Life, the one we must eat from in order to live forever."

There was a pause as Eli considered all this.

"Yeah, I see what you're saying and I agree, but what about this real presence of Christ in the Eucharist? Aren't we just asked to 'do this in remembrance' with the Lord's Supper? It's a symbolic memorial, isn't it?"

"We weren't *asked* to do it."

"You're right, *told* to do it as a memorial," Eli corrected himself.

"Just because it's a memorial doesn't mean it's symbolic, does it?"

"No, it doesn't," Eli had to admit after thinking for a moment.

No one said anything for awhile. Michael was thankful to be able to discuss the Bible, and explain Catholic beliefs, without hostility and confrontation.  Elijah took no offense that it challenged what he had always thought.

"In Corinthians somewhere, I forget which chapter, Paul writes a long letter about how the Lord's Supper is supposed to be conducted.  He rebuked them for not celebrating the breaking of the bread properly.  Somewhere in there he warns them about not taking it seriously, I mean about the Lord being really present.  You can look it up at home."

"Don't worry," Eli assured him, "I will."

He was anxious to find another, perfectly plausible, explanation for what Christ and later the Apostle Paul meant.

Later that night at home, Elijah took the Bible off his shelf and crawled into bed with it.  He read the different parts that were discussed that day.  He read about the Passover from Exodus Chapter 12...

"Your lamb shall be without blemish... they shall eat the flesh on that night; roasted in fire, with unleavened bread and with bitter herbs they shall eat it... and what remains of it until morning you shall burn with fire.  It is the Lord's Passover."

He looked in Leviticus and read the instructions for the various Jewish rituals.  He read...

"When you come into the land which I give to you, and reap its harvest, then you shall bring a sheaf of the firstfruits of your harvest to the priest. He shall wave the sheaf before the Lord, to be accepted on your behalf; on the day after the Sabbath the priest shall wave it. And you shall offer on that day, when you wave the sheaf, a male lamb of the first year, without blemish, as a burnt offer-

273

ing to the Lord. Its grain offering shall be two-tenths of an ephah of fine flour mixed with oil, an offering made by fire to the Lord, for a sweet aroma; and its drink offering shall be of wine, one-fourth of a hin."

## From the Gospel of John Chapter 6...

"Whoever eats My flesh and drinks My blood has eternal life, and I will raise him up at the last day. For My flesh is food indeed, and My blood is drink indeed. He who eats My flesh and drinks My blood abides in Me and I in him."

## From Mark...

Jesus took bread, blessed and broke it, and gave it to them and said, "Take, eat; this is My body." Then He took the cup, and when He had given thanks He gave it to them, and they all drank from it. And He said to them, "This is My blood of the new covenant, which is shed for many."

He thought about the things his cousin had said that day, especially that the Passover lamb *had* to be eaten. His head spinning, he continued paging through the Bible. He had become more anxious after reading some of these passages. It was one thing to listen to his cousin quoting the Bible in a public place. It was another to sit and read Scripture in solitude. He began searching Paul's letters to the Corinthians to find the part that Michael couldn't remember. He began skimming the letters. At Chapter 11of First Corinthians he slowed down...

For I received from the Lord that which I also delivered to you: that the Lord Jesus on the same night in which He was betrayed took bread; and when He had given thanks, He broke it and said, "Take, eat; this is My body... Therefore whoever eats this bread or drinks this cup of the Lord in an unworthy manner will be guilty of the body and blood of the Lord... For he who eats and drinks in an unworthy manner eats and drinks judgment to himself, not discerning the Lord's body.

As Elijah finished the last sentence, and the last part of the last sentence, a shock coursed through his entire body and settled in the pit of his stomach where it sat like a large stone.

# 13

So Hank Brown wants to come by and see me, thought Les. He knew it had to do with Michael. He had heard about the exchange at the auction. Even if Eli had not been there, he'd have heard about it. The town was small enough and Hank Brown had been offended enough for others to take notice. What Pastor Brown would have to say about his nephew, or expect him to say or do about him, Les wasn't sure.

Les sat that night after supper and thought back to the many times that he had locked horns with Hank Brown, who happened to be his pastor years ago. Les had been a deacon in Hank's church. As a deacon he had been energetic and enthusiastic and was well liked by many in the congregation.

*Maybe I had become too popular among the faithful for Pastor Brown's taste,* Les speculated now. *Maybe that's why he had given me such a hard time.* Les almost laughed about it now. *It got to where he contested every little thing I did. He tinkered with my sermons, criticized the counsel I gave to those who sought my guidance, and took offense at my suggestions about how we should spend some of the collection money.*

Pastor Brown had often encouraged Les to develop a more "professional" image and had been willing to provide the money from the tithes to enable him to do so. Les just couldn't reconcile buying a newer model car using other people's money with how he understood the Gospel message. All of the petty differences, though, Les had negotiated. He had been willing to be patient and long suffering. He had successfully checked his pride at the door for a few years. But when they started having irreconcilable doctrinal differences, things began to fall apart. He had felt as though he couldn't even discuss his questions about doctrine with Hank. Hank perceived such questions as dangerous, not only theologically, but to his position as pastor. Les had seen no alternative but to resign his position in the church as he had done before in another church for the same reason, and would do again before founding his own church.

*What will Hank Brown have to say about my nephew? Is he coming here to recommend something? Is he going to chastise me for what Michael O'Shea believes?*

Les was anxious to hear what was on the pastor's mind. His own plan, to reach Michael by way of Bible study, had failed. He had never heard some of the things Michael had explained about Catholic beliefs and was somewhat at a loss to counter them. He was confident that all of what Michael explained could be refuted, but between planting and harvesting, upkeep of the farm, and his own church duties, there simply wasn't time.

He saw that Michael had had a very enjoyable summer and it was his hope to have them all down again next summer. Les sat and continued to rationalize his inability to do what was necessary to evangelize his sister's family. He was committed to his sister and had truly come to enjoy the children. Perhaps the conversion of the O'Sheas would be a multi-year project. Maybe it would become easier for them as time passed. Of course, Michael's sense of loyalty to his father, which was admirable in itself, made the entire possibility of conversion this summer unrealistic.

The knock at the door interrupted Les's thoughts.

Pam left for the kitchen. She knew Hank Brown well enough to know that he preferred not to have women involved in such discussions. That alone, though, would not have caused her to leave. She wanted to leave. She had had a hard time liking Hank Brown since the day she met him. Worst of all, he had not been good to her husband.

One of Hank Brown's strong points, however, was that he did get right to the point.

"Your nephew has sown seeds of division amongst the brethren," he informed.

Les was unsure how to react. He remembered Pastor Brown warning him about "sowing seeds of division" when they were bumping heads so many years ago.

"How so, Hank?"

"Deception, Lester, deception. A young man like that fosters confusion and doubt amongst the brethren."

Les was tempted to ask why he couldn't just set straight all those who were confused.

"I'm sure he wasn't trying to," Les answered casually. Then for a little fun, "In fact, I understood it was you who started the discussion the other day at the auction."

Hank Brown struggled to maintain his composure.

"I am concerned, as the pastor of my church, for the spiritual well-being of my flock."

Les wondered how concerned he was about his own image and reputation in the wake of his meeting with Michael.

"As a pastor myself, I can certainly appreciate that, Hank."

"I have a suggestion for how we might illustrate the numerous errors of Romanism... for the benefit of those who don't know better."

"Of course," Les agreed. Naturally the greatest concern was for those most likely to succumb to deception. "What did you have in mind?"

"I'd like to ask your nephew if he'd be kind enough to come to our church to answer some of our questions about the Catholic Church."

*Hank wants some serious payback for being caught flat-footed at the auction in front of other people,* thought Les. What Hank was talking about, Les understood, was trotting Michael out in front of a bunch of people at his church and grilling him mercilessly. He thought for a moment before responding. *Would this benefit Michael? Would Hank be able to challenge Michael on some of Romanism's basic errors? It wouldn't require my involvement. Michael would probably rather make such decisions for himself.*

"Well, I appreciate your coming to me, Hank, but I'd have to leave that up to Michael."

A big smile split Hank Brown's face.

"Good. I think it would be good for everyone, Les."

"Anytime the Bible is opened it can't help but be a good situation," agreed Les. "The O'Sheas are leaving in about ten days, though," he added.

"I was thinking next Tuesday night over at my church."

"Talk to Michael. I'll send him over your way tomorrow with Eli." Les was already becoming more excited about the prospect. If Michael left with some doubts, or even just serious questions about his faith, that would be a start.

◆ ◆ ◆

The next day, Les sent Eli and Michael over to Hank Brown's in the truck under the pretense of helping Hank move some furniture. Pastor Brown extended the invitation to Michael.

"I really don't think I'd be much help trying to answer many questions," Michael insisted. There was so much he realized that he didn't know. "If you'd like, I'll get the name of a priest or even a nun who'd be much better than I am at explaining things."

"No need to go to all that trouble," the pastor assured him. "I'm sure they lead such busy lives. There's just some real basic things some folks are curious about. You'll do fine."

"Anything I can do to prepare? Any areas in particular that people want to know about?" Michael asked, wanting to be helpful.

"No. Just bring yourself," the pastor assured with a smile.

"Okay," agreed Michael tentatively.

Eli's antennae had definitely picked up something strange. He was unaware of the meeting between his father and Pastor Brown, but sensed that something more was going on.

"You don't have to try and answer all kinds of questions," Eli advised him in the truck on the way back home. "You told him that you didn't know everything."

"I'll answer what I can."

"You don't have to."

"I said I'd give it a try," Michael said, trying to convey that he felt a bit obligated at this point.

When they got home, Michael told his Uncle Les about the invitation to answer some questions at Pastor Brown's church.

"Do you mind if I come?" asked Les, pretending not to be in the know.

"Doesn't matter to me," Michael said. "I think it's just going to be a couple of people from his congregation."

"Well, if it's okay by you, I don't think Pastor Brown would mind." Les knew it was going to be more than a couple of people. He imagined Hank Brown luring Michael by implying it would just be some kind of casual get-together. *Michael's old enough to handle such decisions,* Les rationalized quickly to himself before he started having second thoughts.

◆ ◆ ◆

On the evening of the meeting, Eli excused himself after supper. "Michael and I are goin' to walk over to Pastor Brown's church."

"Good to see you spending extra time with your cousin," remarked Pam. It was a two-mile walk over to the church, and Pam suspected that her son was trying to maximize the time he spent with Michael, who would be leaving in a few days. Then she reminded herself that her own son would be leaving for Marine Corps boot camp in just five weeks, and melancholy enveloped her.

Michael said good-bye to his mother when he saw Eli approaching the front door.

"Now, where is it you're going?" she asked.

"Over to some local church," Michael began. "One of the local preachers wants me to try and answer some questions about what we believe.

"I don't know why," he added in response to her quizzical look. "I'm going to tell them that they can get a Catechism to answer their questions."

"Just do your best and remember you're never alone," she smiled at him. It was something she used to say to him when she tucked him in as a little boy. She suspected that he'd be well challenged this night, but didn't want to shield him. She doubted that any local pastor would invite a young Catholic because he was sincerely curious. She remembered pastors knowing plenty about Catholicism, or at least thinking they did.

Michael let Eli in.

"Hi, Aunt Tammy," said Eli, then turning to Michael, "Ready to go?"

"I guess so."

"Got your flak jacket on?" he asked as he gave Michael a mild shot with the back of his hand right in the ribs. He was smiling, but, like Tammy, he sensed that curiosity was not the driving force behind this request for an interview.

"Hey, I'm just gonna tell 'em what I know."

"That's all you can do," Eli reassured as they headed out the door.

They walked about a half-hour, conversing sporadically before reaching the church at twenty minutes before seven. Some cars were in the lot.

*There must be something else going on now,* thought Michael. They were greeted at the door by a thirty-something, well-groomed man.

"Mr. O'Shea? Hi, I'm Drew Davis, an associate minister here at True Gospel Church."

"Hi," responded Michael awkwardly. "Good to meet you. This is Elijah McGuffey, my cousin."

"I believe we've met before, Eli," he said, putting out his hand.

"Mr. O'Shea, Pastor Brown wanted me to show you to his office where you can wait."

"All right," he said, after looking at Eli for direction. It was obvious that Eli was as much in the dark as he was.

Michael walked with the minister up the carpeted center aisle. Eli stayed behind, then found a place in one of the pews by himself.

The church was bigger than his uncle's and air-conditioned, but still so unlike a Catholic church. It was the size of what Catholics would call a big chapel, Michael decided. Yes, it was like a chapel, minus the statues, he reminded himself, and the altar, and holy water, the stained glass, kneelers, the Stations of the Cross, and especially the tabernacle with the small red candle ever present to indicate whether or not it was occupied.

There was a disproportionately large pulpit up front on the right. It was elevated and made of dark wood. There were steps, spiral-like, rising from the floor. Like an enormous oak on the bank of a stream, the pulpit seemed to hang out over the pews. It looked to Michael as if someone had taken it out of a great cathedral and transplanted it.

Upon reaching the front Michael had to resist the urge to genuflect. Strangely, his catching himself before going down on one knee stirred a profound realization. *Jesus isn't here,* he remembered. *Or anyway, not physically present.* He felt a sadness mixed with something else, a kind of shame... Sadness for what so many were missing — the real presence of the Lord — and shame for taking His presence in the tabernacle for granted.

Drew Davis led Michael to a door that was tucked behind the pulpit structure. It led to a corridor. They passed a room with small desks. Michael noticed crayons and a children's book about Noah on one of the desks. They walked by some offices and finally to the corner office. The nameplate above the door read, *Hank Brown—Pastor.*

"Please make yourself comfortable, Mr. O'Shea," the young minister invited. "We're going to wait until a few minutes after seven, to let the latecomers be seated, before beginning the program. I'll be back when we're ready. Do you have any questions?"

*Program!?* Michael thought. *You're going to let latecomers get seated? What is this, some kind of a show? Am I at the right church? Are you getting me mixed up with a performer that you had invited for another night?*

"No, thank you," answered Michael. With that, the minister closed the door and left Michael by himself in Pastor Brown's office. He sat in one of the two soft chairs in front of the pastor's desk. The clock on the wall said ten minutes before seven. Out the window he could see cars pass by. There was a bookcase against the wall to his right. Michael focused his eyes so as to be able to read the titles vertically.

He looked back to the desk. It was then that he first noticed a folded paper. There was about a three-inch gap between the two ends of the paper, as if it had been straining to straighten itself and had become frozen in that position. From where he was seated he could read the end of the title, which was spelled in bold letters... **olicism:**. He straightened up in his seat and read the part of the second line that he could see... **or Fantasy?** Michael struggled momentarily with the ethical question of reading something on someone else's desk even if it was in plain view.

He stood up, ostensibly to look out the window, and his curiosity overwhelmed him. *This might have something to do with me,* he rationalized, and zeroed in on the cover of the flyer...

**The Bible vs. Catholicism**
You Are Invited to a Discussion
Day: Tuesday, August 6
Time:  7:00 P.M.

His heart began to race. *What are they doing? They didn't say that this was going to be a program!* He breathed deeply to try and settle his pounding heart. Suddenly he was distracted by the traffic out the window. The cars approaching the church were sluggish. He stepped closer to the window and craned his neck to see the parking lot. He couldn't see the lot itself but saw car after car pulling in, which was causing the stop-and-go traffic. The anxiety within him raged and he tried to will himself to calm down before it flowed over into full-fledged panic. He was unable to still his heart. He had prepared nothing to say or explain. He hadn't even brought a Bible. *Is this really happening?* he asked himself. He had a strange feeling momentarily that he might just wake up from this terror. Things this bad usually were the stuff of nightmares.

Then he considered crawling out the window. He could crawl out, run home in twenty minutes, lay low for the next couple of days, and by the end of the week be on the train for Philadelphia where no one would be the wiser. *They didn't tell me it was going to be like this!* he thought, rationalizing his temptation to flee.

The clock on the wall said two minutes to seven. He felt the dread that those on death row must feel as they watch the second hand

285

sweep steadily across the face of the clock, plowing away the time that remains between now and their destiny. As he watched the clock the feeling of dread did not dissipate even as the red second hand dropped to its lowest point and began ascending again toward the seven o'clock hour. He continued watching as it swept past the twelve at the top of the dial. The door to the office was still closed, but instead of relieving his anxiety it heightened the terror. He was on borrowed time now, he realized.

At two minutes after seven there was a knock at the door. A smiling Drew Davis appeared.

"Pastor Brown's decided to lead the folks in some hymns before we get started. You can just relax in here a little longer. I'll be back in ten minutes or so." Then as quickly as he appeared he was gone.

*How could they imagine that I could relax in here?* Trying to be charitable, he decided that they just didn't understand. They didn't realize how nerve racking it was for him.

*"Good evening brothers and sisters..."*

The voice startled Michael.

*"... Thank you for joining us this evening."*

It was coming out of the wall, from a speaker located behind the pastor's desk. It was Pastor Brown's voice.

*"We are hopeful that we can all learn something from our guest."*

Michael, sitting alone in the office, wasn't flattered by the statement. There was something about how he said it that was disturbing.

*"I believe our guest will give us a testimony of his personal relationship with Jesus before he explains some things to us..."*

*Personal relationship with Jesus?* He had heard that phrase a few times since arriving in Kentucky but never fully grasped what it meant.

*"Let's begin with a few hymns to put us in the right frame of mind to discuss the Bible...*

*I have decided to follow Jesus*

*I have decided to follow Jesus*
*I have decided to follow Jesus*
*No turning back*
*No turning back...*

*Though none go with me, still I will follow*
*Though none go with me, still I will follow*
*Though none go with me, still I will follow*
*No turning back*
*No turning back...*

Now Michael could hear the thunderous singing through the walls and over the speaker. He thought about climbing out the window again. *No one would ever know in Philadelphia,* he said to himself... *except me.* He abandoned that idea.

Les McGuffey, who was early enough to get a seat next to his son, was tempted to walk back to find Michael. *This is too much,* he told himself. *It's not right. Hank didn't have to hype this thing to prove anything. This is about payback.*

"Do you think Michael can handle himself?" he whispered to Eli. It was a strange question, he realized. On the one hand he didn't want Michael to be able to respond *too* well to Hank's attack, but he didn't revel in the thought of his nephew being humiliated either.

"I don't know," replied Eli. He, too, was overwhelmed with how far Pastor Brown had gone. He had found the flyer, the same one that Michael had seen on the desk in the office, in the pew just after he was seated. He looked down at the title on the inside again:

**Catholicism:**
**The True Faith or Fantasy?**

Eli looked around the church. There were people standing in the back and up the sides. It was obvious that they did a good job of distributing this around town, he concluded.

"I guess he's going to have to give it his best try, though," Eli finished.

Les decided to hold off, but vowed that he would end this whole thing himself if it got out of hand.

The first hymn ended and Pastor Brown started right in again...

> *Amazing Grace, how sweet the sound*
> *that saved a wretch like me!*
> *I once was lost*
> *but now am found*
> *was blind, but now I see...*

Michael sat and listened to what seemed like five thousand voices. He was beginning to resign himself to the humiliation, so his attention began to turn toward minimizing it. *I'll say what I can, then get out of here.* He prayed that it wouldn't take long. *I'll let them have their victory by forfeit.* His resignation to defeat allowed him to settle down and almost enjoy the hymn they were singing now...

> *... And through this life of toil and snares*
> *If I falter, Lord, who cares?*
> *Who, with me, my burden shares?*
> *None but thee, dear Lord, none but thee...*

*I know that one,* Michael thought, *but from where?... I've heard it before in my own house on Dawson Street.*

> *Just a closer walk with thee*

*Grant it Jesus, hear my plea*
*Daily walking close to thee*
*Let it be dear Lord, let it be...*

*That song's from "Cool Hand Luke" with Paul Newman and George Kennedy! Dad loved that movie.*

He remembered his father's fondness for that most famous line in that movie, and in his mind's eye saw him in their row home back on Dawson Street saying it... "What we have here is a failure to communicate." *I wish you could help me here, Dad.*

*And when my weary life is o'er*
*Time for me will be no more*
*Guide me safely, gently on*
*To thy kingdom shore, to my home.*

Michael sat listening to the last chorus and longed for his father.

There was a knock at the door that swung Michael around in his seat. Drew Davis's head popped in.

"Ready, sport?"

*"Sport?" What happened to Mr. O'Shea?* The minister, he could tell, was almost giddy with anticipation... a willing executioner.

"Yeah, I'm ready." *The sooner we start, the sooner I'll get out of here,* he told himself. The hymn singing had stopped and an eerie silence reigned. *Maybe everybody went home,* he joked to himself weakly.

Drew Davis stepped aside and let Michael lead the way.

*They don't want me making a run for it now,* Michael mused as he stepped past the minister to walk back into the church.

As he opened the door, he almost lost his breath at the sight of the crowd. It was as if someone had kicked him in the stomach. The anxiety surged and his knees weakened as he was escorted to a chair sitting in the middle of the carpeted platform, the altar area if it would have been a Catholic church. There he sat trying to look calm and collected, his eyes turned down. He was too nervous to look up at the crowded pews in front of him and was still unsure what to expect.

*How are they going to do this? Do they want me just to start talking? Just sitting here in this calm is torture.*

"Thanks for being with us tonight, Mr. O'Shea."

Michael's head snapped upward toward the source of the microphoned voice. A black-robed Pastor Brown was in the pulpit above him. One of the spotlights on the wall behind the pastor's shoulder was shining right into Michael's eyes.

*I've answered his questions before,* an astonished Michael said to himself. The thought, though, was preposterous. Before last week he had never seen Pastor Brown. Yet the feeling, that he had been through this before, helped him to relax.

"Before we begin discussing your faith — *Catholicism* — I'd like to invite you to give the people your personal testimony."

Michael considered his options. He didn't have any "story" to tell.

Tammy sat on what had become her favorite large stone by the stream. It was beginning to cool off and she noted how the days were already getting shorter. The two boys played in the creek and Kateri was happy on a blanket watching her brothers. She was thankful for the tranquility of the evening, as well as for the peace the visit in Kentucky had provided her and the family. She pulled the blue rosary from her jumper pocket. She fondled the smooth wooden beads, then holding the crucifix, she began...

*"I believe in God, the Father Almighty, Creator of Heaven and Earth, and in Jesus Christ, His only Son, our Lord; who was*

*conceived by the Holy Spirit, born of the Virgin Mary, suffered under Pontius Pilate, was crucified, died, and was buried. He descended into Hell. The third day He rose again from the dead; he ascended into Heaven, and is seated at the right hand of God, the Father Almighty; from thence he shall come to judge the living and the dead. I believe in the Holy Spirit, the Holy Catholic Church, the communion of Saints, the forgiveness of sins, the resurrection of the body, and life everlasting. Amen."*

"That's all right, we can get right on with whatever you wanted to do tonight," Michael replied as casually as he could.

"You don't want to share your testimony?" Pastor Brown was incredulous.

"Not particularly."

"Do you *have* a testimony, son?"

"I'm not sure. What I mean is that I'm not exactly sure what you mean by that."

"Well, have you been born again!? Born again as it says in John three three?... Where's your Bible, son?" He had just noticed that Michael didn't even have a Bible.

"Mr. Davis, would you please get a Bible for our guest."

*This is too easy,* Pastor Brown grumbled to himself. *He's not even prepared to defend himself.*

Presently Michael was handed a Bible. *New King James Version* was printed on the spine in gold letters.

Pastor Brown began to read while Michael found John 3:3...

Jesus answered and said to him,

"Most assuredly, I say to you, unless one is born again, he cannot see the kingdom of God."

"Have you been born again?  Have you accepted Jesus as your personal Lord and Savior?"

"Yes, I've been baptized, which is what that passage is dealing with," answered Michael.  Michael remembered studying this chapter in a commentary by a recent convert.

"Explain yourself," the pastor invited.

"The Greek term is 'anothen'... *"you must be born anothen."*  It can mean 'again' or it can mean 'from above.'  In this context it seems clear that Jesus meant it to mean 'from above.'"

"And how does it seem clear?" asked the pastor.  He was not convinced that Michael knew what he was talking about.

"Right down in verse five Jesus says...

"Most assuredly, I say to you, unless one is born of water and the Spirit, he cannot enter the kingdom of God."

"Then in verse thirty-one we have...

"He who comes from above is above all; he who is of the earth is earthly and speaks of the earth. He who comes from heaven is above all."

"The term used for 'from above' again is *anothen.*  Jesus meant born 'from above' the first time, but Nicodemus understood him as saying 'born again.'  Then Jesus explained what he meant.  The other thing is that this chapter has in it the part where John the Baptist and Jesus' disciples are baptizing."

"Baptizing with water?"

"Yes."

"And the Spirit?"

"Both.  Baptism includes both.  Peter said, in the book of Acts somewhere,

"Reform and be baptized...that your sins may be forgiven; then you will receive the gift of the Holy Spirit."

"How can an infant repent?" Pastor Brown asked.

"An infant can't repent," Michael admitted. "Peter was talking to adults." He saw where the pastor was going.

*Got 'im!* thought Pastor Brown.

"Then why do you, in your church, baptize infants? You've confessed with your own mouth that infants can't repent."

Michael paused. He let the anticipation build.

"Infants can't repent," Michael repeated, "Peter happened to be talking with adults when he said 'Repent and be baptized,' but the Bible doesn't say anywhere that only adults can be baptized. There were no Christian infants yet."

"How can an infant accept Jesus as his personal Lord and Savior?"

Michael's head was in the Bible.

"I'm sorry. I don't see where it says that in the Bible — the thing about accepting Jesus as your personal Lord and Savior," he said, lifting his head.

The Pastor did not respond, so Michael continued.

"Verse five says 'Unless one is born of water and the Spirit, he cannot enter the kingdom of God.' You'd have to agree that an infant, one who can't repent or profess any belief, can be the recipient of the Spirit.

"In the early Church, the Book of Acts, it talks about entire households or a whole families being baptized. It's likely that those households included young children or even infants."

"Nowhere does it say that infants are to be baptized," the pastor pointed out, seemingly ignoring what Michael had just said.

"No, it doesn't," Michael agreed. "Jesus did say, though, I think in Matthew's Gospel...

> "Let the children come to me. Do not hinder them. The kingdom of God belongs to such as these."

"Little children who are able to walk by themselves?" he asked.
"Yes."
"Not infants?"
"No, it doesn't say infants," Michael agreed again. "The Bible doesn't have anything explicit to say about infant baptism."

Tammy was ready to offer her petitions. She asked the Blessed Mother to petition her Son to provide spiritual protection and guidance for Michael. She sought the intercession of others as well: *St. Dominic, founder of the Order of Preachers, who went forth to answer the heresy of those times, St. Cecilia, St. Thomas Aquinas, St. Albert the Great, St. Catherine of Siena, Pope St. Pius V, St. Martin de Porres, St. Rose of Lima and all the spiritual sons and daughters of Dominic, pray for us.*

"But in your Church infants are baptized?"
"It's not *our* Church, but yes, infants are baptized into the Catholic Church," Michael answered.
"That is part of your tradition?"
"It has been handed down to us, yes," Michael explained hesitantly.
"And you have many traditions and rituals which have been handed down to you," the pastor stated.
"Yes." Again Michael saw where he was headed.
"Matthew fifteen, verse three reads, and this is Jesus saying this...

He answered and said to them, "Why do you also transgress the commandment of God because of your *tradition?*"

The pastor emphasized the last word.

"And verse six reads... 'Thus you have made the commandment of God of no effect by your *tradition.*' That was *Jesus* talking, Mr. O'Shea." Then he paused and asked solemnly, "Why do you place your traditions on the same par as the Word of God?"

"Can you give me an example, Pastor?" Michael asked as he formulated his response.

"Your churches are full of graven images — *idols,* Mr. O'Shea! Is that not part of your tradition? Does not that practice negate the very Word of God?"

"Let's discuss the idea of tradition first," began Michael. Mixing issues would only make things more complicated, Michael realized as he paged through the Bible.

"Jesus wasn't condemning all tradition, just corrupt human tradition. In second Thessalonians two fifteen Paul wrote...

> Therefore, brethren, stand fast and hold the traditions which you were taught, whether by word or our epistle.

"And later, again to the Thessalonians, second Thessalonians three six...

> But we command you, brethren, in the name of our Lord Jesus Christ, that you withdraw from every brother who walks disorderly and not according to the tradition which he received from us.

"And about the statues, Mr. O'Shea, the ones all over the place in your Church?" the pastor asked, seemingly unimpressed with what the Apostle Paul had to say about tradition.

295

"We were given an image of God with the Incarnation," Michael explained. "Before Christ, men didn't know any image of God and were forbidden by God at Sinai to make one. But not making images of any kind was not an absolute commandment—"

"Excuse me, son!? Let me read, for your edification, from Exodus..." He flipped the pages of his Bible quickly back to Exodus. "From the twentieth chapter of that book, verse four...

> You shall not make for yourself a carved image — any likeness of anything that is in heaven above, or that is in the earth beneath, or that is in the water under the earth.

"But God also told Moses to make a serpent and mount it on a pole to cure those who had been bitten by snakes," Michael replied.

"Has he told you or anyone you know to fashion statues for your place of worship?"

"We hang on our walls the fulfillment of Moses' serpent."

Pastor Brown didn't respond. He wasn't sure what Michael's last statement meant.

"Christ on the cross — the crucifix — is the fulfillment of that bronze serpent of the Old Testament," Michael explained.

"Christ as the serpent?" The pastor was incredulous again.

"Christ was lifted up onto the cross as a criminal, an insurrectionist," Michael reminded him, "but like Moses' serpent He wasn't evil, but good and capable of healing."

He continued. "The instructions for the building of the Ark of the Covenant included winged creatures – angels — to look over and protect the mercy seat. The point is that men built images in Old Testament times that were not a violation of that commandment." Michael's voice was calm and his delivery dispassionate, which irritated the pastor even more.

"And your tradition allows for the building of statues?"

"You know we have statues," Michael answered.

"Statues of Mary, the mother of Jesus?"

"Yes."

"Dead men and women?"

"Saints? Yes."

"I am going to read from Paul's letter to the Colossians, second chapter, verse eight," Pastor Brown said slowly and deliberately...

Beware lest anyone cheat you through philosophy and empty deceit, according to the tradition of men, according to the basic principles of the world, and not according to Christ.

"We've already seen that the Bible does not condemn all tradition," insisted Michael, "only human traditions which are corrupt." Now it was his turn to be frustrated.

The pastor continued to look down on him with a mask of pity on his face.

"That town just south of here in Tennessee has a big statue of Andrew Jackson in its town square," stated Michael. "Is that wrong?"

"That's a question of rightly dividing Scripture," the pastor returned. "It's a secular statue for secular purposes."

"Do you approve of the statue? When people look at it and think about Andrew Jackson and his life, do they benefit?"

"Yes," the pastor affirmed.

"It makes people feel proud to be from Tennessee, I bet," Michael agreed. "I would have to believe that people who took the time to consider the virtues of men like Andrew Jackson would tend to be better citizens."

The pastor held his tongue but Michael could see he followed the argument at this point. Nonetheless Michael drove it home for those listening who did not follow it. "If we honor secular heroes and teach schoolchildren to imitate them, then shouldn't we do the same for the heroes and martyrs of the Faith?"

Tammy finished her Rosary as she prayed ...

*O God, whose only-begotten Son,*
*by His life, death and resurrection,*
*has purchased for us the rewards of eternal life;*
*grant, we beseech Thee,*
*that meditating upon these mysteries*
*of the most holy Rosary of the Blessed Virgin Mary,*
*we may learn to imitate what they contain*
*and obtain what they promise,*
*through the same Christ our Lord.  Amen.*

"I'll answer that by reading from first Timothy two, verse five... 'For there is one God and one Mediator between God and men, the Man Christ Jesus.'"

*That doesn't answer my question*, Michael said to himself, *and he's not going to try*.

"Mediation is another issue."

"You pray to these statues, don't you?" Pastor Brown asked.

"To the men and women the statues represent," Michael clarified. *He knows better*, thought Michael.

"Then it's not another issue, is it?  I mean, I don't pray to Andrew Jackson, but you pray to the statues in your Church even though it's contrary to Scripture."

Michael was going to point out again that the Church didn't tell people to pray to statues but decided against it.  He resisted the temptation to get caught up in the games the pastor was playing.

"Has anyone, maybe someone in your congregation, ever asked

you to pray for them, Pastor?"

"Of course."

"Did you assure them that you would?"

"Certainly."

"Why?"

The pastor was confused.

"Why didn't you tell them to go straight to Jesus themselves? Why didn't you quote second Timothy to them?" Then as Pastor Brown absorbed the shock... "Did you point out to them their error?"

"We're instructed to pray one for another," Pastor Brown insisted with passion.

"To intercede for one another, right? Well, that's all we're doing when we pray to the saints and to Mary."

"To dead people!"

"'I am the God of Abraham, the God of Isaac, the God of Jacob.' He is 'the God of the living not of the dead,'" quoted Michael. "Jesus said that in Matthew's Gospel."

"I know what Jesus said, thank you," thundered Pastor Brown. Then he was silent for a moment.

"The same Jesus you sacrifice every time you gather together in church?" he asked. "I'll read from Hebrews, chapter seven, verse twenty-seven...

> Who does not need daily, as those high priests, to offer up sacrifices, first for His own sins and then for the people's, for this He did once, when He offered up Himself.

*"'For this He did once,'"* he repeated while looking at Michael. Then slowly, "And you sacrifice my Lord daily."

His accusation made Michael shudder. He was trying to impress upon Michael his indignation, his hurt, his pain... the tragedy that some deceived group would insult the body of his personal Lord and Savior. Michael shuddered, though, not because he felt guilty of re-sacrificing Jesus or that he was doing something that was hurtful to such devout men. Rather the shudder was an involuntary reaction to his first glimpse right through the pastor. It was affected, Michael felt — the whole pained look of indignation was put on for effect. It was a lie. And he recognized, for the first time, this figure that posed as a man of God. It was the robed figure on the parapet, the one that haunted him in his dreams.

"No," Michael denied calmly, "I think there's a misunderstanding."

"You sacrifice my Lord daily all over the world!"

"We don't re-sacrifice Jesus, not in the way you're claiming it," Michael said, still formulating his thoughts.

"You call it the sacrifice of the Mass, don't you?"

"Yes we do, but what it is, is *re-presenting* the sacrifice of Christ. It's the same sacrifice, the everlasting sacrifice."

"It's blasphemy!" Pastor Brown thundered back. This time his emotions were sincere, his frustration at not being able to trap his prey evident. He stood wild-eyed and caught his breath. "A man is not saved by offerings, rituals, and works," he continued, "but by faith is he justified... Romans five one." The newest grenade had been tossed.

"That's not what the Bible says." Young Michael's response flabbergasted the pastor and rendered him speechless.

"That's exactly what the Bible says," he insisted, thinking now that he was beginning to close on the wily boy. "Let's turn to Romans five."

"I misspoke," Michael acceded quickly. "The Bible does say that, but by the same token one could say that a chair is made out of wood."

Pastor Brown paused for a moment but did not appear to understand the point.

Michael continued. "Ours deeds or our works are presumed. I

could say that this chair that I'm sitting on is made out of wood and you'd accept that. I wouldn't have to say that this chair is made out of wood, glue, and metal."

Michael paused for just a moment to let his illustration sink in. "We can assume the screws and the glue and we even assume the craftsman's labor."

"Now we hear the Jesuit in you," the pastor scoffed.

"And was James a Jesuit, the James who wrote the epistle in the Bible?"

No answer was given and Michael, not expecting one, read James 2:24... "'You see then that a man is justified by works, and not by faith only.'"

"So you busy yourself with works like a good Catholic?"

It was Michael's turn not to respond.

"And you're never wrong? Your Pope is infallible!"

"Are you asking me?" Michael wasn't sure if it was a sincere question or just the start of a new stage, one where he would content himself to endure and offer no response.

"Your Church, the executioner of millions in the Inquisition, is infallible? Need I ask?"

Michael sat unperturbed in his chair. *This is not a test of wills or of knowledge,* he reminded himself.

"You won't respond?" Pastor Brown was finally seeing the light at the end of the tunnel. He perceived that he had found a soft spot with his probing.

"Your argument is not with me," Michael answered softly, "but with the Church."

"The Church of the Inquisition?" he taunted.

"Infallibility means that in matters of faith and morals the Church is protected from teaching error," Michael explained as if he were reading the Catechism. "That is not to say that the Church does not include sinners, even evil men, or that those men haven't reached positions of authority in the Church."

"Indeed more than a few have," Pastor Brown remarked as if he had scored a hit.

Michael again noted that the pastor didn't address the relevant part of his explanation.

"And what of your infatuation with Mary?"

"What of it?" Michael returned to the taunting cleric.

"What of it!? It is perhaps the most grotesque example of Catholic mythology."

"We honor Mary," Michael said innocently.

"Yes, you honor her, at the expense of Jesus. All praise and glory to God and his only Son, Mr. O'Shea!" He shouted it at the rafters.

Michael didn't try to counter the pastor. He knew that honoring Mary didn't take away from God but was unsure about how to articulate it.

"What about it, Mr. O'Shea? Should we pray to Mary?"

"If we want her to pray for us."

"Should we believe in her perpetual virginity, that she had no more children, and in this so-called Immaculate Conception?"

Michael didn't respond.

"Do you believe, Michael, in the Immaculate Conception, that Mary was born without sin?"

"Yes."

"Do you believe that she remained a virgin as your Church teaches, that Jesus had no siblings?"

"Yes."

"I'm open to an explanation." Then reaching his arm out with an open hand toward the throng in the pews, "I think we're all open to an explanation."

Michael followed his arm and looked out toward the people for the first time since sitting down, the people who, ostensibly, were open to an explanation.

*Open to an explanation?* It seemed that nothing could be further from the truth, he mused.

Perhaps it was because he looked out at the crowd and it broke his train of thought, perhaps it was merely fatigue, but Michael couldn't find his voice. He tried to think of how to answer, where to begin. It all seemed overwhelming to him, to explain the Immaculate Conception from scratch in a couple of sentences. He couldn't think of one Scripture passage. His mind raced, searching the files in his mind. Nothing.

"Do you believe that Mary had no other children, that she remained a virgin?"

"I've said so."

"And why do you believe that?" *Is this his Achilles heal?* the pastor asked himself as he noted his adversary's delay. He began to smell victory while Michael sat pondering the obstacle.

"The Church teaches me that it is so." Michael cringed within himself as he finished saying it, yet he felt almost compelled to so answer. *Have I just handed it all over to them?* he asked himself with a feeling of dread. *I don't know what else to say. Have I just confirmed all too well their impression of Catholics as pathetic sheep following blindly?*

"I understand," Pastor Brown replied with a most sympathetic voice. "If your Church is wrong about one doctrine that it teaches then doesn't that call into question everything it teaches?"

"Yes, it does."

Pastor Brown was impressed with how quickly and honestly Michael had made this admission. *This boy's just greased the skids that will lead to his own downfall,* the pastor thought. "I read from the Gospel according to Matthew, chapter twelve, verse forty-six and following...

*While He was still talking to the multitudes, behold, His mother and brothers* stood outside, seeking to speak with Him. Then one said to Him, "Look, Your mother and Your brothers are standing outside, seeking to speak with You."

But He answered and said to the one who told Him, "Who is My mother and who are My brothers?" And He stretched out His hand toward His disciples and said, "Here are My mother and My brothers!" For whoever does the will of My Father in heaven is My brother and sister and mother."

*Now I'll smash this bug,* the pastor thought, as he prepared to unleash his barrage...

"You believe in the 'perpetual virginity'" — *he used his fingers to make quotation marks* — "of Mary because the Church teaches that it is so." His voice was restrained. "You believe that she was conceived without sin because the Church teaches that it is so, at least since the eighteen fifties," he added parenthetically. "Who knows what she'll teach fifty years from now?" he asked with shoulders shrugged at the crowd he was just beginning to entertain. "You believe in baptizing infants..." — *he pulled out the thumb of his left fist with his right hand so as to count as he proceeded* — "...because the Church teaches you it is so. You believe in the power of relics, holy water, and incense because the Church tells you it is so. You believe that some man in colorful capes can call an invisible Savior down onto the altar to put himself into bread."

Michael lowered his eyes after the pastor pulled out his second finger. *He won't stop when he runs out of fingers*, Michael realized as he girded himself for the onslaught.

"You believe that the Pope is Christ's representative on earth" — *again the fingers used as quotation marks* — "because the Church teaches that it is so. You believe in confessing sins to a man, lighting candles to statues, not eating meat on Fridays, and calling men Father... all because—" He slowed his pace and said each word deliberately. "— the... Church... teaches... you... that... it... is... so.

"You believe in praying to Mary on little beads, reciting in vain repetition the same words. You believe that Mary has come back to talk with a peasant man in Mexico, and with gullible children in Portugal, France, Spain, and all over the place. You believe in the 'fires of purgatory'"— *again the fingers curling into quotation marks* — "and you believe all of this because the Church teaches that it is so. I'm curious..." Now he looked directly at Michael, who lifted his head to make eye contact. "Why hasn't Mary come down to consult with your popes or maybe some of the cardinals at their fancy estates?"

*This is what I was afraid of,* Les said to himself, *an uncharitable free for all.* And, he recognized, Hank Brown had not addressed the issues raised. He had been slipping punches like a well-trained boxer and throwing counter punches, many below the belt, as he continued to bob and weave, never giving Michael the opportunity to respond to one issue before throwing out another.

Les was wondering if his nephew was crying; he couldn't see Michael's face clearly. *I can't jump in at this point, though,* he rationalized. *Michael has been able to answer for himself quite ably and I've let it go to this point. Besides, I have to respect the fact that this is not my church. He's a smart kid who has all the answers. Maybe this is what he needs, a thorough drubbing, to get him on the right track.*

Elijah felt Michael's humiliation vicariously. He had been engrossed, as had the entire congregation, as Michael gave answer to everything thrown at him initially. Now he looked at his cousin, who had been rendered speechless by the imposing Hank Brown who stood above him in a full length black robe. *He's trapped with nothing to say.*

Pastor Brown continued... "Ah, who knows? Maybe she does. Oh, Holy Mother Church teaches many things. She teaches that dead people can pray on our behalf, that tradition is on the same par as the Holy Bible, that we need to earn our way into eternal life, that Jesus needs to be sacrificed time and again, that Mary was a woman without sin, that it's acceptable to have statues in our places of worship, that we need to confess our sins to men and so much else that is error... Here is the Word, Michael!" He held out the Bible and paused as Michael looked up. Then solemnly he said, "Will you commit yourself to Jesus now and be saved?"

*He's going for it all*, marveled Les, who had to admire Pastor Brown's sheer boldness. *Maybe I was too quick to judge his tactics.*

*What's he going to do?* wondered Elijah, echoing the thoughts of everyone else gathered there. *He has no choice. Either he accepts the Pastor's invitation or he crawls out of here defeated and lost.* Eli himself was unsure about what he would rather see Michael do.

*What can I say?* Michael asked himself. He remembered, of all things, the short conversation he had had with the Dominican sister down in Nashville and the question she had asked, *"Why the Bible at all?"*

He finally rose from his chair slowly. *Is this how Uncle Matty would do it?* He prayed for help as he took a few steps toward the pulpit.

"Minister Davis, would you please come forward to assist us," Pastor Brown requested, barely able to contain the thrill of victory. He thought it would be appropriate to have his assistant pray over Michael first before asking him to renounce the Catholic Church and receive baptism.

"Pastor," Michael spoke as he looked up. He was so nervous that he barely got the word out.

"Yes, son."

"Why do we believe the Bible?"

The question surprised the pastor. It was so simple and spoken with humility. It was evidence that he was ready to accept Jesus and begin looking to the Bible. It was evidence that he was ready to eschew the superstitious rituals of Catholicism, and though this was no time for lengthy instruction, he felt compelled to suckle his brand new child in Christ.

"The Bible is the inspired Word of God, son."

"But how do we know that?" Michael persisted like an innocent child.

"'Faith cometh by hearing and hearing by the word of God.' As you read the Bible your faith will grow," he said, continuing to indulge the child.

Les was in awe. Pastor Brown, his old nemesis, was implementing his own strategy to perfection. The pastor had confronted and challenged his nephew and now was making the transition to consoler and teacher.

"And the Word of God is contained in the Bible?" Michael persisted.

"Yes." The questions were beginning to get tiresome but Pastor Brown tried to be magnanimous.

"All of God's Word?"

"Yes."

"Where does it say that?"

"It doesn't say that in so many words," the pastor replied. It's a matter of faith. Your faith will grow, son. Don't trouble yourself with things you're not capable of understanding yet." Pastor Brown, like a bow-hunter waiting for a browsing deer to step within range of his tree stand, struggled to maintain his composure.

"I hope it will, Pastor Brown, and I'm sorry for asking so many questions. It's just that what we're doing here is extremely important and I know you understand that. I have to know... Really, we all have to appreciate what we're doing here."

"Yes, we do," agreed the pastor, "and it's a point worth making." He was impressed with Michael's sincerity. He chastised himself for getting impatient with the young man.

"Do you believe," began Michael solemnly, "that the Bible..." He lifted the Bible still in his hand up to the side of his face. "...is the pillar and foundation of truth?"

307

"Yes, I do," answered Pastor Brown with a solemnity that surpassed Michael's. He was proud and flattered that he had not only won the boy over, but was getting a disciple, someone who would credit him for his conversion and look to him for instruction.

"But that's not what the Bible says," countered Michael evenly. "It doesn't make that claim."

"'Scripture is given by inspiration of God, and is profitable for doctrine, for reproof, for correction, for instruction in righteousness.' Second Timothy three sixteen," the pastor thundered at the impudent boy.

"I believe that," Michael responded.

"Then what is the problem?" He had given up trying to restrain his impatience.

"The problem is that the Bible tells me in first Timothy three fifteen that, well let me just read it."

The pastor waited, a smoldering volcano, as Michael paged through the Bible. Those in the congregation waited, transfixed on the drama playing out in their midst.

"Here it is...

> These things I write to you, though I hope to come to you shortly; but if I am delayed, I write so that you may know how you ought to conduct yourself in the house of God, which is the church of the living God, the pillar and foundation of truth.

The silence after Michael finished reading was deafening until he lifted his head, this time toward the assembly for the first time, and spoke. "The inspired Word of God claims that the *Church* is the pillar and foundation of truth."

Pause.

"Which Church?" Someone called out the question from the congregation.

"The Church in the book of Acts, the one fathered by the Apostles. The one that saved and protected the parchments that Paul, John, Luke and the others used to write the Gospels and epistles. The one that commissioned councils at the end of the fourth century to determine which writings were inspired and should be part of the canon of Scripture. The one that re-produced Scripture by hand for centuries and protected its integrity. The one that still has all the original books in the canon, even the ones that have been discarded by the so-called reformers.

"You see, Pastor Brown," Michael looked back to the robed man, "I believe that the Bible is the inspired Word of God."

The pastor just stared.

"I believe it is because the Church, the one that compiled it, protected it, and teaches from it, teaches me that it is so."

Pastor Brown remained silent for a moment.

"I should have known better than to cast pearls before a swine," the pastor began with a calm veneer. "Remove yourself from my church."

Michael hesitated. He had not expected to be asked to leave.

"Get out!" the pastor screamed.

With that, Michael turned on his heel and made his way out, straight down the center aisle, in silence.

*Martin de Porres Kennedy*

# Epilogue

George pulled his Chevy into the church lot. *It must be almost two months since that O'Shea boy rolled out of town,* thought George as he stepped out into the brisk October morning. It was Sunday and the sky was a beautiful deep blue. Two weeks had passed since Eli McGuffey had shipped out for the Marine Corps training depot at Parris Island.

*It must have been a whirlwind of a summer for that family.* He was sympathetic when he reminded himself that Les was only acting in Christian charity when he invited his sister's family to come and stay.

He recalled with fondness having been asked by Les to be a founding member of their church. He had enjoyed listening to the sermons he had heard Les preach over the years. He still considered Les a brother in Christ, but remained disappointed and disheartened by how Les responded to, or rather didn't respond to, the many challenges posed by his young nephew.

*We've got to stand strong against false teaching lest we be taken captive ourselves,* he had insisted to himself. Such a strong deception it was that he hadn't been able to work it all out. He still wasn't sure about some of the issues raised by Michael O'Shea and wasn't even sure it was profitable to consider them. *Perhaps,* he told himself at times, *it was dangerous. Perhaps it would be better to ignore deception altogether.* He consoled himself with the knowledge that even his new pastor had not been able to give answer to all that was asserted.

"Good morning, George!" Drew Davis greeted with enthusiasm as George approached the door.

◆ ◆ ◆

Matty O'Shea was nervous as he drove back from the Phillies game along the Schuylkill Expressway. He always savored the last few weeks of the season.

He had invited his nephew to the game so that he could discuss some things, things that in this day and age, were important for young people to understand. He doubted his brother had ever broached such subjects. In fact, he was sure he hadn't. It would have been contrary to what his brother believed passionately. *Nevertheless, Michael has a right to know, for his own health and well-being,* Matty had rationalized. *He's just started his senior year. Nowadays it can be a matter of life and death.*

They had enjoyed the game and each other so much, though, that he had squandered nine innings and even the time they had sat in the stadium traffic. Matty O'Shea was not one to hesitate, but he had been searching for exactly the right words to express his thoughts to Michael.

Should he focus on barrier protection and the cold, clinical side of the whole issue?

*No, that's not my style and it doesn't resonate with young people,* he decided.

Should he relate the horror stories, how painful the symptoms of sexually transmitted diseases, and how much more excruciating the treatment?

*No, kids don't respond to scare tactics,* he told himself. Besides, he had no heart for it.

*Best just to try and talk with him, just try to relate on his level,* Matty finally decided and ordered himself to settle down.

"I hope you realize what a great future you have, Michael."

"Uh-huh."

Pause.

"I mean, you've got your whole life in front of you, a good head on your shoulders, and you're a good-looking kid."

Michael didn't respond, so self-conscious was he, but he appreciated his uncle's trying to build him up. It was well intended he knew.

"You've got to watch out for the pitfalls that some young people can fall into, though. Do you understand what I'm talking about?"

"Yeah," Michael lied. It wasn't really a lie. He did understand the words clear enough. Was he missing something? Was this an anti-drug message?

"Do you have a girlfriend?"

"No."

"Just as well. You've got enough to concern yourself with."

Pause.

"If you did have a girlfriend, do you feel confident you'd know what to do? ... I mean, you know, about protecting yourself."

Now Michael was embarrassed. *Is he talking about what I think he's talking about?* He didn't know what to say.

"I guess so."

"There are some good organizations if you ever have any questions. Planned Parenthood has an office right near our firm down town."

*Planned Parenthood!* Michael cried to himself. He remembered his Dad railing against that organization. *Do you know what they do, Uncle Matty? Who they are? Now what should I say? It wouldn't be right to let that go unchallenged.*

He prayed quickly for guidance and wisdom to St. Thomas More, the patron saint of lawyers.

"Thanks, Uncle Matty, but Dad taught me everything I need to know, I think long ago."

Matty was startled.

"Yeah, the Church teaches very clearly that sexual intercourse before marriage is a grave sin."

Pause.

"Good," Matty said, turning to his nephew. They were just passing boathouse row on the Schuylkill. The lights that framed the boathouses shimmered on the dark surface of the river. "I just wanted to make sure you understood what the Church taught."

◆ ◆ ◆

Eli's eyes opened and from his bottom rack ("bunk" just a few days ago) he noticed a hint of natural light in the barracks that housed the platoon of Marine recruits.

*It's Sunday,* he remembered. *I wonder what we'll do on Sunday.* Just three days ago they had gotten off the bus in the receiving area in the middle of the night and entered into the organized insanity that was Marine Corps boot camp. It was as if a bunch of maniacs wearing "Smoky Bear" state trooper hats had been sleeping peacefully until the bus arrived to wake them up and they took it quite personally.

Elijah thought back to that night and marveled that it had occurred so recently. It seemed as if it were part of another time. *Have I been here forever?*

He heard some movement. A few of the recruits were up and making their way to the head. In minutes the lights would be on and the beehive would be active.

Elijah looked up to his left and saw Montoya's bare feet hanging down from the top bunk next to his. Elijah had talked with him on the bus ride onto the island. He had noticed this lean, brown-skinned guy fingering beads and had wondered if they were Rosary beads. He had wanted to ask about them on the bus but had hesitated. Last year, before all that he and Michael had talked about, he would not even have noticed.

314

"And God said... Let there be light."

It was spoken in a bass voice an instant before the bright overhead lights came on. The recruits scrambled to stand at attention in front of their racks as the lean drill instructor's heels clicked down the squad bay.

"God!!!... Country!!... Corps!... in that order."

He continued clicking down the squad bay.

"Today is the Lord's Day..." *(It was not a suggestion.)* "...You will get this squad bay squared away and fall out for breakfast formation in forty-five minutes.

"You will have the opportunity to attend religious services today... Your vacation in the receiving area is about to end... Tomorrow you will move to the Delta company area and begin boot camp..." *(He had walked the entire length of the squad bay.)* "Do not waste God's time by praying for deliverance from this island..." — *in a low voice as he turned to walk back* — "...You will not be delivered... I suggest that you pray for the strength to endure the next twelve weeks... you will need it."

His clicking heels continued past the remaining recruits and out the door.

Recruits scrambled around their bunks and into the head. Elijah noticed that Montoya stood near his locker momentarily with the Rosary beads in hand.

"Them beads ain't goin' t'do you no good down here, boy."

It was a big-framed, country-boy looking recruit who playfully taunted the lean Latino.

"They ain't goin' t'stop no bullet and save your ass in a war."

*How will he react to this kind of a taunt?* Eli wondered.

Montoya raised the beads to his lips and kissed the small crucifix, then proceeded to put them into his locker. He turned to look at his taunter who sported a big-toothed grin. "Listen, 'Big Country,' I can't talk right now, I gotta go wash my hair."

They had all been sheared like sheep the first morning on the island. "Big Country" smiled after him, "They done took everyone's hair down to the skull and my hair was really my best feature."

Eli was impressed with Montoya's style. He had gained an ally in the big recruit.

After breakfast they were released back to the squad bay and given the chance to write letters home until summoned for church formation. Back at their lockers Eli couldn't resist asking about the Rosary beads.

"Do you really think that using those beads to pray will help protect you?" he asked in a low voice.

Montoya looked up and ascertained that it was indeed a sincere question.

"From bullets? I don't know... Maybe—"

Eli nodded in appreciation for his candor.

"—But there's more to lose than your life," he finished.

"That's true," Eli agreed as he turned toward his bunk to begin writing a letter to his family back home. He was unsure of how much to tell his parents about the various things going through his mind.

"All those going to the Catholic Mass fall out," a voice came from beyond the squad bay doors.

Eli watched for a moment as Montoya and a good portion of the other recruits made their way toward the door. Then he rose to join them.

Montoya, noticing Eli, raised his eyebrows slightly. He had assumed that Eli was of some other faith, based on his inquiry about the Rosary.

"You Catholic?" Montoya asked.

"Not yet."

# Resources

*A Philadelphia Catholic in King James's Court* presents Catholic responses to several questions posed by Protestant fundamentalists. The Church has preserved and protected the Deposit of Faith for nearly 2000 years. To help guide you in your exploration of the faith we highly recommend the following resources:

**Envoy magazine**
New Hope, KY 40052
502-325-3061
www.envoymagazine.com

**Catholic Answers/This Rock magazine**
*Where We Got the Bible,* by Henry G. Graham
P.O. Box 17490
San Diego, CA 92177
888-291-8000
619-541-1131
www.catholic.com

**The Coming Home Network**
P.O. Box 4100
Steubenville, OH 43952
614-283-6320

**St. Joseph's Communications**
(tapes by Dr. Scott Hahn and others)
P.O. Box 720
West Covina, CA 91793
800-526-2151
626-331-3549
www.saintjoe.com

**Ignatius Press**
*Rome Sweet Home,* by Scott and Kimberly Hahn
*Catholicism and Fundamentalism,* by Karl Keating
*Born Fundamentalist, Born Again Catholic,* by David Currie
800-651-1531

**Basilica Press**
*Surprised by Truth,* by Patrick Madrid
888-396-2339

**Providence House**
(comprehensive source of books, tapes, and gifts)
Jim and Felicia Coffey
610-949-9131

To order more copies
(Please do send a copy to someone you know)

To order more copies of this book, call

**Lilyfield Press at 800-932-3051**

or write to:

**Lilyfield Press
W5180 Jefferson St.
Necedah, WI   54646
Fax: 608-565-2025
Email: familytrad@aol.com**

For a single copy send $12.95 + $3.95 shipping.

Bulk quantity discounts are available.
Special discounts for religious education, churches, and schools.

• • •

**NEW! Discussion/Study Guide $3.95**

Over 50 pages of in-depth questions and answers for
*A Philadelphia Catholic in King James's Court.*

Provides supplemental information and  supporting  references from
Scripture and the Catechism of the Catholic Church.
Especially useful for religious education classes, RCIA,
confirmation, bible studies, homeschoolers, as well as group
and individual study. Perfect for teens and adults.